D0723367

Raising Your Child in a Digital World

Finding a healthy balance of time online
without techno tantrums and conflict

Dr Kristy Goodwin

FINCH PUBLISHING
SYDNEY

Raising Your Child in a Digital World

First published in 2016 in Australia and New Zealand by Finch Publishing Pty Limited, ABN 49 057 285 248, Suite 2207, 4 Daydream Street, Warriewood, NSW, 2102, Australia.

16   8 7 6 5 4 3 2 1

There is a National Library of Australia Cataloguing-in-Publication entry available at the National Library.

Edited by Megan English
Editorial assistance by Teaspoon Consulting
Text typeset by Meg Dunworth and The Creative Workshop
Cover design by Ingrid Kwong
Printed by Griffin Press

Permissions: The image on page 225 is used with permission from Ergo Break 4 Kids (www. ergobreak4kids.com)

The paper used to produce this book is a natural, recyclable product made from wood grown in sustainable plantation forests. The manufacturing processes conform to the environmental regulations in the country of origin.

Finch titles can be viewed and purchased at **www.finch.com.au**

Contents

Introduction

The increasing role of digital technology in children's lives has left many parents concerned and confused. Deciding on the right amount of screen time and the appropriate level of access to televisions, touch-screen devices, mobile phones and video games – as well as issues of addiction and cyber-safety – are just some of the digital dilemmas facing modern parents.

When asked about our childhood memories, most of us reminisce about long days spent climbing trees, roaming the local neighbourhood unsupervised or playing with cardboard boxes and cubby houses. This is distinctly different to the digitally saturated world in which we're raising our own children. *And for many, this is scary.*

As parents, it's impossible to use our own childhood as a point of reference for some of the parenting situations and decisions that we're confronting in relation to technology. We spent our childhoods staring at the sky, not at screens! Our parents simply didn't experience the same digital dilemmas that we now face. The only decision many of them had to grapple with was how much television we could watch. And that screen was permanently affixed to the wall, with only a handful of programs to watch – not smuggled into pyjama pants or stashed in mum's handbag!

Today, television is just one of many digital devices parents have to help their children manage. There is a digital smorgasbord for them to choose from. In addition, technology is constantly changing and evolving, which further contributes to our confusion and sense of overwhelm as parents. Just when we finally feel we have a handle on the technology that captivates our children, along comes a new one that entices them further.

To make matters worse, we're bombarded with conflicting advice from health professionals and the media. Popular advice is often grounded in ideology, not research, so myths and misnomers flourish. On the one hand, we're told to avoid or minimise young children's exposure to screens and devices because of the perceived harm it may cause developing brains and bodies. On the other, we are urged to introduce them to all forms of technology at an early age so they don't fall behind at school or later in life.

Even when we try to find out what is best for our children (often online), the amount of advice is overwhelming, contradictory and, more often than not, inaccurate. As a result, cycles of techno myths are perpetuated and circulated among well-meaning parents, such as:

- technology causes ADD and ADHD
- TV, touch screens and video games are bad for children
- baby DVDs and Mozart will boost brain development and enhance language skills
- children don't learn from video games
- leaving the TV on when no-one is watching is okay
- there are safe amounts of screen time.

As a parent, researcher and former teacher, I've personally wrestled with these techno myths and more, trying to decipher how technology intersects with child development. I've spent countless hours devouring and digesting the latest research from a range of disciplines to build a comprehensive picture of what digital practices and habits are effective and conducive to young children's learning and development – and which are potentially harmful.

I must admit that at times my discoveries have both surprised and scared me. This doesn't mean we need to ban or fear technology completely (our kids would hate us if we did this anyway), but we do need to think carefully about how it is shaping our children's early experiences.

Whether we love it or loathe it, our children are already living in a digital world. Digital abstinence isn't an option. Together, we need to find healthy and helpful ways to leverage technology in their lives while at the same time preserving the sanctity of childhood.

What this book offers parents

In order for us to make informed choices about how we use technology with our children, we need access to the latest information and research on how child development and neuroscience intersects with the exploding world of technology.

That's exactly what this book will provide: research-based information, coupled with lots of practical tips to help parents understand how to raise children in this digital landscape (*without* having to ban the iPad, disconnect the wi-fi, or unplug the TV).

This book won't tell parents what they *should* do with young children, aged 0–12 years, in terms of technology – no-one likes to be should on! Instead, it will help parents make informed, everyday decisions about how to navigate this digital world.

I'll also share the seven essential building blocks of child development and outline how technology can either support or stifle each of them:

1 relationships and attachments
2 language development
3 sleep
4 play
5 physical movement
6 nutrition
7 executive-function skills.

Ultimately, my hope is that this book will provide parents with the peace of mind that our children's digital habits are not detrimental to their health and development. An array of tips, tricks and tools – grounded in research – will ensure that our young children have every chance to learn and thrive in this digital world that they've inherited.

1

Obstacles and techno myths

While technology isn't necessarily toxic or taboo for young children, we are flirting with danger if we don't use it in ways that are aligned to their developmental needs.

As parents of young children, we're trying to balance claims of an impending digital apocalypse with the practical reality of wrangling smart phones and gaming consoles from our children's hands. We're trying to ensure we balance our children's screen time with green time, while keeping them safe online. We're trying to navigate the ever-changing digital terrain with our little ones, but we're also scrambling to keep up.

There is an ongoing debate about whether technology is appropriate for young children. Entrenched philosophical beliefs about the sanctity of childhood have been used to discourage the use of technology with young children, but it is here to stay. We can no longer debate whether or not we use it. Instead, we have to think about the best ways to use it with young children.

This chapter will outline some of the obstacles and techno myths parents encounter in the digital age, such as:

- why parents are bamboozled trying to raise young children in the digital world
- how misleading media headlines and conflicting advice has resulted in techno myths being perpetuated
- why we have no role models when it comes to being a modern parent.

It will also explore the potential dangers of excessive or inappropriate use of technology on young children's development as well as the positive outcomes that technology can offer.

Bamboozled parents

As parents, we're completely confused and wholeheartedly concerned about raising children in the digital age. While we struggle to keep up with the abundance of screens that surround us and captivate our children, they live out technologised childhoods that are completely different to our own. The memories we have of our childhoods are of swinging in trees and riding bikes, not tapping and swiping screens!

In addition, the technology they're using is constantly changing and often foreign to us. Combined with the increasing pressure to introduce technology to young children due to false and misleading advertising claims on toys and gadgets, it feels overwhelming!

We thrust digital devices into our children's hands so they don't fall behind while we fret about what all this exposure is doing to them. Still, the marketing claims on baby smart phones, toddler laptops and educational apps suggest they'll boost our child's brain development. But, we wonder, is this digital overload impairing our children's development?

As parents, we often feel grossly unprepared to deal with the digital onslaught facing our children. The intense pull and obsessive nature of what the digital world offers young children terrifies many parents because we know we've been sucked into the digital vortex, too, constantly checking emails and social media on *our* smart phones.

We seek guidance about how to leverage technology in healthy and helpful ways, without having to digitally amputate our children. Many of us acknowledge that fearing technology or banning it altogether is not a long-term solution. We realise that if we adopt this head-in-the-sand approach, we're missing important opportunities to help our children develop esssential, lifelong skills. But for many of us, we're simply unsure of the best ways to guide our little ones.

Technologised childhoods

As mentioned, today's children are growing up in a world where digital devices dangle from their prams, tablets are thrust into their hands in restaurants and touch screens are hidden under their pillows. They look at us vaguely when we ask them to 'hang up' the phone or 'tape' a TV program.

Screens and devices are a ubiquitous part of everyday life for most children. Many tap, swipe and pinch screens before they've learnt to ride a bike or tie their shoelaces. In fact, research conducted in 2014 by AVG confirms that many children meet their digital milestones before they meet traditional physical and developmental milestones![1]

Having a daily dose of digital as a child is something completely foreign for us as parents, yet our children have quickly become immersed in it. They're bombarded with screens and, as parents and educators, we're understandably worried about their technology habits.

This is the modern parents' dilemma. While we marvel at our children's technological proficiency and intuition – toddlers

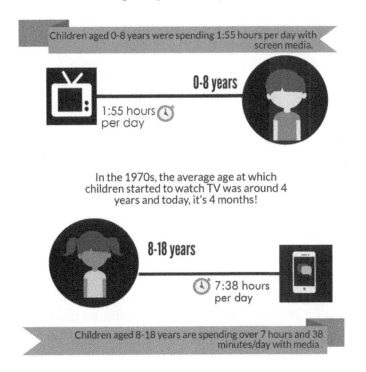

Children aged 0-8 years were spending 1:55 hours per day with screen media.

0-8 years

1:55 hours
per day

In the 1970s, the average age at which children started to watch TV was around 4 years and today, it's 4 months!

8-18 years

7:38 hours
per day

Children aged 8-18 years are spending over 7 hours and 38 minutes/day with media.

manipulate smart phones with ninja-like speed and confidence – we find it terrifying. We fret about the possible adverse impact this digital exposure has on their bodies and wellbeing (we've experienced the meltdowns when we ask for *our* smart phone to be returned, or their irritable and sometimes aggressive behaviour when we tell them that they can't play Minecraft for another hour. (We also fret about their exposure to wi-fi given that it's now omnipresent.)

Children today are using devices for increasing amounts of time (see the infographic from Young Children and the Media, on p3). This data was yielded from studies conducted by the Kaiser Family Foundation in 2010[2] and Common Sense Media in 2013[3] and the figures are likely to increase over time as children's access to mobile technologies increases.

Technology is evolving at such a rapid rate that parents and educators are scrambling to keep up. Just when we feel like we have a handle on the technology our children are obsessed with, along comes something else to supersede it!

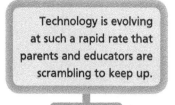

Technology is evolving at such a rapid rate that parents and educators are scrambling to keep up.

And it's little wonder. Consider the penetration rate, which describes how long it takes a technology to reach 50 million users worldwide. The radio (the original wireless!) took 38 years, the telephone took 20 years, television took 13, mobile phones 12 and the internet four. Facebook took two years, YouTube just one year and Angry Birds 35 days!

Many aspects of childhood have become technologised. Toy manufacturers have observed young children's infatuation with technology, in particular the 'pass-back effect', a term coined by Carly Schuler, where parents hand over their digital devices to entertain, educate or pacify their children in waiting rooms, restaurants and at home – and they're manufacturing digital toys and products geared towards parents from baby smart phones to toddler laptops to touch screens for preschoolers.

Through careful marketing, we're often led to believe that these techno-toys and digital products are superior to more traditional toys. We reason, *a modified laptop must surely be superior to a set of blocks for my 4-year-old?*

Often these products are directly marketed as educational with packaging and promotional materials that suggest they will give children the academic head start they need to thrive in the twenty first century. However, many of these marketing claims are *not* substantiated by research.

There are also a wealth of gadgets and products geared towards parents of infants. We now have baby mobiles that take photos of babies in the cot and automatically upload them to social media on our behalf. There are modified baby jumpsuits with built-in technologies to monitor our baby's temperature and track their sleeping habits.

We now have baby mobiles that take photos of babies in the cot and automatically upload them to social media ...

There's even the iPotty, a potty with a tablet attachment that is intended to lure and reward them for using the potty. (Personally, the thought of toilet training with a touch-screen device terrifies me – think of all the extra cleaning up required, let alone the hygiene implications!)

The Fisher-Price Apptivity Seat was another traditional baby product that was technologised. Designed for children aged approximately six months and older, this baby bouncer with a tablet attachment hovered over the baby's face. The apps that came with the device claimed to teach young babies concepts such as numbers and colours. Thankfully, the seat has been discontinued.

As parents we're led to believe that these digital devices offer educational advantages for infants because they have been manufactured by reputable brands that we've trusted in the past.

Advice and confusion from the media

The harmful effects associated with young children's use of technology are often disproportionately represented in the media. We're bombarded with media headlines that demonise technology and claim it will harm children's development. The headlines frequently decry the negative effects of technology for young children, especially as it relates to cyber-safety, cyber-bullying, obesity, video games and overall screen time.

The shock tactics employed in media headlines that attract parents' attention (as they're designed to do), convince us that *all* technology is harmful for young children and, as a result, should be avoided. The research behind the story is not always accurately represented in the media though, and as busy parents we often don't have time to read further on the topic. This can lead to us becoming misinformed.

Rarely are the positive impacts of technology on young children reported, either. Instead, the advice given can be conflicting, which inflates parental concern and increases fear and guilt, resulting in confused and angst-ridden parents.

Parents are also struggling because we're given conflicting advice from health professionals, educators and other parents. This has resulted in the perpetuation of techno myths. These are the common myths, misnomers and misinformation that surround young children's technology use, many of which will be explored and debunked throughout this book in TECHNO MYTH-BUSTER boxes (see below).

TECHNO MYTH-BUSTER

MYTH: There are 'safe' amounts of screen time.

FACT: We do have screentime recommendations that prescribe recommended amounts of daily screen time. In Australia these are:

- 0-2 years: zero screen time
- 2-5 years: 1 hour/day
- 5-12 years: 1–2 hours/day

Parents are given conflicting advice when it comes to screen time. Health professionals often caution parents about excessive screen time while schools (and even preschools) are introducing more and more technology into the classroom. This can leave parents bewildered about what amount is harmful.

It's important to note that the current recommendations aren't empirically tested or scientifically validated. They're based primarily on the opportunity cost associated with screen time. They're also based on research on passive forms of technology like TV and DVDs. (Research with more interactive types of screens are still in their infancy.)

Current recommendations also consider all screens equal. This simply isn't the case: one hour spent creating a story on the iPad is qualitatively different to an hour spent playing a violent video game. Talking to Grandma via Skype is not the same as watching TV. They're qualitatively different experiences. As such, it's impossible to prescribe precise, quantifiable amounts of time that are safe for all children, based simply on their chronological age. This isn't an exact science. There aren't safe levels of exposure.

Moreover, the current Australian recommendations are considered rigid and outdated in the digital age. From my experience (speaking to parents and educators throughout Australia), many people *are* unaware that such guidelines even exist. If parents or educators are aware of the recommendations, they're often considered untenable and unrealistic, and are often disregarded. (Details regarding the current screen time recommendations are explored further in Chapter 10.)

A very different childhood

As we've seen, as parents we're struggling to make confident decisions about how our children should use digital devices. We have no reference point from our own very different childhoods, and we don't have any other parenting role models to rely on – we can't ask our friends with older children for guidance because, in most instances, their children didn't have access to the same gadgets and devices ours do.

As adults, we often have romanticised notions of our own childhood. We hanker for the same types of experiences we had for our own children. But we seem to forget that many of us did in fact encounter technology when we were growing up. We certainly didn't have as much of it, or such easy access to it as our children do today, but we didn't grow up in a completely screen-free world.

We forget that we watched TV or played Pac-Man or Space Invaders on the Atari, listened to music on our boom box or Walkman, played educational games on our Spell and Check or snapped photos on our Polaroid or disposable Kodak camera. (Admittedly they probably weren't selfies, and it took weeks to get our over-exposed photos developed.)

Still, there's a natural human tendency to worry when new technologies are introduced to society. Indeed, in 1440 there was social panic when the printing press was introduced (it was feared it would erode storytelling and verbal communication). Similar concerns were also echoed when televisions were introduced.

Indeed, in 1999 when Douglas Adams wrote *The Hitchhiker's Guide to the Galaxy*, he proposed that the internet would change the world. He also wrote:

1 Everything that's already in the world when we're born is considered *normal.*
2 Anything that's invented before we turn thirty is incredibly *exciting and creative* and we can hopefully make a career out of it.
3 Anything that's invented after we're thirty is *against the natural order of things* and the beginning of the end of civilisation as we know it – until it's been around for about ten years when it gradually turns out to be alright really.

Childhood is just so different now. When we grew up, taking away TV privileges was often a form of punishment. However, that's no longer the case. According to a 2015 study conducted by Miner & Co, making children watch TV (instead of playing video games or using a touch-screen device) is a modern way of disciplining children. TV is now considered an inferior screen.

Childhood is a very sacred time. It's a unique period in our life span and one that needs to be treasured and protected, so it's only natural that we're concerned about digital devices encroaching on this precious time.

TECHNO MYTH-BUSTER

MYTH: Technology causes ADD or ADHD.

FACT: Research does not conclusively prove that screen use causes ADD or ADHD.

There's a common assumption that frequent scene and content changes can disrupt children's attention. While there's some research that proves a correlation (or connection) between excessive and/or inappropriate screen use and attention issues, we don't have any evidence to confirm that technology itself *causes attention issues*.

However, research by Zimmerman and Christakis in 2007 showed that while violent and non-educational programming *is* associated with later symptoms of attention deficit, exposure to educational content has not been related to attention problems.

Do children with attention issues seek out screens because of the fast-paced, rapid-fire input they offer? Does the on-screen pace and frenetic energy appeal to these children as it satiates their appetite for activity and action or do screens, with their bells and whistles, cause children to have attention issues? This is still unknown.

Techno-guilt

The lack of accurate and consistent information about young children and technology has resulted in a sense of moral panic and overwhelm among parents. This has resulted in techno-guilt and techno-shame among many parents.

I coined the term techno-guilt to describe a phenomenon I witnessed firsthand as a parent. I often talk with other parents at the local park or beach (it's a great unofficial source of research). If the topic of technology comes up, I often detect a sense of guilt or shame. 'Oh no, my child doesn't watch TV.' Or, 'I've banned the iPad. It's just not good for them.' And, 'We *never* let our children play video games.' (And no, I often didn't disclose what I do for work at this point in the conversation!)

There's often a stigma associated with young children using technology, which is often seen as bad for children and should be avoided at all costs. Many parents also feel guilty about acknowledging their child's use of technology. I often hear parents secretly confessing,

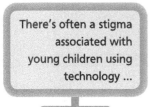

There's often a stigma associated with young children using technology ...

'I'm a bad Mum; I let my child watch TV.' Or, 'I feel so guilty when I let my child use the iPad.'

There's also a lot of public scrutiny from other parents and older adults who look back nostalgically on *their* parenting journey. I refer to this as techno-shaming. Some parents fear that they'll be judged as a bad parent if they allow their child to use a screen or if they use their mobile device around their children.

Moral debates also play out on social media about whether parents should allow their children to use technology and whether they should be using technology around their children. Blog posts and social media posts also often condemn parents for allowing their children to use technology, which has led to parents feeling unnecessary guilt about their own – and their children's – digital habits.

Case STUDY

Why we can't be too quick to techno-shame ...

Brad was made redundant eleven months prior to his son's birth. As the sole income earner, he felt an immense sense of financial pressure to support his family. Brad had been actively seeking work since his redundancy and things were looking promising. He'd been shortlisted for a second round of interviews and was relieved.

Brad had decided to take his son to the local park to play. An email notification appeared on Brad's phone and he quickly checked his email to read the promising news. He was successful in gaining a second interview. Brad discovered that the interview had been scheduled for the next day and he quickly began to SMS his mum to organise childcare for his son for the next day, all the while watching his son crawl around on the equipment.

A grandmother at the park had observed Brad on his phone. She uttered a nasty comment to Brad under her breath and used her iPhone to snap a photo of him, posting it on social media. She claimed he had been a neglectful father, glued to his device.

This was obviously an inaccurate representation of what had actually happened, but the post went viral and Brad was publically vilified on social media – this grandmother clearly didn't know the full story.

Digital parenting

Our gadgets perpetually distract us. Digital devices are cornerstones in our lives and, as adults, many of us have a dependent relationship with our smart phone. We can even suffer from nomophobia, the fear of not having our phones on us. In fact, a 2013 study estimated that we're checking our phones in excess of 150 times per day. This equates to spending over three hours on them a day, on average, of which 1.72 hours are spent on social media.

We feel compelled to instantly respond to every ping and notification. We reach for our smart phones and check email and social media often before we've hopped out of bed. We're snapping photos of our kids and sharing them on social media sites and rely on Dr Google and not our family GP to make medical diagnoses.

We're living in a constant state of distraction. This is changing how we parent and is an often-overlooked part of how technology is changing childhood. We assume that technology is primarily and directly exerting an influence on our children, which it certainly is doing, but it's also impinging on our parenting by:

- **sharenting** – over-sharing our children's milestones online
- **techno-glect** – when we're so consumed by our digital devices that we aren't paying sufficient attention to our children
- **suffering from FOMM (fear of missing memories)** – we want to capture *every* moment of our child's development on our smart phone and end up not living in the moment fully.

Each of these modern parenting habits will be explored further throughout this book.

Why *our* screen habits are important

A recent neuroscience discovery of mirror neurons helps to explain why our babies and children imitate, or mirror, everything we do. Our mirror neurons are a network of nerve cells run along our motor nerves and their prime function is to emulate, or mirror, everything seen. The observed actions are stored in our brains to access later when we need to perform that task or action.

This is why, as humans, we acquire skills as quickly as we do. We're wired from birth to interact with other humans and emulate what they're doing. In fact, studies have shown that babies as young as 15 minutes old are able to copy one of their parents poking out their tongue (and *not* because they're hungry).

This is also why our little ones role-play superhero and fairy characters from movies – and why we have to be very careful about *what* our children consume through TV, movies, video games, websites and apps. Their brains are primed to imitate.

Our children's ability to role model behaviour impacts so many aspects of parenting in the digital age, but especially our technology use around our children. Our digital habits (constantly checking our smart phone or spending hours binge-watching TV) are being absorbed and emulated by our kids *all the time.*

Potential dangers of technology on children's development

The first five years in a child's life are absolutely critical for brain development (see Early Brain Development, below). The neural pathways that are used and repeated are strengthened, and those that are not used are pruned away.

Given that children are being introduced to technology at earlier ages and for increasing amounts of time, we need to think carefully about how this digital exposure is altering their basic brain architecture. We need to consider that a child's digital experiences in the early years will exert a powerful influence on their *overall* development, health and wellbeing.

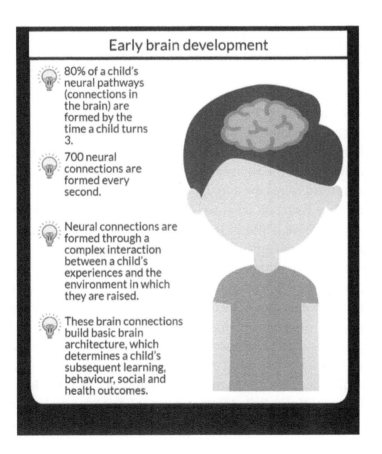

Early brain development

- 80% of a child's neural pathways (connections in the brain) are formed by the time a child turns 3.
- 700 neural connections are formed every second.
- Neural connections are formed through a complex interaction between a child's experiences and the environment in which they are raised.
- These brain connections build basic brain architecture, which determines a child's subsequent learning, behaviour, social and health outcomes.

Early brain development

There's little doubt that digitally overloaded childhoods can pose developmental risks to our children. While technology isn't necessarily toxic or taboo for young children, we're potentially flirting with danger if we don't use it in ways that are aligned to their developmental needs as the overuse or inappropriate use of technology can derail a child's development.

Children have voraciously adopted a range of digital devices, many of which we know little about. We don't yet have a complete picture of exactly how every type of technology can shape a child's development (remember, the iPad was only introduced in 2010). Many questions still remain unanswered about the long-term physical, mental, emotional and social consequences of young children and their parents using digital devices. In some regards, we're conducting a bit of a living experiment. That's why we have to adopt a cautious and considered approach to introducing technology to young children.

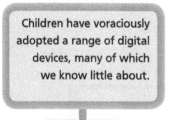

Children have voraciously adopted a range of digital devices, many of which we know little about.

Warren Buckleitner, an expert on the relationship between children and technology proposes, 'Technology is like fertilizer [sic]. Use a little bit at the right time and the plant will blossom. Use too much or the wrong type and you will burn the plant.'

But if we focus on what we *do* know, we discover that we have a comprehensive platform from which to make informed decisions about how technology is impacting childhood.

Firstly, we've ample evidence about how children use and respond to some forms of technology, especially when it comes to more traditional types of technology, including TV and video games. We're often drawing on this research base to hypothesise about the possible impact of more interactive screens, especially as it relates to screen time and content design of media. However, more interactive, sophisticated screens (like tablet devices and interactive gaming consoles) elicit different types of thinking and responses from children. This means it's not always appropriate to transfer research with more traditional types of technology to the current digital climate where interactive technologies dominate.

Secondly, we have a significant corpus of research on childhood development from the developmental science and neuroscience fields. We have a consistent and comprehensive picture of children's basic, unchanging, developmental needs. I refer to these as the seven essential building blocks for a child's development and each of these will be explored in this book. When we match a child's technological experiences to their developmental needs, we can be assured that their screen time won't compromise their wellbeing or development.

A precautionary approach to using technology with young children ... is advised.

Psychologists, parents, child development experts, educators, medical professionals and allied health professionals are united in their calls for concern. A precautionary approach to using technology with young children (particularly those children under two years of age) is advised.

Until we have a more comprehensive picture about the impact of screens on children's development, we must be careful and intentional about young children's screen habits. There are possible risks associated with unrelenting and omnipresent screens in our young children's lives including adverse impacts on their physical, social-emotional and cognitive development. Technology can:

- **interfere with the traditional developmental trajectory** – as the next chapter will explore in more detail, the brain is built from the bottom up. Development starts in the sensory and motor regions of the brain (the primal region of the brain) and gradually, over time, moves to the prefrontal cortex (the part of the brain where higher-order thinking skills such as impulse control and working memory reside). Experts are concerned that technology may potentially overstimulate the sensory region of the brain before the prefrontal cortex is ready to deal with the digital onslaught of sounds and visuals.
- **displace essential developmental experiences** – our children's relationships, language exposure, sleep, play and physical movement

can all be compromised if technology isn't used appropriately with and around them. (Remember that how we, as adults, use technology is just as important as what our kids do with it.)

- **exposure to toxic content** – children are often playing in digital playgrounds that aren't being adequately supervised by adults because of our time restrictions or a lack of understanding of what children are actually doing online and the inherent risks. Exposure to inappropriate content such as pornography, violent media, scary content or unhealthy body images can adversely impact our children's development.

- **health risks** – there are a host of physical and developmental risks that technology may pose to young children. While we don't yet have conclusive scientific evidence, there are possible risks associated with excessive or inappropriate use of screens on children's weight, sleep, vision, hearing and posture (all of which will be explored throughout the book). There are also mounting concerns about potential health consequences associated with young children's constant exposure to wi-fi (this is explored more in Chapter 11).

We have to ensure that technology is carefully selected and managed when it comes to young children. We need to provide strong role models ourselves while leveraging the technologies available in ways that are commensurate with how young children learn and develop.

The positive impact technology can have on children's learning and development

It's important to acknowledge that there are many benefits to young children using technology. Technology provides new opportunities for young children's learning. As the joint position statement from the National Association for the Education of Young Children (NAEYC) and the Fred Rogers Center for Early Learning and Children's Media at Saint Vincent College in the US reveals, there's a swell of research that confirms that when used intentionally and in developmentally appropriate ways, children benefit from technology.

Ways in which technology can support young children's learning include:

1 **catering to visual preference** – it's often said that a picture tells a thousand words. This is especially true for today's learners who are predominantly visual learners. They're growing up in a highly visual world, surrounded by images from TV, computers, mobile devices, advertising displays and traditional media.

   As humans, the visual cortex in our brain is five times larger than the auditory cortex: we're literally wired to gravitate towards visual images. Technology offers unique opportunities to cater for this visual preference by allowing children to view and create their own visual images.

   Today's children also have a keen eye for aesthetics and know what looks good, so they're keen to create visually pleasing work. Technology allows them to easily do this (for example, preschoolers can make digital stories with animated characters using apps like Book Creator and Toontastic).

2 **compensating for emerging skills** – technology can be a wonderful tool to compensate for and support young children's emerging skills. It can also provide assistance to children with additional learning needs. For example, technology can allow children to create a digital story where they narrate it with their own voice (using the two apps mentioned above).

   This is empowering for young learners or for children with additional learning needs as it allows them to create work that's commensurate with what they're capable of producing. This often isn't the case if children are required to use more traditional learning materials like pencil and paper.

3 **allowing choice** – whether it's picking which YouTube clip to watch, making a choice within a video game or selecting the correct answer in an app, children love choice. Technology provides a smorgasbord of choices for children. This freedom to choose is one of the appealing factors for children, especially given that so many live very regimented and timetabled lives where their choices are predominantly made for them.

4   **editing made easy** – technology makes it very easy for children to create and edit digital work. It's much easier to press delete and retype something than it is to erase and rewrite something.

   Children are much more likely to revise and improve digital work than they are more traditional forms of work. I've observed many children edit their voice recordings or movies because there were errors, omissions or the work wasn't of a pleasing quality. Very rarely do we see children use the same level of persistence or revision with more traditional forms of media like pencil and paper.

5   **providing instant feedback and gratification** – today's children crave instant gratification. They want to know straight away if they're right or wrong. They want instant access to information. They have grown up in a world where they download and listen to music online rather than saving up their pocket money to buy records, tapes or CDs.

   When children use technology that provides instant feedback, it allows them to confirm (or reject) their understandings. It also prevents them from perpetuating mistakes. For example, when a child is playing an app and they receive instant feedback that tells them that 6 x 9 does not equal 56, they're instantly forced to reconcile their error.

   This form of instant feedback provides cognitive conflict for the learner and means that children can learn concepts more quickly and accurately, especially where there is factual content to learn (like mathematics facts, phonics and spelling).

6   **allowing interactive learning** – young children can learn from interactive, educational media such as apps, websites and video games. When children interact with content on a screen, they have the chance to experiment with their ideas, make predictions and confirm or reject their hypotheses by manipulating objects or data on a screen.

   This dynamic interaction supports learning. For example, using the app Motion Math Hungry Guppy, children can learn about basic number facts by feeding digit bubbles to a fish. If the child feeds the fish the correct digits that add up to the total specified on the fish's back, the fish swallows the bubble and grows bigger. If the child feeds the incorrect numbers to the fish, then the fish rejects the answer and spits the bubbles out.

In this example, children are manipulating ideas and dynamically testing out their thinking and receiving instant feedback. This is a very interactive experience and quite different to simply answering maths algorithms on a worksheet or textbook.

7 **providing opportunities to create content** – technology gives young children powerful tools to *create* digital content (and not just consume it as they've previously done with TV and DVDs). Today's digital kids are creating, uploading and sharing digital work in online spaces.

In my work as a researcher and teacher, I've seen preschoolers record, edit and share videos. I've seen kindergarten students create their own digital books with animations, background music and narration. I've seen primary school-aged children plan, create and edit their own animations or augment reality productions using apps like Aurasma and FETCH! Lunch Rush. And they're doing all of this with common technology tools: tablets, laptops and digital cameras.

8 **providing instant access to information** – children can quickly google information and have it at their fingertips within seconds. This can enable children to instantly access information and extend their learning at critical moments in their learning, rather than delaying or hindering their learning because they need to locate information in books or other traditional sources.

9 **allowing differentiation** – educators and parents are spoilt with an array of choices when it comes to children's educational technology. We can find apps, websites, games, videos and animations that meet children's precise learning needs and preferences. For children with additional learning needs, they can revise concepts and consolidate their learning (often in a fun and engaging way).

Unlike more traditional forms of instruction, where we relied on textbooks and worksheets, we now have quick and affordable access to digital resources that can support learning.

New ways to play and communicate

Children are now playing in cyber worlds and digital technologies offer exciting opportunities to enrich children's play experiences. While techno toys and digital play experiences are no substitute for more traditional toys, they can offer new ways of playing. From interactive TV to apps and gaming consoles, young children's play experiences can expand as they enter and explore new worlds and create music, books, videos and animations (see Chapter 6 for more details).

Technology can also broaden children's opportunities to communicate. Video-chat capabilities allow children to have meaningful conversations with distant family members, which enriches their relationships and develops their language skills. Parents can see and send photos and videos of their children to other family members to facilitate interaction while young children can watch and share photos and videos of themselves and their family members allowing them to revisit and discuss important family events. They can also interact in real-time by playing online games.

In short: be alert, not alarmed

We can fear or ignore the technological invasion in our children's lives – or we can guide our children to learn healthy and helpful habits about how to live and thrive in a digital world. Our children need us to be technology mentors. We need to accept that when technology is used intentionally and in developmentally appropriate ways, it can support and promote young children's development.

In order to navigate the appropriate use of technology and guide our children, we need to be armed with evidence-based information and facts, not techno myths. As parents and educators, we need to focus on the positive potential technology offers young children, while also mitigating any potential adverse impacts on their development.

We also need to be mindful that children's screen time isn't displacing other critical aspects of childhood. There are simple things that we can do to ensure that they're developing sustainable and healthy technology habits that won't compromise their long-term health and development (without having to ban the TV or unplug the gaming console).

It sounds relatively simple, but the most important thing that we can do as parents raising children in a digitally saturated world is to provide them with a balance of experiences. Children need to climb trees, build sand castles, run around with their friends, ride their bikes and experience the many wonderful things that childhood offers. Technology must not interfere with or compromise these experiences. Instead, we need to find ways to weave technology into childhood in ways that complement and enhance these more traditional aspects of childhood.

It's critical that we teach our little ones how to form healthy and sustainable habits with technology. To do this effectively, we need to model healthy media habits ourselves – easier said than done, I know! – and teach our children how to unplug from devices. We want them to use technology intentionally and appropriately so that it *supports*, not *stifles*, their development.

> It's critical that we teach our little ones how to form healthy and sustainable habits with technology.

The next chapter will give an overview of the seven essential building blocks for a child's development and highlight how technology can stifle and/or support each of these building blocks, depending on how it's used.

At a glance

Modern parents and educators are facing many obstacles and myths when it comes to raising and teaching children in the digital age:

- We're bamboozled by the overwhelming amount of information on technology and the rapid pace of technological change.
- Misleading media headlines and conflicting advice scare and confuse us and this has resulted in the perpetuation of techno myths.
- We don't have any frame of reference for raising digital kids. We have no role models to fall back on and guide us or our parenting decisions

because we didn't grow up in a digital landscape. It can be difficult for us to make parenting decisions because childhood today is so foreign to those of us who grew up experiencing analogue childhoods.

- While there are potential developmental dangers associated with the overuse or inappropriate use of technology with young children, it can also positively impact children's learning and development when it's aligned to their developmental needs.

2

The seven essential building blocks for young children's development

What is it that developing children need to thrive – and not just survive – in this digital age? You might be pleasantly surprised ...

This chapter will provide a brief overview of how brain development occurs (think neuroscience 101 for parents). It will then explore the seven essential building blocks for a child's healthy development and outline how technology can encroach on, or be used to support, our children's development. This is the basis for the following chapters where these ideas will be discussed in more detail.

Why the early years are critical

Thanks to advances in neuroscience and developmental science, we're gaining a more comprehensive picture about what young children *really* need to thrive in a digital age.

We know, for instance, that the early years are absolutely critical for a child's development, particularly their brain development. We also know that a child's brain will grow *more* and *faster* in their first five years of life than at any other time. Child development researchers Fox, Levitt, and Nelson suggest that 80 per cent of brain development occurs in the first three years of life with 90 per cent by age five.

These statistics are a powerful reminder that we need to get the early years right. The early experiences our child encounters – the things they see, hear, touch, smell and taste – stimulate their brain. This stimulation creates millions of neural connections which are the foundations for learning, health and behaviour throughout life.

Children's and parents' screen-use during these early years is pivotal in shaping their brain architecture and developmental outcomes. A digital overload or poor digital habits can impair their social, emotional, intellectual and physical development. Equally, when it's used appropriately technology can support children's development.

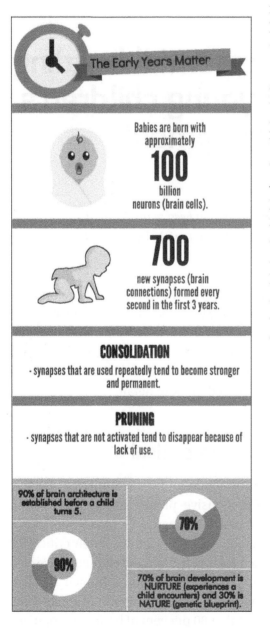

The Early Years Matter

Babies are born with approximately

100

billion
neurons (brain cells).

700

new synapses (brain connections) formed every second in the first 3 years.

CONSOLIDATION
- synapses that are used repeatedly tend to become stronger and permanent.

PRUNING
- synapses that are not activated tend to disappear because of lack of use.

90% of brain architecture is established before a child turns 5.

90%

70%

70% of brain development is NURTURE (experiences a child encounters) and 30% is NATURE (genetic blueprint).

Neuroscience 101: How do children's brains develop?

Typical brain development is determined by the interplay between a child's genes and the experiences they encounter. Normal brain development starts in the sensory and motor regions of the brain (the posterior brain). This is considered a primal part of the brain, as it was responsible for our human evolution and allowed us to survive. It is also where a baby's orienting response originates. This explains why they startle when they hear a loud noise, or turn their head to watch the TV – their attention is alerting them to a change in their environment and their senses are heightened.

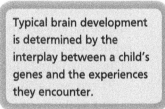

Typical brain development is determined by the interplay between a child's genes and the experiences they encounter.

Over the next three to four years, with the right types of experiences, typical brain development shifts from the primal region to the prefrontal cortex (located behind the front of the skull). Higher-order thinking skills like impulse control, working memory and mental flexibility develop here. The prefrontal cortex is sometimes referred to as the CEO or air-traffic control system as this is where executive-function skills are recruited. This part of the brain doesn't fully develop until the early twenties for females and late twenties for males.

This progressive development of the brain is one reason why some health professionals and educators are concerned about the possible impact the early introduction of screens might have on a child's development. In particular, there are concerns that our noisy, busy digital world may adversely impact our children's attention and overstimulate the sensory region of the brain before the prefrontal cortex has adequately developed. Young children are experiencing a sensory overload before their brains are ready to process this type of input.

As adults, we understand the intense pull of technology on *our* attention and its addictive potential. When a screen involuntarily captures our attention, it activates the sensory (primal) region of the brain and strengthens the neural pathways in this region. In contrast, when we *voluntarily* direct our attention on something (perhaps it's another human or an object in our environment), we're strengthening a completely different set of neural pathways in the prefrontal cortex (impulse control and working memory, for example).

Given that the prefrontal cortex is not yet fully developed in infants and young children, they don't yet have the impulse control required to direct their attention. Instead, their primal orienting response may be dominating and directing their attention. So if we're thrusting young children into a digital world that's constantly grabbing and vying for their attention, we're *potentially* changing the ways that their brains are wired. This *may* compromise their prefrontal cortex development. In particular, there are concerns that children's attention spans may be compromised if they're being immersed in digital worlds that perpetually overload their senses. (This is explored in more detail in Chapter 9.)

There are also concerns that the development of the motor region of the brain, where basic movement skills are learnt, may be compromised if our children's screen time is constantly displacing their opportunities for physical movement. Movement is vital for brain development, but if children are spending too much time tapping and swiping at screens, then they're not having sufficient time developing these essential physical skills. This is particularly concerning for infants aged under two years, as the early years are an essential time for learning basic movement skills that are essential precursors for later development and learning. (This is explored in more detail in Chapter 7.)

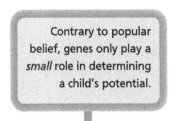

Contrary to popular belief, genes only play a *small* role in determining a child's potential.

Nature or nurture?

We often blame our partner's genetic pool for some of our children's attributes or behaviours. 'He's good at maths like his dad,' or, 'She gets her stubbornness from me.'

Contrary to popular belief, genes only play a *small* role in determining a child's potential. Their genes provide a blueprint for their development, but their experiences determine *when* and *how* their milestones are reached. In fact, a child's genes and environment work *together* to determine their capacity to learn and develop.

Work by the National Scientific Council on the Developing Child suggests that a child's experiences can determine if their genes are turned on or off, or whether they're activated at all. It's estimated that 70 per cent of a child's development is attributed to the experiences they have and approximately 30 per cent to their genes. Therefore, the experiences they encounter early in life, and the environment in which they encounter them, can significantly shape their developing brain architecture – and powerfully affect their development.

For example, the way in which a toddler responds to a stressful situation depends on their temperament, which is determined predominantly by their genes, and the relationships they have with other people in their environment, in addition to the role modelling that they've encountered (usually from their family or carers).

Digital childhoods

Given what we know about typical brain development, it's vital that we closely and critically examine the digital environment in which we're raising our children. A digital world that beeps, pings and booms will exert a powerful influence over our children's development. As discussed, the ways in which we, as parents, interact with technology around our children will also significantly impact on *their* development too.

When parents are perpetually plugged in to their devices, they cannot provide the type of interaction that their children need for optimal development. Children need a type of to-and-fro interaction that develops their relationships and language skills (as Chapters 3 and 4 will explore). To develop, they also need eye contact, and serve-and-return type interactions. This simply cannot happen when a parent is *constantly* staring at a screen. We need to ensure that we're present when parenting.

I'm not suggesting that we *never* use phones around our children, that's certainly not the case. (I do use my phone around my children from time to time.) But we must be careful that we're modelling healthy technology habits around our children. Too much of our time spent on technology can potentially damage and erode the relationships that we form with our children. Failure to pay attention to our children can send them powerful messages about the role of technology – and them!

Case STUDY

Steve was *constantly* obsessed with his smart phone. He'd read emails at the breakfast table (after also checking them upon waking). He'd take his 4-year-old daughter, Ellisa, to the park and would push her on the swing, scrolling through his social media feed. He'd stop mid-way through a conversation with Ellisa if he received an email alert. Ellisa would plead for his attention and Steve would respond *after* he'd done 'just one more thing' on his phone. While Ellisa was only 4 at the time, she was very aware of Steve's actions and often quite upset by his phone obsession.

Ellisa was in tears one day at preschool after she'd been dropped off *without* a kiss from her dad. He was unable to kiss her goodbye because he was 'on an important work call'. Ellisa very eloquently said to her teacher, 'My dad doesn't have a smart phone. It's a stupid-phone. He thinks I'm boring because all he wants to do is talk and read on his phone.'

TECH TIP ✂

Establish phone-free times. Identify specific times in the day when phones will be used. This is often easier than specifying when we *won't* use our phone. Perhaps check social media in the morning, lunch and night and email twice a day. If we establish boundaries, we're much more likely to adhere to them than if we didn't establish any.

So what exactly do developing children need?

Despite living in a digital world, our children's basic developmental needs remain unchanged. Optimal child development still requires very simple things. Children need opportunities to play with objects, toys and other children. They need opportunities to move, interact, explore, build relationships, sleep and eat nourishing foods. This is often called 'ancestral parenting' as it refers to the basic, inherently good ways our grandparents parented.

So while child development is much the same as it always been, we now have digital devices to contend with. Children don't necessarily need flashcards, DVDs, apps, early learning lessons and digital toys to learn and thrive. When carefully selected and used in the right ways, digital technologies can assist young children learn and develop, but they're not essential.

Technology does, however, have the potential to derail a child's development, particularly if it displaces many of the more traditional childhood experiences that *are* essential for development. There's no denying this displacement effect is one of the chief concerns associated with young children using and being immersed in technology. When children use screens, there's an opportunity cost.

The good news is that technology can be used in ways that *support* these essential experiences. Technology can be a valuable aid in supporting children's learning and development. It can enrich and expand a child's development, providing unique and exciting opportunities for them.

> Technology can be a valuable aid in supporting children's learning and development.

It's important to note that this is not about hothousing children and trying to *accelerate* their learning and development. It's about ensuring that each child is provided with experiences in this digital age that will *support*, not *stifle* their learning and development.

Given that we know that experiences account for about 70 per cent of a child's development, it's critical that we provide them with the *right* types of experiences. I call these essential experiences 'building blocks'. These basic, unchanging developmental needs that children require to thrive are outlined below.

Building block #1: Attachments and relationships

For healthy development to occur, babies and young children need to form strong attachments to caregivers. Warm, predictable and loving relationships allow children to feel secure – when they feel safe, they're able to learn.

Regardless of their intellectual capabilities, when children don't feel safe and secure, or experience chronic stress, they can't learn and develop because their cognitive resources are dedicated to ensuring that their basic needs are met, not on learning. Stress also releases cortisol that impacts on neurons in the amygdala, the part of the brain that helps with learning and memory consolidation.

Technology can both *help* and *hinder* children's relationships with parents and carers and also their social skills, depending on how it's used. (We'll explore this in more detail in Chapter 3.)

Building block #2: Language

Babies and young children need ample opportunities to hear and use language. A 2012 study published in the Journal of Vision observed that babies' serve-and-return interactions with adults (that's lots of talking and direct eye-gazing with adults) actually lights up particular parts of the brain that aren't activated when they look at objects.

Language literally wires and builds brains. Parents and educators play a critical role in developing children's language skills. Unfortunately, technology can *hamper* this building block. We know, for example, that the use of background TV can have an adverse impact on children's language development. We also know that baby DVDs, contrary to their marketing claims, can negatively impact on infants' language skills.

Technology can, however, also promote language development if it's used in *healthy* and *helpful* ways. For example, co-viewing can help build children's language skills. (This will be explored in Chapter 4.)

Building block #3: Sleep

Sleep is vital for children's emotional, physical and mental development. During sleep memory consolidation occurs, which is essential for optimal cognitive development to take place. Insufficient or poor-quality sleep can result in poor behaviour and concentration and can impact on children's impulse control and immunity.

The use of digital devices before bedtime and in children's bedrooms is adversely and seriously impacting children's sleep habits. (Practical tips for minimising the impact of technology on children's sleep will be detailed in Chapter 5.)

Building block #4: Play

It is through play that babies and young children develop a host of skills critical for childhood development. Play has been positively associated with improved cognitive abilities and communication competencies as well as enhanced creativity, physical development and emotional skills.

Children need opportunities to experiment and explore with real materials, such as blocks, sand and water. No screen experience, regardless of how sophisticated the graphics are, can ever replace real hands-on experiences (see TECHNO MYTH-BUSTER Box below).

Sadly, digital toys and time spent with screens are displacing traditional play opportunities. Conversely, carefully selected technology can support and enhance young children's play opportunities when used in developmentally appropriate ways. (The concept of play will be more fully detailed in Chapter 6.)

TECHNO MYTH-BUSTER

MYTH: Babies and toddlers can easily learn from screens.

FACT: The research identifies a phenomenon called the 'transfer deficit'. Basically, it explains that digital experiences are no substitute for hands-on experiences with infants. The transfer deficit is believed to persist until children are approximately 30 months of age. Technology can support children's learning, but we know that young children learn more from hands-on experiences than screens, particularly in the first three years of life.

Think about how a 14-month-old baby might learn about the concept of an orange (piece of fruit). She *could* use a flashcard app or watch a DVD that shows her a picture of an orange. It might also tell her the word and perhaps even the colour (and no, we don't need to be in a hurry to teach babies colours as that's not developmentally appropriate).

She might start to recognise oranges in her everyday environment. She might point to oranges when asked by her parents, or if she's a little older, she might even start using the word orange to label real life objects. But has she *really* understood what an orange is?

To have a complete understanding of what an orange is, she needs to touch the rough skin and taste and feel the juicy inside of an orange. She needs to smell the citrus odour, feel the juice run down her hands as she bites into an orange. This is a real understanding.

Children typically develop symbolic competence between 2–3 years of age. This is why it's so much easier for young children to learn from adults and real experiences and objects, than from screens.

Building block #5: Physical movement

Physical movement is critical for a child's intellectual development and overall wellbeing. As the brain is built from the bottom up (remember the sensory and motor regions are developed first), children need to have mastered basic physical skills in order to develop more sophisticated, higher-order thinking skills later on. Much like a builder needs a foundation slab before he builds the second storey or roof, so too do children's brains need the basic foundations to be developed first.

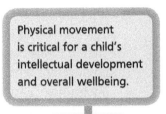

Physical movement is critical for a child's intellectual development and overall wellbeing.

There can be a cascade effect if basic physical milestones (like crawling or rocking) are bypassed.. For example, children who haven't spent enough time rocking, rolling and swinging often have under-developed vestibular systems, which they need for a sense of balance. Therefore, it's almost impossible for children with under-developed vestibular systems to sit in a classroom and pay attention to the teacher. As such, we have to ensure that children's screen habits don't encroach on their opportunities for basic physical movement.

Technology can be used in *healthy* and *helpful* ways to support and promote children's physical movement. For example, we now have interactive TV, exergames, apps that require physical movement and fitness trackers for children. While they're certainly no substitute for outdoor and physical play, they can be a wonderful complement to more traditional physical activity, or a great way to entice more sedentary children to move.

However, due to the opportunity cost, *excessive* technology can be detrimental to a child's physical development. *Excessive* screen time is a contributing factor to childhood obesity and can delay the development of critical physical skills. Excessive or inappropriate use of screens can also impact on children's eye health (and vision) and cause musculoskeletal problems (repetitive stress injury and postural concerns from sitting with a gaming console).

Today's digital children still need to hang off monkey bars, ride bikes, roll down hills and climb trees. It's essential that technology doesn't supersede or displace these experiences. (These factors will be more fully detailed in Chapter 7 and the physical health risks in Chapter 11.)

Building block #6: Nutrition

Quality nutrition is vital for optimal development. For example, there's increasing evidence to confirm that children's diets need to be rich in foods containing essential fatty acids to facilitate optimal brain development.

Technology can help parents access healthy recipes and advice online. However, technology use can also compromise our children's nutrition. The prevalence of food advertising in children's media (and we're not just talking about TV ads anymore) can exert a very powerful influence over their food choices and preferences. Children also tend to snack on unhealthy foods when using screens and screen use during meal times is also impacting on children's eating habits and taste preferences. (Details about nutrition in a digital age will be explored in Chapter 8.)

Building block #7: Executive-function skills

The final essential building block for a child's optimal development is executive-function skills, a suite of generic skills and behaviours that children need to develop in order to become effective learners.

Executive-function skills are developed in the prefrontal cortex of the brain, which is the last part of the brain to be developed (it's the CEO of the brain). Executive-function skills are higher-order thinking skills such as attention, working memory, inhibitory control and mental flexibility. While these aren't new skills, they're imperative skills that children will need to thrive in this digital age.

Technology is certainly changing the development of executive-function skills in both positive and negative ways. For example, we know that children's memory and impulse control skills are being shaped by the use of technology as many children now suffer from digital dementia. (This phenomenon and others are discussed in more detail in Chapter 9.)

In the digital age, children also need to have good inhibitory control (also called impulse control), to know where to direct their attention. But it's difficult for children to be masters of their attention when they're constantly tethered to devices that flash and buzz, causing their attention to be constantly re-oriented. (Executive-function skills will be explored in Chapter 9.)

At a glance

What do children need to thrive in a digital age?

- The early years are vital for a child's optimal development (80 per cent of brain architecture is established before a child is 3 years old and 70 per cent of this development can be attributed to the experiences they encounter). Digital technologies are shaping this process.
- Developing brains and bodies need simple things. Also called ancestral parenting, the way our grandparents parented is an ideal model.
- There are seven essential building blocks for a child's development. Each building block can be supported or stifled by the use of technology.

The next chapter will examine the first building block for development in a digital age: attachments and relationships.

3

Building block #1: Attachments and relationships

It's vital that we protect and value relationships in the digital age.

It's a fundamental, universal human need to connect with others. From the moment we're born, we're literally wired to interact. Depending on how it's used, technology can either *support* or *stifle* our ability to build authentic relationships with others.

When it's used in the right way, technology can help young children build and sustain important relationships. As parents, when we use technology in intentional ways, we can support our children's relationships. For example, helping communicate with family members living afar thanks to advances in video–chat technologies or creating treasured memories of important events and milestones thanks to digital cameras.

On the flipside, if technology is used excessively or if we don't selectively and intentionally use technology *with* and *around* young children, it can potentially interfere with the relationships they form. In this virtual world, face-to-face contact can be displaced and new technologies can dehumanise us in some regards. For this reason, it's vital that we protect and value relationships.

We're wired to connect

Children need to form secure attachments to parents (or a consistent caregiver) for many reasons, but in particular, for optimal brain development. There's been an explosion in research from a range of disciplines such as the neurobiological and social sciences as well as behavioural disciplines that have led to major advances in our understanding of how children's early relationships with parents and/or carers determine their overall development. The good news is that cuddling and loving your children actually builds their brains.

Healthy, reliable, secure relationships literally build children's brain architecture and enable them to learn and develop. When children form loving and predictable relationships with their parent/carer, their brain is able to learn. When their basic needs are met, their brain has the cognitive capacity to focus on other aspects vital to their learning.

However, if they don't form predictable and loving relationships early in life, this can cause toxic stress. This results in the production of cortisol (an adrenal, or stress, hormone) that inhibits brain activity. If all of their attention and cognitive resources are focused on ensuring their safety and security, they don't have the bandwidth to learn effectively – even if they're intellectually capable. In short, feeling unsafe and unsure compromises a child's capacity to learn.

Tips when feeding newborn babies and using screens

In the early days, newborn babies spend a lot of their awake time simply staring at faces. This is called facial mapping. It might appear very innocent and like they're not doing a whole lot, but they're actually engaging in some important visual and cognitive tasks that are a critical part of their development. It's one reason why we need to spend lots of time holding and playing with babies.

Research published in 2012 revealed that infant brains respond to faces in similar ways that adult brains respond, even though the rest of their visual system is still developing. Babies, even newborn babies, will stare at faces for longer periods than any other object. They *want* to stare at our faces. We also know that unique regions of their brain light up when gazing at faces. Therefore, real face-to-face time is vital to their development.

This is why we must be mindful about how we use technology, *especially* around babies when we're feeding them. The term 'brexting' (breast-feeding plus texting) has been used to describe the phenomenon of feeding babies whilst using a mobile device. It's a polarising topic. Some people suggest that mothers have always been distracted when feeding (reading books, or magazines or watching TV) and this is an attempt to make mothers feel guilty, whilst others say that our screen habits are more sinister and may be harming our babies. I sit in the latter camp and believe that we need to carefully consider our brexting habits based on the research at hand (and how I feel instinctively as a mum).

Early on, given their limited waking hours, feeding time is a unique opportunity for this facial mapping to occur. If we're *always* glued to our smart phone or tablet or *always* watching TV while feeding our little ones, they aren't getting the direct gaze that their brains need. They want to stare into our eyes, not watch our faces be illuminated by a screen – they need our direct gaze not our glazed look as we scroll through our phone. We don't want our babies thinking that our phone is part of our visage.

Researchers from the University of California found that fragmented and/or chaotic maternal care may potentially disrupt brain development and lead to emotional disorders in adolescence and adulthood. The study found that erratic maternal care can increase the likelihood of mental disorders such as depression later in life. It's vital to note that the study did not specifically examine mothers' use of mobile devices and nor did it involve human participants (it involved rodents). However, the findings from this study are important to consider and give weight to claims that fragmented maternal care may impair emotional development and wellbeing – I don't think we need to wait for human studies to prove this.

The study found that it's not how much maternal care that impacts on later mental health, but the avoidance of unpredictable and fragmented care that's important. In a digital world where smartphones are vying for our attention, we can see that there are possible risks about constantly being distracted by our devices when caring for babies. Babies' dopamine receptor pleasure circuits are not developed and they require predictable sequences of events for these circuits to mature. Without such predictability, babies' pleasure systems don't mature and this can result in adolescents finding it difficult to feel happy and/or seeking happiness from risky behaviours, or drugs and alcohol.

Obviously I'm not suggesting that we should *never* use our smart phone around our babies, or that we're a bad parent if we watch TV while we're feeding our child. That's certainly not the case – I used my phone and watched TV (or read a book or magazine) while I fed my babies from *time to time*. There's no need for techno-shame – that doesn't serve anybody. Remember, our parents probably read magazines and books when feeding us and we turned out okay! We just have to make sure that we're not scrolling our Facebook feed all the time when feeding our little one. Our babies want direct face-to-face time with us. They need this time for healthy development.

It has been found that warm relationships with parents/carers can help build brain architecture. A 2012 study found that children with responsive, warm and caring mothers (this study *only* examined relationships with mothers) had a larger hippocampus than their peers who didn't receive the same sort of responsive attention. (The hippocampus is the part of the brain that's responsible for memory, learning and stress responses.)

This study showed that a mother's nurturing can literally shape a child's brain anatomy, providing powerful, scientific evidence that the types of relationships we form with our children in the early years of life is absolutely vital for their overall, long-term development. Our love and affection literally builds their brains.

How technology can help our attachment to, and our relationship with, our children

Serve-and-return interactions between us and our child are vital to establishing optimal brain architecture. Colloquially referred to as ping-pong exchanges, they involve us interacting in a conversational manner with our child. While seemingly very natural and simple, this to-and-fro interaction with babies and young children can actually help them develop their language and emotional skills.

The good news is that technology can be used to facilitate these interactions. Here are some common ways that technology can support ping-pong interactions:

1 video–chat technologies
2 interactive technologies
3 character relationships
4 using photos as a stimulus to build memories.

Video–chat technologies
Many modern families now have family members living overseas or interstate, and some have parents who travel for work. Skype and other video–chat platforms like FaceTime have become a common tool for parents and family members to connect. These are amazing technologies that allow us to *establish* and *maintain* relationships, which may otherwise not be as easily maintained by phone calls alone.

A 2010 study published in *Infant and Child Development* confirmed that video–chat platforms can help young children form and build meaningful relationships as well as develop language skills. To maximise the benefits of video–chat technologies:

1 **Pick a good time of the day** – be mindful and avoid times when little ones are tired or hungry. Video–chat platforms require children to sit quietly and focus. This may not work well for them at the end of the day when their concentration is low. Also, make sure that they're well fed or have snacks on hand so that they're not distracted.

2 **Use mobile devices like tablets, smart phones and laptops where possible** – so it's easy to move around different places in the house.

3 **Prepare props** – encourage children to have some toys, books or artwork they've created to share on the call. This keeps it relevant and meaningful and gives young children something concrete to discuss. Also, encourage the other person to bring some props too. Reading a book to a grandchild is a great way to build authentic relationships.

4 **Plan some topic ideas** – before starting a call, brainstorm some possible topics that children can chat about. Have they been somewhere exciting recently? Have they learnt something new? This helps in case they are stuck for ideas or the conversation stalls.

5 **Use gestures** – encourage the other party to use lots of gestures. This will sustain the child's attention throughout the call and prevents them from thinking the other person is simply a talking head, making it a more natural conversation.

6 **Use familiar welcome rituals** – is there a fun greeting that can be used or a song that can be sung at the start of each call? This is particularly important for babies and toddlers. They thrive off repetition and routine and can quickly learn to associate voices and songs with people. It also helps with recognition because little ones typically rely on touch and smell to determine familiarity, but in a video–chat they need to rely on sight and sound.

7 **Encourage some movement** – little ones, particularly babies and toddlers, will tire quickly if required to sit in front of a screen for

extended periods of time. So have realistic time expectations. Try having a shared dance break or encourage children to get up and move around if they're fatigued.

8 **Have closing rituals** – it's important to close the conversation, just like we do when we have a real conversation. It's a lovely and often very special way to build relationships with family members too. I fondly remember my grandmother finishing her Skype conversations with my son when he was a toddler with, 'I love you little lad. Be a good boy for mummy,' followed by a big, virtual smooch. This was played out every time and Taj came to really enjoy this special little ritual, asking Grandma for it if she ever forgot to do it.

Case STUDY

Carly and her fiancé Ben lived in the UK for several years and had regular Skype dates with their niece Charlotte, who was 2–3 years of age at the time. When they arrived home from their international trip she greeted them at the airport with a very puzzled look.

After a couple of moments she said, 'How did you get out of the computer?' She went on to explain, as only 3-year-olds can, that she thought that they lived *inside* her family's desktop computer; she didn't know they were real people!

TECH TIP ✂

Children sometimes assume that the other person lives in the computer because they haven't yet developed object permanence (the ability to understand that an object exists, even if it can't be seen).

Explain to children that it's a real person on the other end of the call, especially if they've never met in person. Perhaps show them photos of the other person in other contexts beyond the video–chat.

Interactive technologies

There's an incredible range of new technologies that are allowing children to experience live ping-pong interactions. These to-and-fro types of interactions are essential for young children, as it engages them cognitively (as opposed to passively). Remember, as previously mentioned the 'video deficit' means that it's much harder for young children to learn from 2D images than from live face-to-face interactions. However, more interactive technologies (like tablet devices and responsive video games) may prove to be better in engaging young children and helping them to extrapolate meaning from what they see on a screen (research in this area is still in its infancy).

Many book apps now offer the capacity to record our own narration to accompany the story. For example, The Wrong Book app allows users to record their voice within the digital book, so that each page is narrated accordingly. This is a great feature for parents who need to travel for work and who want to be there for the night-time book routine. It's also a great way for grandparents (or other family members or friends) to record their voice on an app.

Case study

Kindoma is a book app that has two pop-up windows in the top corners of the screen. By using this app Jan, from Sydney, can read in real time with her grandson Lucas who lives in Canada. She can simultaneously see Lucas while reading with him and her on-screen gestures (perhaps she touches the screen to tap on a character's face) are also replicated on Lucas' screen. They can turn the pages and experience reading using the app. Another example of a similar app is Quality Time (by Quality Time App Pty Ltd).

Character relationships

Children often form relationships with characters on screen. They might talk constantly about Dora or Elmo or Peso. While this might seem quite innocent, it can actually be quite significant in the eyes of a young child. These are called para-social relationships and they can have a positive impact on a child's physical and cognitive wellbeing and development.

On-screen characters are familiar because of repeated viewings. Exposure to them can literally act as an educator to young children. We know that young children often repeat what Dora or Big Bird has told them on a TV episode, but this familiarisation can also enable young children to learn educational content with these characters. This was confirmed by a 2013 study published in *Media Psychology* that found familiarising toddlers with an on-screen character improved their performance on a mathematical task.

Using photos as a stimulus to build memories

I often remind parents and educators that one of the best features on their smart phone or tablet is the camera. Not only can we easily capture photos and/or videos when we're out and about, but we can also revisit these photos/videos with our children *after* the event. This can help to consolidate important memories and hooks for our child to recall positive, past events.

For example, a family trip to the zoo, special moments from a family holiday or a birthday party can be captured on a smart phone. These photos can later be retrieved and viewed by the children. This is a great way for young children to recount, describe and reflect on the experience. They often recall far more details after they've looked at photos and/or videos than what they would have if we had simply discussed the event from memory. Photos or video can also be a great stimulus if we want to explain an event to a friend or family member who wasn't at the event.

In our fast-paced, busy world, we have less and less time to pause and reflect. But scrolling through photos and/or videos on our device's camera roll can allow our child to develop their reflection skills and also retrieve or cement important memories.

As I explore below, however, we do have to be mindful that our preoccupation with capturing moments on our smart phones doesn't interfere with our ability to meaningfully experience the moment.

How technology can hamper the development of children's relationships

When technology is used inappropriately or excessively, it can hamper children's relationships and their ability to connect with others. Following are some of the ways that technology can be detrimental to a child's capacity to build relationships:

1 techno-glect
2 FOMM (fear of missing memories)
3 self-regulation skills
4 social skills deficit
5 bullying
6 exposure to violent content
7 pornography
8 social networking.

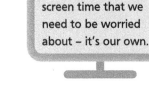

Techno-glect

In some instances, it's not our children's screen time that we need to be worried about – it's our own. In fact, the more we're connected to our devices, the more disconnected we can become from our children. Some of us are so absorbed by our devices that we're parenting without presence. Screens don't only distract us as parents, they can also potentially shape how we *are* as parents.

Sometimes *we* can be so consumed with our devices that our children feel neglected or overlooked. A large-scale global study (with over 6000 participants) by online security company AVG found that 32 per cent of Australian child respondents said their parents spent equal or less time with them than on their devices. Many parents recognise that this is a problem as 54 per cent of parents acknowledged that they checked their devices too frequently.

We have a wealth of screens at our disposal, many of which we carry in our pocket or handbag. We have laptops, tablets and smart phones at an arm's length. For many of us, we can barely remember a life before the invasion of digital devices and it can be very easy to become engrossed in our email or checking our social media.

But we need to be mindful that we're not so engrossed in our devices that it's to our children's detriment. I understand that from time to time we may need to use our smart phone at the park when our little ones are playing, or we may quickly need to take a call for work when we're playing with our kids. That's a modern reality. We just have to be careful we're doing this intentionally and not in ways that distract us from our core role of parenting.

> ... one child attempted to lift his mother's face while she used her tablet, but with no success.

An ethnographic study in 2014 from the Boston Medical Center observed parents in a food court. The study found that many parents were so consumed by their devices that it adversely impacted their children's behaviour. Moreover, the parents who were absorbed by their devices also tended to have more negative interactions with their children. The researchers believed that this was because the children felt like they were competing for attention with their parents' gadgets.

The data revealed that one child attempted to lift his mother's face while she used her tablet, but with no success. Another mother kicked her children under the table after they tried to gain her attention while she used her smart phone. The research showed that there was either very little interaction, harsh interaction or negative interaction between the adults and the children observed.

As parents, our own digital immersion can adversely impact the relationships we form with our children. If we are preoccupied by our gadgets, it can be difficult to be present and emotionally available. We need to be able to switch off from technology at various times of the day and meaningfully interact with our kids.

The ubiquity of technology means that we've been lulled into believing that we need to be tethered to our devices. As a parent I understand that sometimes it's necessary to reply to an email while we're at the park. Perhaps we're responding to a friend's urgent SMS. This isn't about filling parents with techno-guilt (or techno-shame). We never really know anyone's full story so we shouldn't judge or shame other parents who elect to use their gadgets around their children.

But we do need to be mindful about how and when we're using our smart phones and tablets around our children. Are our gadgets robbing our attention? Are we doing Google searches or replying to emails that we could deal with later on when our children aren't around? It's critical that we ensure that our children's safety isn't being jeopardised by our screen obsession.

Tips for preventing techno-glect

In order to be fully present when we are with our children, consider the following suggestions.

- **Assigning tech-free zones** – which specific places can we avoid using technology? Dinner tables, play rooms and bedrooms are recommended as it can minimise any potentially distracting effects that smart phones and other technologies can have on parent–child interactions.
- **Establishing specific tech-free times** – our children need to know that there are sacred times when we won't be using technology. Kids love to know that they have our undivided attention. Children learn important social cues and behaviours through real interactions so we need to ensure that our screen time isn't interfering with these opportunities. Perhaps we could get up early and use devices before our children wake up, or have a policy of no checking email or social media once we walk in the door.
- **Recognising when our child is trying to gain our attention** – scrolling through Facebook or Instagram or replying to an email while our children are vying for our attention isn't fair to them. It can also potentially change the nature of our relationship with our child as we're subliminally sending them the message that they are not as important as our device.

FOMM (fear of missing memories)

Susan Pearse and Martina Sheehan, authors of *One Moment Please*, have coined the term fear of missing memories (FOMM) to describe how we're obsessed with digitally capturing moments using digital devices. From our family vacation snaps to the cute things our children do or a school concert, as parents we're often so fixated on curating the moment digitally that we're not truly absorbing and relishing the experience at hand.

Ironically, we're often so busy composing the right shot, or trying to re-create the moment (where we ask our child to pull the funny face again, or sit looking enthusiastic by their sand castle because our previous photo was blurry) that we're actually missing the moment. As Susan Pearce and Martina Sheehan say:

> *'A live performance used to attract applause, but now it's muted. Hands are busy with a device trying to capture the moment. At school concerts, kids no longer see the faces of their proud parents instead, it's the back of the device as they snap a moment to share, rather than sharing the moment as it happens.'*

For many parents, being able to capture their baby's first steps or their child's sporting victory on their smart phone's camera is priceless. It's a permanent record capturing a precious milestone that we may have otherwise only been able to experience once or on our own (instead of being able to share it with proud grandparents or other family members and friends).

But we need to be mindful of the digital habits we're powerfully teaching our children. Do we need to digitally validate *every* experience? As they observe us scrambling to record events on our smart phone screen, they learn to emulate our digital habits. We want our children to mindfully and authentically experience moments in life – we don't want them to pause or re-create moments to simply have a digital record. And we need to be good role models so our children won't suffer FOMM.

As parents, it's difficult to try and find the right balance between using screens to record and capture important moments while at the same time, not forget to actually enjoy and experience the moment. I don't have the answer here. We need to try and strike a balance (whatever that might mean for us). And we need to ensure that we're not so preoccupied with recording moments that we actually miss them. We need to commit things to our own personal hard-drive as well as to our phone's camera roll.

Case STUDY

I have a confession. When my second son was learning to walk, he took his first steps while my husband was at work. In an attempt to re-capture the moment so as to share it with his dad, I quickly grabbed my phone so I was ready to record a video as soon as he took his next steps.

As a proud mum, while filming I excitedly declared, 'Look ... Billy's taking his first steps!' Only to have my 4-year-old interject in the background with, 'No Mum, these are his second steps. He just walked before. Weren't you watching?' Oops!

Self-regulation skills

It's very tempting to hand over an iPhone to a screaming toddler when every other trick, distraction and strategy has failed to calm them down or ease their frustration. Many modern parents admit to using iPads and iPhones to avert a meltdown or tantrum. In a 2015 poll conducted by the *American Speech–Language–Hearing Association,* nearly 50 per cent of parents of children aged 8 years reported that they often rely on technology to 'prevent behaviour problems and tantrums'. I admit that I have done this too!

But we need to think carefully about the long-term implications of *always* using gadgets as digital pacifiers. If we're constantly wielding screens at our kids to avert or diminish an emotional outburst or ameliorate them when they're bored or frustrated, then they're not developing self-regulations skills. To function effectively in society our children need to learn to deal with emotions in appropriate ways. We don't want to teach our little ones that we reach for technology whenever we're feeling uneasy or dealing with a difficult emotion.

Learning how to self-regulate and deal with our emotions is a critical life skill. It's a skill that children can only learn from experience. Children literally need to experience emotions first-hand in order to learn how to respond in socially appropriate ways.

Case STUDY

Sophie was a very content 8-year-old. She loved playing outdoors with her siblings and playing inside with her doll collection and Lego sets. When Sophie's older brother received an iPad for his birthday, Sophie's parents decided to add some apps on the device for Sophie to use every now and then.

Sophie's brother was happy to share his device with Sophie (so long as he wasn't playing Minecraft). Initially Sophie started playing on it before school, once she was dressed and ready for the day. However, she soon started asking to use it more and more often. She demanded it first thing in the morning and the minute she walked in the door when she arrived home.

When she was told 'no' by either her parents or her brother, a techno tantrum would ensue. Much like a typical toddler tantrum, Sophie would throw herself on the floor and beg to use the device. Sophie's tantrums were becoming so intense that one day, she threatened to punch the wall. Her mum was at her wit's end – she gave in and allowed Sophie to have the iPad.

From that moment forward *every* time Sophie demanded the iPad she would have a techno tantrum until her parents gave in and handed her the device. Her mum described her hideous tantrums as 'worse than when she was as a toddler'.

Sophie had quickly learnt to self-soothe with a screen. Every time she was bored, upset or frustrated she expected (and received) the iPad. Sophie's behaviour deteriorated and her parents ended up taking her to a psychologist. Over time, Sophie's family were able to help her self-regulate without a device, but it took several months to do so.

TECH TIP ⚒

Establish and enforce limits for screen time and stick to the rules. A one-off 'yes' or giving in to their demands for more screen time can quickly become a very slippery slope!

Social skills deficits

There are concerns that screen time is impacting children's face-to-face interactions. Children need real face time to develop essential interpersonal skills and learn to read body language and emotions.

A 2015 study published in the *Journal of Developmental & Behavioral Pediatrics* showed that toddlers who watched a lot of TV were more likely to be victimised by their peers as adolescents. The study followed children from birth to sixth grade and showed that those who watched more TV at 29 months of age reported more instances of being bullied years later.

While this study didn't *prove* that TV viewing causes children to be bullied, it suggests that children who've watched excessive TV may be more vulnerable to bullying. The study's authors proposed that children's communication and social skills might be hampered by their screen habits.

Another study conducted in 2014 and published in *Computers in Human Behaviour* showed that just five days away from screen media improved preteens' recognition of non-verbal emotional cues. The study's authors suggested that increased opportunities for real social interaction *and* time away from screen activities were the reasons for the preteens' improved recognition of emotional cues.

Moreover, it appears that less time for social interaction is likely to result in social skill deficits. The early years are a critical time for building basic social skills and we have to be careful that children's screen habits aren't jeopardising their social skill development.

Cyberbullying

There are also increasing numbers of young children being subjected to cyberbullying. Defined as children sending or receiving hurtful or abusive images, videos or SMS messages over the internet, it can also include imitation of someone online and exclusion from online groups. A 2014 study from the *Social Policy Research Centre* at the University of New South Wales found that around 20 per cent of young children aged 8–17 report being cyberbullied.

Unlike offline bullying, cyberbullying follows children *everywhere*. It's omnipresent and this unrelenting nature means that it's more serious for young children. Repeated exposure can have serious implications including depression and self-harm. Equally, young children who are victims of cyberbullying lack the emotional skills to adequately cope with such scenarios. Some children feel that their parents are ill equipped to deal with such situations because of their limited technology knowledge and often don't report such behaviour.

Young children can also lack the social skills to know what's appropriate online and the anonymity and instant access means that young children aren't thinking about the long-term ramifications of their online actions. Because it's not face-to-face, it often doesn't feel like real bullying. Many young children lack hindsight and empathy and simply don't understand the implications of engaging in cyberbullying.

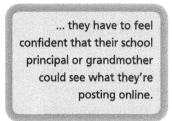

... they have to feel confident that their school principal or grandmother could see what they're posting online.

To prevent our children from being perpetrators of cyberbullying we need to encourage them to pause before they post. Remind them that they have to feel confident that their school principal or grandmother could see what they're posting online. This is often a good filter for children to think about before pressing send or post, as they often lack the hindsight and catastrophe scale to predict the consequences of their actions.

Just like we wouldn't throw children into a pool and expect them to know how to swim, nor should we toss children into the digital river and expect them to know what to do to keep their heads above the water, let alone confidently swim. Our children need our guidance when it comes to using technology in safe and appropriate ways – and so do we as parents and educators. We need to keep informed about how to keep our children safe online and how to teach them appropriate online behaviour.

If our children *are* subject to cyberbullying, we must insist that they:

- **stop** responding to the bully
- **block** the bully (but keep evidence of the incident)
- **report** the incident to the website administrator or school
- **support** our child through this time.

Don't overreact if your child reports bullying. In fact, praise them for seeking help and reporting the incident. Blaming our child will not help – they need our nurturing during this time. Find practical ways to help them cope with the situation at hand and then look to implement preventative measures to reduce the chances of it happening again.

Remember, banning technology is not necessarily a long-term solution to prevent our child from being bullied. Instead, ongoing and transparent conversations will allow our child to feel comfortable reporting any concerns or issues to us in a timely manner, without the incident escalating.

Exposure to violence

Sadly, our young children are increasingly exposed to inappropriate content in the media. A study conducted by Emm found that young children are only three clicks away from accessing explicit material such as nudity or violence when viewing popular TV episodes like *Sesame Street* and *Peppa Pig* on YouTube. This is why co-viewing, which is using technology *with* your child, is essential. (This will be explored in Chapter 4.)

There's a clear cause-and-effect relationship between media violence and children's aggression and other antisocial behaviours. Children who consume more violent media tend to be more aggressive and demonstrate anti-social behaviours.

Further, in 2003 a meta-analysis by Anderson provided clear evidence that aggressive video games can be particularly problematic.

This is especially the case for boys (who tend to play more of these types of games than girls), and are therefore more susceptible to some of the adverse effects.

Video games with violent content can be harmful to children because:

- **Their mirror neurons predispose them to emulating the actions of characters** – this means they may become more aggressive in their play or leisure activities.
- **They elicit an active response** – children are not passively observing violence, but instead are actively participating in it.
- **They are characterised by repetition** – this is like a behavioural rehearsal of violent activities.
- **Violence is often rewarded** – advancing or progressing often requires violent actions.

It's important to note that video games per se are not inherently bad (or good, for that matter). Like all technology, they're just a tool. How they're used will determine if they'll support or stifle a child's development. There are plenty of examples where video game content can promote pro-social behaviours and even academic learning!

Tips for managing distressing or violent news

News coverage of natural disasters or senseless violence is often upsetting for adults, much less our children. In a world with 24/7 news coverage, it's sometimes difficult to shield children from these distressing global events as shootings, missing people, natural disasters and violence flood our screens.

Unlike adults, young children don't have the hindsight or rational-thinking skills to filter this incoming information. They need help understanding and contextualising the events they're witnessing.

While very young children may not be able to process the language presented on news and current affairs programs, they're still absorbing graphic or distressing images. As a result, frightening media coverage can have lasting adverse effects on our children's emotional development.

Children may not have the language skills to articulate their concerns or angst, but they can still be internalising and processing these images. As such, they might feel worried, anxious, upset or angry, but not be able to convey these emotions.

If children have seen or heard about distressing events reassure children that they're safe. Help them to rationalise and localise the experience. Explain that it's one-off and a rare occurrence. (Often when natural disasters or violent world events occur, news footage is limited so the same images are replayed over and again. Young children can therefore mistakenly think that the event is re-occurring, so reassurance and explanation is vital.) Be mindful of your own reaction, too, as children can often sense if parents are upset or anxious.

Other considerations include the following three things:

1 **Minimising news exposure** – turn off the TV when distressing world events occur. There's no rush to introduce distressing events to children before they have the emotional skills to cope with them. (Many children under seven are still trying to distinguish between what's real and what isn't, and frightening images can confuse this distinction.) If we want to stay up-to-date, we can use more passive forms of media (newspapers or social media) away from little ones.
2 **Not dismissing their fears** – provide children with the facts about world events if they've heard about them from peers or siblings. Again, reassure them that they're safe.
3 **Knowing what your child can cope with** – as parents, we know our children best. Some children can cope with learning about upsetting world events while others don't have the emotional bandwidth to deal with them.

Pornography

Children are increasingly accessing pornographic material. According to research conducted by Sydney University psychologists Sitharthan and Sitharthan, children are starting to view pornography between 11 and 13 years of age.Moreover, a 2012 publication from the St. James Ethics Centre reported the worrying trend that young children are *intentionally* accessing porn, sometimes as young as eleven years of age.

There are also reports that there's an increase in youth-produced child pornography, according to a study conducted by Bobkowski, Brown and Neffa in 2012. Young children under 15 years are creating and curating explicit pornographic material using popular online sites and social media. Some tweens are also engaging in self-generated pornography too, taking nude or semi-nude photos or videos of themselves engaging in erotic or sexual activities and electronically sharing these on social media and instant messaging sites like Instagram and Kik.

> ... it's too late to wait until children are teenagers to start having these conversations.

It's imperative that teachers and parents have open discussions with young children about viewing and creating pornographic content. Young children are often unaware that it's not appropriate for them to engage in sexual activities, especially if they're consuming pornography – and it's too late to wait until children are teenagers to start having these conversations. As uncomfortable as this may make us, it's vital that we start these conversations with our tweens.

Case study

Cara, a 9-year-old girl reported 'an itchiness' on her genitals. Her mother took her to the family doctor and it was discovered that Cara had a sexually transmitted disease. Her mother was horrified to learn that Cara had been engaging in what she described as 'sexing' with her friends.

Cara's mum had been vigilant about what Cara was watching at home and used internet filters to prevent Cara and her younger sister from accessing inappropriate material on the home computer and tablet. Cara had been given a smart phone when she turned nine, and although her mum had disabled the internet app on the device, she had allowed Cara to set up a Snap Chat account. (She felt that it was okay as many of Cara's friends' parents had allowed their children to use the app.)

Unfortunately, it was via Snap Chat that Cara and her friends had been able to view (and in some instances upload) pornographic material – resulting in the experimentation that caused the sexually transmitted disease.

There's been a disturbing trend where young children, sometimes younger than Cara, are engaging in sexual acts and in some cases sexually abusing each other. Treatment services are reporting that increasing numbers of young children are engaging in sexual behaviour too and there are concerns that easy access to pornographic material is partly to blame.

Children are exposed to highly sexualised content in the media. Some TV and movie characters, protagonists in apps and video games are often portrayed in very sexualised ways. This is impacting on the formation of children's body image and is causing the premature sexualisation of children.

It was previously thought that the onset of puberty was when children started forming ideal body images but research from the Australian Institute of Family Studies now suggests that this occurs much earlier. This is supported by research published in *The British Journal of Psychiatry* that children as young as eight years of age are expressing body dissatisfaction. This can result in social problems, depression symptoms, poor self-esteem and eating problems, which can put our children at risk of eating disorders in their teens.

Tips for minimising the access of inappropriate content

While some of the facts above are frightening, again, it is worth being alert, not alarmed. Here are some of the things you can do to minimise exposure and harm.

1 **Install filters on the internet** – we can filter websites that we don't want our child accessing and specific domains we want to block. I highly recommend Family Zone.

2 **Set up parental controls and filters on computers, smart phones and tablets** – using the settings, we can create user accounts and set up different protections for each user.

3 **Turn on SafeSearch on Google** – this filters out sexually explicit videos and images from Google search results and results that can possibly link to explicit content.

4 **Turn on Safety Mode when using YouTube** – this blocks inappropriate materials such as pornographic or objectionable language. (It's important to note that this feature is not 100 per cent accurate as it relies on other users flagging content as inappropriate.)

5 **Use kids' browsers** – these browsers are designed specifically for children with games, pre-approved websites, email and other age-appropriate activities. Popular examples include Zoodles, Kidoz and Kidzui. They typically have a monthly membership fee.

6   **Create playlists on YouTube** – use an app like KidsVideo: Kids YouTube Playlist to create a playlist of appropriate videos. This minimises the chances that our children can access inappropriate content.

7   **Have open conversations** – talk often and openly about what your child is doing online. (We'd much prefer our child learn about sex from us than from their peers or online sources.)

Note: while these strategies can help reduce the chance our children will access inappropriate content, no filter or setting is 100 per cent effective and *active* parental supervision is still essential. This is why it's important to have clear rules about *where* technology can be used in the family home – devices should only be used in high-traffic areas of the home like the kitchen, living room or lounge room (and be kept out of bedrooms).

Social networking

It's been estimated that over half of all ten year olds have used an online social media site. Children are forming more and more online relationships and can chat and interact on online forums within websites and some apps and video games like Minecraft and Club Penguin. Parents are frequently shocked to learn that these are examples of social media for young children.

While these online forums can be great ways for children to interact and connect, it's critical that parents monitor their children's use of these platforms. In many instances, these chat rooms are not policed or adequately supervised and children can be subject to cyberbullying or cyber-safety risks.

Case study

James was a responsible 10-year-old boy who'd recently become infatuated with Minecraft. He'd spend hours crafting a variety of materials and building his online world with his online friends using the multi-player mode. Using the chat facility, James regularly interacted with his friends and other users playing on the server.

James had a falling out with one of his international friends. The disgruntled friend accessed James' passwords and in turn accessed his parents' credit card details and identities and posted highly sensitive information about James' family including their address and phone number on the internet. James' distraught parents had to call the police to intervene.

TECH TIP ✂

Monitor young children's online activities and talk to them about what information is appropriate (and inappropriate) to view and divulge online.

As parents and educators, we need to teach children what's safe and appropriate to share on social media sites and how to interact appropriately online. Many of us falsely assume that children, being digital natives, will know how to behave online, but children still need to be *explicitly* taught the skills for online etiquette, interaction and safety: they're not learnt via osmosis.

We need to be very careful not to introduce social media sites to our children prematurely. (It is illegal for a start: the required age limit in most instances is 13 years of age.) If social media sites are not carefully managed, even when our children are above the age limit, there's a risk they can promote narcissistic tendencies and cause unnecessary social anxiety at an age when children are eager for external approval and validation.

We also need to be mindful that we're not over-inflating the importance of social media sites with our own children too. Children absorb our digital habits and if we're constantly posting images of our children on social media sites and telling them how many likes or shares or comments our posts received, we can convey very powerful messages to our children about their perceived value.

Technology's no substitute for real connection and a child's ability to form and sustain relationships is critical for their development. No app or social media site is anywhere near as rich and meaningful as what in-person connections offer. Children need to connect in real life (ironically our tweens and teens use the acronym IRL to describe this phenomnenon).

If we use technology carefully, we can support and build our children's relationships with both ourselves and other important people in their lives. However, if used excessively or inappropriately with or around children, it can potentially diminish the quality of our relationships, resulting in a disconnect with our loved ones.

At a glance

How to build relationships in a digital age:

- **Use technology *with* children** – where possible, use technology *with* young children. Watch TV, play a video game or use the tablet with them. This not only develops their language skills and capacity to learn, but it also shows them that we're interested in what they're doing with technology. (This will pay dividends years later when we want our child to have an open relationship and frank discussions with us regarding technology.)
- **Look for interactive technologies** – Skype and interactive book apps are a great way to leverage technology to build relationships with family members who travel or live overseas. Use these tools to build or maintain relationships.
- **Be mindful of our own technology habits** – children naturally emulate our behaviour so it's essential that we think very carefully about how we use technology around our children. We also need to establish tech-free times and places and avoid placing too much importance on social media.

- **Set up parental controls and filters** – to determine what content young children can view and consume. Actively supervise what they're doing online (even when you have controls and filters set up).

The next chapter will examine the second block for development, language, and the ways in which technology can help and hinder this building block.

4

Building block #2: Language

Technology can support children's language development if it's used appropriately and if it doesn't infringe on opportunities for real face-to-face interaction.

Language allows children to name people, objects, feelings and places. It also gives them more information to bring to new learning situations. It's through language that children make sense of the world.

Language acquisition begins before birth – long before babies utter their first words even. The early years are a sensitive period for language development as it is when the neural pathways for language are cultivated, facilitating later learning.

It is during the first three years of life that a child makes the most dramatic gains in language – there is literally an explosion in their vocabulary and sentence use. (At 12 months, babies have a vocabulary of up to 50 words, but by the age of 6 this has expanded to about 5000 words.)

As research has consistently identified, it is imperative that babies and young children both *hear* and *use* language. A study conducted by Hart and Risley showed that 86–98 per cent of the words used by children by the age of three were derived from their parents' vocabularies. It is therefore critical that parents immerse young children in language-rich environments at home. It is also vital that technology doesn't stifle this process.

Interacting with babies is critical

Through her studies, language acquisition researcher Patricia Kuhl has shown that babies and toddlers benefit from serve-and-return interactions with parents and/or carers. These serve-and-return interactions allow babies to develop critical language skills such as expressive and receptive language.

Infants naturally attempt to interact with others through babbling, gestures, vocalising and facial expressions, and these simple acts build and nurture relationships with parents/carers (as identified in the previous chapter). Importantly, they also form and strengthen brain architecture.

> Babies and toddlers need our direct gaze, not our glazed look from our screens.

New brain-imaging technologies have provided clear evidence of what happens neurologically when adults interact with babies. A 2015 study found that it is the combination of *both* infant-directed speech from parents and direct gaze that leads to enhanced brain activation.

A critical period for sound development is between 8–10 months of age, as this is when babies can recognise and distinguish the special sounds of their own native language. Those neural pathways for sounds that are not heard in the infant's environment are pruned back, or completely diminished at this time, so it's critical that infants and young children have opportunities to engage in back-and-forth communication with us. This serve-and-return interaction is vital for their development.

It's essential that as parents we're not constantly tethered to technology and distracted by our devices when interacting with infants. Not only do they want to hear us use language and interact with us, they also rely on visual cues to interact and want to watch our mouth movements. If we're too absorbed by our screens, or not fully immersed in these interactions, it could potentially interfere with our infant's language development. Babies and toddlers need our direct gaze, not our glazed look from our screens.

Is there a good age to use my smart phone with my infant?

There's no safe or ideal age at which to introduce technology to little ones and there's absolutely no hurry to do so either. I advise parents to err on the side of caution. In the early months and years, young children really only need simple things to thrive: lots of exposure to language (including plenty of serve-and-return interactions with adults) combined with lots of opportunities to move, explore their world and see what their bodies can do (see Chapter 7 for more details). Screen time can interfere with these skills: young babies and children need laps, not apps!

Infants and toddlers learn less from TV and touch screens than from live demonstrations because it's difficult for them to understand how information depicted on a screen relates to the real world. This is the transfer deficit. Research by Anderson and Pempek has shown that babies and infants learn half as much and recall it for much shorter periods of time when using touch screens.

Now before we fret or worry that we've exposed our baby to TV or other screen time in the first two years, rest assured that a little bit of technology is unlikely to be harmful. Small amounts, of around 15–30 minutes/day is likely to be fine. I simply encourage parents to limit the time children under two years spend on screens, and use it intentionally.

If we do want to use technology with our little one, we should try to use it together. Use it as a way to cement our relationship with them and immerse them in language. For example, watch videos and photos from smart phones and discuss what's observed. Explore new words or ideas, sounds and images online. Try to connect what they're watching on DVDs and TV to their life and experiences (to compensate for the video deficit).

We need to make screen time a social and interactive experience with our child and ensure that time spent *with* screens doesn't replace or substitute time spent with us or another caregiver.

Word gap

Roben, Cole and Armstrong have conducted longitudinal research that's shown that a word gap emerges around 18 months of age and continues to widen and exacerbate as children get older. Moreover, Hart and Risley's work found that 4-year-old children from language-rich environments (whose average word exposure was approximately 45 million words at age 4), had been exposed to 30 million more words than children from poor language environments (whose average word exposure was approximately 15 million words at age 4).

It is therefore paramount that we spend as much time as possible building our children's language skills in the early years. This means that as parents we need to be careful that we're not missing vital opportunities to interact with our children because we are distracted by our devices. It's also another reason why we need to be careful that young children's screen habits are not adversely impacting their language skills.

Simple ideas to boost children's language skills in a digital age

- **Use parentese with infants** – *Brain Rules* author John Medina claims that the high-pitched, exaggerated, long-vowel sounds and short-clipped consonant sounds we use when talking to babies is exactly what their brains need to learn language.
- **Sing** – songs are an ideal way to build children's language skills (and lots of fun).
- **Recite nursery rhymes and poems** – children love hearing rhymes and respond positively to rhythm and they help children develop language skills in a playful manner.

If you can't remember the words to songs or nursery rhymes, check out YouTube, or the Baby Karaoke page and app (http://raisingchildren.net.au/baby_karaoke/baby_karaoke_landing.html).

How technology is changing children's language skills

When children use screens, there's an opportunity cost – they're *not* doing something else. With infants and toddlers, the displacement effect associated with screen use can be quite substantial given their limited waking hours each day.

If we consider a young child's screen time as a percentage of their waking hours, we can see that it can sometimes displace other important developmental opportunities. For example, a youngster might only be awake for 10 hours a day, so if they're watching 1–2 hours of TV/day this is 10–20 per cent of their waking time spent with a screen. This clearly limits the time available to them to engage in language-rich experiences.

A British government study found that teachers and health professionals are reporting increasing numbers of children are entering kindergarten with under-developed language skills. This study found that there was a 71 per cent increase in the number of school children requiring expert help for speech and language difficulties between 2005 and 2011. Anecdotally, paediatric health professionals are also reporting similar concerns in Australia and other developed countries.

Case study

Michelle is a speech pathologist. She has noticed a decline in young children's language skills and is treating increasing numbers of young children who present with communicative difficulties including language delays and poor receptive language skills (hearing and processing language).

She and her colleagues have been speculating that children's screen time is encroaching on their opportunities for direct conversation with parents. She explains, 'Young children are spending less time engaging in face-to-face interactions with adults, siblings and peers and more time with screens. They're not spending time sitting down at meals and actually talking, and kids aren't singing songs and nursery rhymes like they used to do with their parents.'

Michelle is concerned that children's language skills are impaired due to their screen habits. She continues, 'The first three years are a critical period for brain development. Children primarily learn through verbal communication in ways that technology can't replicate. Young children *need* interactions with humans. Screens can't provide this type of interaction. Don't get me wrong. I'm not a Luddite. In fact, sometimes I recommend that children use apps as part of their treatment. But it's really important that parents interact too and not rely on the app to do all the therapy alone.'

Increased screen time is not the only reason why there's a possible decline in our children's language skills. While it's highly likely that screens are *part* of the problem, we must also consider other factors that may account for the decline in children's language skills. For example, changes in the pace of family lifestyles (reducing time available for interaction and verbal communication) and the increase in early intervention services (meaning that children who would have once had language delays or difficulties are now being identified much earlier on, often in prior-to-school settings) may also be responsible.

How technology can help children's language development

Technology can support children's language development if it's used appropriately and if it doesn't infringe on opportunities for real face-to-face interaction. It can support language development in the following ways:

1 co-viewing
2 television
3 book apps
4 audio books
5 interactive apps.

Co-viewing

Co-viewing, which involves using technology *with* our children, is beneficial for their learning and language development in particular. Three separate studies published in the *Journal of Broadcasting and Electronic Media* from 1999–2008 provide compelling evidence to support co-viewing, which means using technology *with* our child.

The aim of co-viewing is twofold:

1 **To mitigate the possible negative media effects on children and reduce the chances of exposure to inappropriate content** – it also means that parents can respond quickly to children's concerns and questions if they were to view something unsavoury or violent.
2 **To increase the likelihood of children learning and benefiting from using technology** – over forty years of research with *Sesame Street* has shown greater learning benefits occur when children co-view.

In many modern households, the digital landscape has changed. Co-viewing is no longer restricted to simply watching TV with our child. There is a range of digital technologies being viewed and consumed in family homes, making co-viewing much harder to implement. In response to these changes, a new term has been coined called joint media engagement (JME). It can happen anywhere, anytime and occurs when multiple people interact together with digital (or even traditional) media.

The benefits of JME extend beyond TV viewing alone. Research published in 2009 in the *International Journal of Learning and Media* showed that most children's media activities benefit from adult, or even sibling or peer interactions. Video games, eBooks and touch-screen games are so much richer when children use them *with* someone else. Through verbal interaction children engage in deeper levels with screens, use language and solve and discuss problems.

... most children's media activities benefit from adult, or even sibling or peer interactions.

Parents can provide spontaneous explanations, respond immediately to questions, share their perspectives and encourage children's participation.

Children's learning is supported with JME because parents can provide resources to enable children to make sense of the experience. Research by Leibham, Alexander, Johnson, Neitzel and Reis-Henrie found that children are more likely to engage in a sustained exploration of a topic or idea, which can build their content knowledge, if parents co-view. It also prevents the digital-zombie effect whereby children become so immersed in a game or app that they're oblivious to what's going on around them (that transfixed state where you could be offering them chocolate for dinner and they'd be completely oblivious).

Case STUDY

My 4-year-old son loved watching *The Octonauts*. After one particular episode he explained to me how one of the sea creatures used echolocation to source food. Using sophisticated language, he explained that some sea creatures had this particular adaptation as a way of compensating for their poor eyesight. (Yes, I was just as surprised to hear his explanation!)

We then had an in-depth conversation about what echolocation is and how animals use it (thank goodness for Google!) and discovered that other animals also have this capability. This kind of opportunity is unlikely to have occurred had he not watched the episode.

The hectic pace of modern family life means that it's not *always* possible to use technology *with* our children. Obviously, we want to try to aim for using technology *with* our children as much as possible, but as a mum, I completely understand that sometimes we rely on screens to entertain or occupy our little ones in order to make a phone call, complete some work or prepare a meal. And that's okay. There's no need to be riddled with guilt in these instances.

Tips for co-viewing

It's so important, where feasible, to use technology *with* young children as much as possible. In particular, very young children (two and under) have difficulty making the connection between 2D screens and real-life 3D objects and need our help. (Researchers call this the video deficit.)

For example, children may see a horse on the TV, but may not instantaneously recognise a horse in a book or in real life. Simply talking to them can help with these understandings as well as consolidate and strengthen the neural pathways in the brain responsible for language.

For older children, it's still important that we co-view as we're building relationships and sending powerful messages that we value what they do online. When we create and encourage an open environment around technology, we reinforce that it's not secretive or taboo – and that our behaviour online matters.

Here are some ideas to make co-viewing easy and achievable for all ages:

1 **Keep devices in central and accessible areas of the home** – such as the living room or kitchen. This way you can be involved and set all-important boundaries.

2 **Don't try and go it alone** – engage the help of siblings, peers and grandparents so children can have someone to talk to and with while using technology.

3 **Ask questions** – about what they're doing and what they're watching, especially if you can't sit down and use it with them. Show an interest in their on-screen activities.

4 **Keep talking** – before, during and after tech time. This can prevent the digital-zombie effect, but don't feel you need to do all of this every time they use a screen! Before they use technology, quickly ask them what they plan on doing, or what they expect the episode or app to be about. (This is called cognitive priming and it sets the brain up to tune into what to watch out for.) While they're using the technology, check in with them every now and then. Remember, we don't want to interrupt their state of flow, but try asking them how the characters are dealing with the problem in the TV episode or how they plan on progressing in the game. After they've used technology, encourage them to explain what they did or observed. This can help them – and us! – determine what they understood (or perhaps didn't understand) and we can build on the experience further with teachable moments.

5   **Be prepared** – have a list of TV programs, video games or a folder with apps that you're happy for your child to use when you're not able to co-view. Literally write down the TV program names, create playlists on sites like YouTube, pre-record TV programs or have a physical collection of DVDs.

6   **Lighten up** – our interactions don't always have to relate to the learning goals or content of the show. And we can interact when watching non-educational shows and children will still benefit, for example discussing how characters on TV shows handled social situations. This can be a great platform to have rich conversations about some big issues. Remember, it's ok to just have fun sometimes too!

Television

One of the most common myths related to kids and technology is that TV is bad for them so, as parents, we're often surprised (and elated) to hear that TV can actually be beneficial to our children.

In 2013 Mares and Pan examined a substantial body of research that's investigated *Sesame Street* and its impact on preschoolers. They found that educational and age-appropriate content can help preschoolers learn and enhance their language and cognitive development. Obviously, content is paramount, and it's critical that we provide educational programs for young children while ensuring that their screen time is not excessive.

... TV can actually be beneficial to our children.

Tips on what to look for in quality TV programs for young children

Children's TV programs should ideally feature:

- **repetition** – the human brain literally hankers for repetition. This is why our child wants us to read the same book every single night. And it is why Dora repeats the same language throughout each episode. Children's TV programs employ language repetition to help children learn new vocabulary or concepts.

- **a linear storyline** – TV programs for children should follow a straightforward storyline. There should be an orientation, a complication and a resolution. Too many plot twists or deviations from this format can confuse young children.

- **predictability** – a predictable format allows for familiarity and means children can dedicate their attention to understanding the episode, not anticipating what might happen next.

- **a very slow-pace** – rapid-fire, fast-paced screen action is often too much for young brains to focus on and places extra demands on their attention. This can cause cognitive overload whereby the child tends to focus on the less essential aspects of the TV program (i.e. they might process the animated characters' actions and incidental comments, not the plot).

- **interactivity** – look for programs that encourage participatory interaction such as asking children questions or encouraging them to do something physical while they watch. For example, *Play School* and *Sesame Street* often pose children questions during the episode and suggest off-screen activities at the end of episodes.

TECH TIP ✂

Many media developers describe their programs as educational because they know that parental techno-guilt diminishes if we think we're using educational resources. But not all of these programs are in fact educational.

To find quality TV programs, parents/carers are advised to install the Common Sense Media app (http://www.commonsensemedia. org/mobile) and review the Australian Children's Television Foundation's website (http://www.actf.com.au), where we can keep up-to-date with the best TV programs for children (both educational and entertainment).

Book apps

Book apps and digital stories are no replacement for the traditional book, but they can certainly complement traditional book experiences and boost language skills. Book apps include animations, sound effects, background music and interactive elements. And so long as these are well designed and don't encroach on a child's ability to comprehend the story, they can be a great way to enhance a child's book experience.

Many forward-thinking publishers are now utilising augmented reality capabilities to bring traditional printed books to life. For example, the *Numberlys* book can be brought to life with an accompanying app from Im-ag-no-tron. When the printed book is scanned using a touch screen's camera, background music plays or animated characters appear on the touch screen. These are completely unique ways of reading and are quite different to more traditional books.

TECHNO MYTH-BUSTER

MYTH: Book apps and digital stories are better than traditional books.

FACT: The design of book apps determines if they're more beneficial than traditional books.

Reading book apps and digital books elicit very different cognitive processes than traditional print books. In some book apps, so much of the story is clearly delivered to the child – with animations, background music and sound effects – that sometimes very little cognitive effort is required on their part. For example, they don't have to construct the story in their head like they do with a traditional book.

It's the same experience for us as adults when we've read the book and then go and see the movie version. Rarely is the movie ever as good as the book because we've created the story in our imaginations.

This isn't the case with traditional books and again, this is why a balanced approach to reading is necessary. Children need to read both digital *and* traditional books.

TECH TIP ✂

Look for simple design in book apps. Too many distracting features (like excessive background music or distracting animations) have been shown to compromise children's comprehension.

Audio books

Audio books are a wonderful alternative to both book apps and traditional books. Again, they're no substitute for reading printed books. They develop children's listening, comprehension, visualisation and imagination skills as children conjure up images themselves as opposed to having them delivered or provided to them.

Audio books can also boost vocabulary and teach children the important skill of focus (they have to filter out distracting elements like background music and sound effects sometimes). Audio books can also be a great way to engage reluctant or struggling readers.

Interactive technologies

Touch-screen devices offer new opportunities for children to engage in more interactive screen experiences. Unlike passive types of media, tablet devices encourage children's active participation and interaction (depending on the design of the app) so it has been assumed that this increased engagement *may* enhance learning.

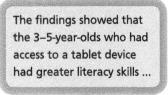

The findings showed that the 3–5-year-olds who had access to a tablet device had greater literacy skills ...

Of the few available published studies regarding preschoolers and interactive apps is a 2012 Australian study of 109 preschoolers and their literacy habits. The study was designed to ascertain if the children's access to tablet devices at home impacted on their literacy skills. The findings showed that the 3–5-year-olds who had access to a tablet device had greater literacy skills (better letter-sound knowledge and name-writing skills) than their peers who didn't have access.

It's important to note that this was a correlational study. It didn't *prove* that tablet devices improved learning outcomes, but did show a connection between tablet device access and literacy skills (it's plausible that parents who invested in tablet devices also spent more time reading with their child, or engaging in literacy-building activities).

How technology can hamper children's language development

Just as technology can support children's language development, it can also hamper their language skills. Technology can interfere with children's language skills in these ways:

- techno-glect
- transfer deficit
- baby DVDs
- background TV.

Techno-glect

As outlined in the previous chapter, our absorption in digital devices is potentially altering the relationships we form with our children. It's also possibly altering our children's language skills because they're not getting the serve-and-return interactions that are vital for language development.

In a 2015 study conducted by the American Speech–Language–Hearing Association, 52 per cent of parents believed they had fewer conversations with their child than they'd like to because of their technology habits. As parents we need to be careful that we're not so immersed in our digital devices that we're not adequately interacting and engaging with our children.

Transfer deficit

Research conducted by Anderson and Pempek and Barr provides evidence that young children learn less from TVs and touch screens than from real, live demonstrations. This phenomenon describes young children's inability to transfer learning from screens to real-life situations.

The transfer deficit is believed to persist until children are approximately 30 months of age. This means that young children need ample opportunities in the early years to engage in rich, hands-on tasks. It also means that if they're to use screens in these early years that we carefully consider what Lisa Guernsey calls the 3 Cs: child, content and context.

> *If we focus on the content and context of children's screen time, we can have a positive impact on their development.*

In particular, if we focus on the *content* and *context* of children's screen time, we can have a positive impact on their development and also help to ameliorate the transfer deficit. In terms of *content*, we need to ensure that we're exposing children to age-appropriate content. (For suggested TV programs and apps check out the Common Sense Media app that curates and reviews the latest technology for families and educators: https://www.commonsensemedia.org/mobile.)

In terms of *context*, we need to minimise exposure to background media (see the next section on background TV) and also co-view where possible (see previous section in this chapter for more information about co-viewing).

It's important to note that screen time for young children (under 2 years) is not necessarily harmful; it's just not likely to be the best use of their time. Basically, we need to be very careful and selective about *what* media we use with very young children (in fact, it's important with *all* children). What they watch and how we interact with them while they're watching is absolutely critical.

Content really is king! But the ways in which children use technology, the context, is just as important too.

Baby DVDs and programs

The baby DVD industry is estimated to be worth over $US200 million per year in the United States alone. New parents and well-intentioned grandparents and friends often purchase baby DVDs as the marketing claims suggest that these educational products give infants a head start on their development and boost brain development and language.

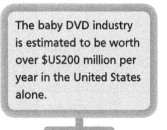

The baby DVD industry is estimated to be worth over $US200 million per year in the United States alone.

Not only are there baby DVDs, but also a range of educational video games, techno-toys and touch pads specifically designed for children under three. As parents we're under increasing pressure to purchase baby media devices and give our little ones a head start.

As parents we're under increasing pressure to purchase baby media devices and give our little ones a head start.

Despite the marketing hype and claims of many baby DVD products, there's an absence of research to substantiate their claims that these devices offer any educational advantages to infants. In 2007 Disney, the owner of the *Baby Einstein* DVDs, was forced to offer a refund on their baby DVD range after the Federal Trade Commission found that their website and packaging claims were not supported by research.

A 2007 article published in *The Journal of Pediatrics* concluded that baby media doesn't provide educational benefits to infants. They're not the teacher in the living room, despite marketing claims that suggest otherwise. Zimmerman, Christakis, and Meltzoff found that for every hour per day that babies aged 8–16 months watched baby DVDs, they knew on average six to eight fewer words than babies who didn't watch them. The baby media, DVDs and videos also had no effects, positive or negative, on toddlers between 17 and 24 months of age. So marketing claims that such products will boost language weren't actually grounded in research.

Many baby media products have a narrative, or story, format. Child development research tells us that infants aren't able to understand narratives until between 18–22 months of age so many educational DVDs aren't actually developmentally appropriate.

> ... many educational DVDs aren't actually developmentally appropriate.

Now before panic sets in because our child *has* watched or uses baby DVDs, let me provide some reassurance. Just because our little one has watched these DVDs it doesn't mean we've failed or messed them up. It's highly unlikely that small doses of these videos and DVDs are harmful. As part of a balanced range of learning experiences, it's unlikely that these products will adversely affect young children.

In fact, the average length of time spent watching a baby DVD is reported to be 9 minutes, so it's unlikely that a couple of minutes here or there will cause long-term problems or adverse effects. But if we do choose to use baby DVDs, we must use them sparingly and use them knowing that they're not going to 'teach' our infant. And when using the DVDs we need to try, where possible, to watch them with our infant and discuss with them what they're seeing on-screen and help them to connect it to their real-life experiences.

Don't be duped into thinking that baby DVDs and media are educational or will boost your baby's IQ or language. This is simply not the case – and there's no clear evidence to support any benefits of baby media. So don't feel pressured to introduce them to your child.

As mentioned, given babies' limited waking hours each day, it's better that they spend their time engaged in activities other than screen time. As a parent, I understand that sometimes we need a break and baby media can be an effective way to entertain little ones (when we need to have a shower or make an important phone call), but we need to be very careful that we don't *always* rely on the digital babysitter.

Babies can very quickly become accustomed to be pacified by screens and technology if we're constantly using baby media to soothe or entertain them. Instead, we need to look for other ways to engage our infant when we need some solo time. Block play and tummy time, for example, are some of the most effective ways to entertain infants *and* build their brains.

A 2014 study published in the *Journal of Educational Psychology* confirmed that babies don't learn to read from baby media. DVDs, flashcards and videos can't teach infants to read either. In fact, we don't need to be teaching infants to read at all – there's no hurry to introduce formal academic skills to infants and it's not developmentally appropriate.

We don't need to purchase products to boost our children's language either. We know from the research that infants benefit most from simple, serve-and-return interactions with parents. In fact, we don't need to hurry childhood.

So why do babies enjoy baby media?

Many parents with colicky babies often report that baby DVDs are their saving grace. Even when their baby is screaming, if the TV is switched on or a baby DVD is played, their child's crying often instantly stops.

The Pavlov effect has been used to explain why babies are drawn to baby DVDs (and why infants quickly realise where the TV screen is and twist their necks to catch a glimpse). The rapid sequencing of images and musical accompaniment is the primary reason why babies are initially attracted to screens as the constantly changing images and sounds cause an orienting response. This is a primitive reflex and so the primitive part of the brain is activated (much like other primitive reflexes like the startle reflex) and is a protective reflex. It automatically alerts us to potential dangers and focuses our attention. The newness and constantly changing images and audio actually *engage* the baby and explains why they appear to be mesmerised by what they see on screen (and forget about the pain associated with colic).

TECHNO MYTH-BUSTER

MYTH: Young children can learn a second language from apps and DVDs.

FACT: Digital devices are no substitute for real interaction. Children benefit most from interactions with real people.

A 2013 study published in *The Journal of Neuroscience* suggests that immersing children in a bilingual environment before the age of four gives them the best chance of becoming fluent in both languages. A child's brain is most receptive to learning another language during this period of time. This has prompted a deluge of digital products being designed and marketed towards parents to captialise on this prime cognitive time for learning a second language.

Many parents are keen to teach their child a second language by using media like TV programs, DVDs, computer software, CDs and apps. However, a study by Kuhl, Tsao and Liu found that young children can't learn language from digital media as effectively as they can from face-to-face interaction. This study found that babies aged 6–12 months of age learnt more Mandarin with pre-recorded audio when there was personal and social interaction than those babies who only were exposed to recorded Mandarin.

Background TV

The term, 'background TV', describes when the TV is on in a room where a child is doing something else other than watching it. While it may seem quite benign, it can have unintended consequences, especially for a child's language development and social wellbeing.

Much like second-hand smoke, second-hand TV can have an adverse impact on children's development, particularly their language skills. Nature Play Western Australia's chief executive Griffin Longley claimed that in households where television (or screens) were on for two hours a day, the occupants will speak 6000 words combined to each other in a day. In a house where screens were on whenever anyone was home, the occupants of that house would speak 500 words combined.

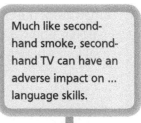

Much like second-hand smoke, second-hand TV can have an adverse impact on ... language skills.

In many homes, having the TV on in the background is common practice and very often the everyday soundtrack. In fact, a 2013 study published in the Pediatrics journal found that children aged 8 months to eight years were exposed to an average of nearly four hours of background TV per day.

Background TV diverts a child's attention from other worthwhile and important activities such as play and learning. In turn, this can impact on their language and social development. We know that background TV has a negative effect on children, disrupting their play and interfering with the development of language skills. It also changes the ways in which parents interact with their children.

Background TV can change infants' and toddlers' play patterns in specific ways. It can make it much harder for infants to pick up on the conversations going on around them, making it more difficult for them to learn new words and tune into speech patterns. The competing sounds from the TV also makes it harder to focus and process what other people are saying.

Background TV can also result in less-focused attention during playtime. Instead of lingering with a toy for several minutes, young children tend to play with one toy, tune into the TV and then move onto another toy. This fleeting attention can diminish their focus.

The ways that parents interact with children is also altered when the TV is turned on as we're often distracted. This can result in less interaction overall with our little ones. A 2009 study published in *Child Development* discovered that background TV impacts on the quality and quantity of interactions with our little ones.

When I speak to parents, they're often shocked to learn that leaving the TV on in the background can have such a harmful effect. So if we're feeling concerned – or even guilty – because we were unaware of the adverse consequences, rest assured that this certainly isn't common knowledge. Remember, as Maya Angelou said, 'When you know better, you do better.'

TECHNO MYTH-BUSTER

MYTH: It's okay for babies to watch sport because they don't understand what they're seeing.

FACT: Watching sport on TV isn't necessarily harmful for babies, but it distracts them and limits the time parents have for serve-and-return interactions, which are essential for their development.

Babies often appear to like the attention-grabbing sound and visual effects from TV – especially when it comes to viewing sports programs – but it's not beneficial for them. Remember, their attention is captivated because of their orienting response. Adult-directed content, whether it's the news, sports or game shows, are not meaningful to infants. When parents are watching TV, their attention isn't always on their baby. Babies can sense this. They also need lots of serve-and-return interactions and watching TV detracts from these interactions.

Every now and then a bit of sport watching is unlikely to harm babies, but given their limited awake time, we don't want this precious time to *always* be dominated by screens.

Tips to minimise the intrusiveness of TV

To minimise any potential harmful effects associated with TV families can:

- **turn the TV off when no-one's watching it**
- **minimise media consumption when young children are around** – we don't need to avoid it completely, but we do need to be mindful that our media habits aren't interfering with our interactions with our children
- **schedule media downtime** – plan times of the day where there's no background media so our children can learn to self-soothe and not always be stimulated by technology. Children need to become accustomed to silence and white noise, at times. These are essential skills for successful school performance.

TECHNO MYTH-BUSTER

MYTH: Background music is harmful for children.

FACT: Slow, soft and familiar background music can support children's development.

Background music that's fast-paced, loud and unfamiliar to young children interferes with their learning and play. It also causes cognitive overload as children's brains have finite resources to process incoming information. If they're trying to process new lyrics or rhythms, this places extra demands on their attention.

A 2012 study published in *Psychology of Music* looked at adults' reading comprehension when listening to music. The study found that fast and loud music disrupted reading comprehension. It's likely that children's cognition would also be adversely impacted by fast or loud music. So slow, soft and familiar background music is advised around young children.

MYTH: Playing Mozart to babies or young children boosts their IQ.

FACT: Playing Mozart won't necessarily enhance our child's IQ. They're not detrimental to our child's development, but they don't accelerate learning.

This neuro-myth has been perpetuated, marketed and resulted in thousands of parents being duped.

A study in 1993 in *Nature* suggested that listening to classical music improves brain function. The problem was that the University of California study involved 36 young adult students – it didn't involve babies or children.

Participants were given a series of mental tasks to complete and before each task they listened to either ten minutes of silence; ten minutes of relaxation exercises; or ten minutes of Mozart's sonata for two pianos in D Major. The study found that the group who listened to Mozart did better at tasks where they had to create a shape in their mind (spatial skills). However the effects only lasted for about 15 minutes.

Now what's really interesting is that the study's authors never used the term, the Mozart effect, and they did not make bold claims. In fact, they were very conservative about their findings. However, a whole baby Mozart industry evolved from this one study.

This is one example of where neuroscience has been misinterpreted and generalisations being made from one study. But parents weren't the only ones being duped. In Georgia, US, the governor proposed that that the state government fund an initiative whereby every newborn baby would be sent a classical music CD.

Further studies have been conducted to test out he Mozart-effect and all have found that while there are *some* benefits, they are not long-term. The benefits accrued from listening to classical music subside over time very quickly and most of the benefits are focused on developing spatial skills.

Overall, most of these studies have shown that music, regardless of whether it's Mozart or even a modern tune, can help activate and engage our brains and this is *why* we can perform better on spatial tasks afterwards (even if it's only for brief amounts of time).

We don't need to throw out the baby Mozart CDs, though. While they won't do any harm to our children, we shouldn't use them under the impression that we're boosting our little one's brainpower.

Music, as one of the few activities that integrates both hemispheres of the brain, can still assist a child's development. It can also impact on children's moods, acting as a circuit breaker (there are very few children that don't crack a smile when their parents sing *If you're happy and you know it*). Music has also been shown to develop children's sense of rhythm and working memory skills (both essential skills for reading) so turn up the tunes (not too loud) because music can be beneficial for young children!

At a glance

How to develop language in a digital age:

- **Don't let screens interfere with our interactions with our children** – engage in lots of serve-and-return interactions with children and put smart phones down when talking with them.
- **Specify tech-free zones in the house** – identify places where technology doesn't go.
- **Have dedicated times when technology isn't used** – for example before school and screen-free Sundays.
- **Co-view (when possible)** – use technology with children as much as possible. Talk about what they're watching or creating before, during and after they've turned on the screen.

- **Offer opportunities to talk** – and promote interaction and discussion with children at home (or in the car). Don't let screens interfere with these opportunities.

Language-rich experiences are critical to our children's development. When used appropriately and intentionally, technology can enhance children's language development, but screens can potentially also interfere with their language skills if they are not carefully managed.

The next chapter will examine the third building block for learning: sleep.

5

Building block #3: Sleep

Our children's sleep patterns and habits are under threat from a range of digital technologies.

This chapter will examine why sleep is critical to children's development and how our children's digital lives are affecting their sleep habits.

Sleep is vital for developing brains

Young children require sleep to ensure healthy brain development and to allow their developing bodies time to recuperate. In addition, growth hormones are released during sleep, making it vital that our little ones have adequate rest.

As adults we know how poorly we function when we don't have enough sleep. Remember those sleepless nights as the parent of a newborn baby and how we would have done *anything* for some much-needed shut-eye?

During wakeful periods, it's too onerous for a child's brain to take in the flood of new experiences and make sense of them at the same time. During sleep, their brains shut out new input and sort through what it's seen and experienced.

When children sleep, their brain performs like a computer defragmenting a hard drive. It formats and tidies up, performing two important tasks: pruning and consolidation. It prunes the synapses (the connections between the brain cells), that *aren't* required. For example, unnecessary memories are dumped.

Sleep also allows the brain to consolidate by processing information it's encountered throughout the day. The brain is highly efficient and knows what to get rid of to be most efficient. The quality and duration of sleep is critical for memory consolidation.

The impact of inadequate sleep

A 2014 Australian report estimated that children's poor sleep habits costs taxpayers an extra $27 million/year in extra doctor visits and sleep clinics and are associated with disruptions to employment and increased mental health issues.

Inadequate sleep has been shown to have many adverse impacts on children's health and development according to research by Sadeh, Gruber and Raviv. It negatively impacts their mood (we've all experienced a toddler emotional-tsunami from exhaustion), behavioural issues, alertness, capacity to learn, memory formation, emotional health, concentration, immunity, reaction times, obesity rates and impulse control.

How much sleep do children need?

As with most childhood guidelines there are huge variations among sleep requirements for children, even of a similar chronological age. The following guidelines indicate suggested ranges of sleep for each age range according to the Australian *Sleep Health Foundation's* guidelines. These guidelines are based on sleep recommendations published in *Sleep Health* in 2015.

Age range	Amount of sleep required/24 hour period
Newborns (0–2 months)	14–17 hours
Infants (4–11 months)	12–15 hours
Toddlers (1–2 years)	11–14 hours
Preschoolers (3–5 years)	10–13 hours
Primary school children	9–11 hours
Pre-teens and teens	8–10 hours
Adults	7–9 hours

Are today's kids really sleep deprived?

Digital insomnia is considered a modern health epidemic. Children's health professionals and teachers are lamenting the fact that many children are chronically tired. Some sleep experts also suggest that some children's behavioural issues and learning problems, such as hyperactivity, *may* in some instances be attributable to chronic tiredness.

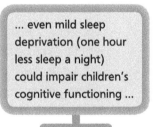

... even mild sleep deprivation (one hour less sleep a night) could impair children's cognitive functioning ...

A University of South Australia study showed that school children aged 10–15 years are averaging at least 30 minutes less sleep than children the same ages did more than 20 years ago. This is a significant sleep reduction. Our biological needs certainly haven't changed over this time span, so this represents a drastic change in our sleep habits.

This finding is also alarming given that a 2013 study published in *Developmental Neuropsychology* showed that even mild sleep deprivation (one hour less sleep a night) could impair children's cognitive functioning, in particular their language skills. The study showed that a loss of just one hour's sleep a night for primary school children was equivalent to reducing their cognitive ability by two grade levels. Therefore, a Year 4 student deprived of one hour of sleep nightly can perform at the same level as a Year 2 student.

Anecdotally teachers are reporting that children are falling asleep during the school day and some health professionals are also reporting similar problems during their appointments. A study conducted in 2000 and published in the *Journal of Developmental and Behavioral Pediatrics* showed that teachers reported approximately 10 per cent of kindergarten to Grade 4 children falling asleep regularly in the school day. A 2012 study conducted at *Boston College* showed that teachers believe that their instruction is hampered by children's sleep deprivation.

TECHNO MYTH-BUSTER

MYTH: TVs are okay in children's bedrooms.

FACT: TV in children's bedrooms can compromise the quality and quantity of a child's sleep and has been linked to obesity.

Watching TV has been linked to sleep problems especially if TVs are in children's bedrooms. The presence of other media – computers, video games or internet-enabled devices – in a child's bedroom is also associated with poor sleep quality and quantity. Screens in bedrooms can delay the onset of sleep and disrupt children's sleep cycles (as will be explored in this chapter).

Young children have increasing access to mobile technologies – gaming consoles, tablets and smart phones – that are often easily transported (or snuck) into bedrooms. It is much more difficult for us to monitor exactly *how much* media our children consume and place limits on what they can access when these devices enter their bedrooms.

Despite guidelines that discourage TVs in bedrooms, there's evidence to suggest that these recommendations are often disregarded. It's estimated that 30 per cent of 5-year-old Australian children have a TV in their bedroom.

It's important that we establish healthy sleep patterns and habits. Removing technology from children's bedrooms means that they're less likely to become distracted by digital devices, which helps prime their brains for sleep and reduce their exposure to blue light (as we'll explore later in this chapter).

TECH TIP ⌘

One of the simplest ways to foster good sleep habits with children is to ensure that bedrooms are designated tech-free zones. Specify a landing zone – a designated place in the house where devices go each night, at a set time, to be charged. This makes it much easier for parents to do a quick head count and check that all the mobile devices are in the landing zone (and not under doonas or pillows).

How technology can help our children's sleeping patterns

There's a range of new technologies that claim to improve children's sleep habits. While there's no doubt that these devices can *sometimes* help children's sleep, we need to be careful that they don't become a digital crutch for little ones. In an ideal world, we don't want to be relying on technology to do something that should be very natural: sleep!

Some technological advancements that can possibly aid children's sleep habits include:

- fitness trackers
- white noise apps
- baby monitors and apps
- screen dimmers
- responsive night-lights.

> ... white noise can help induce sleep or counteract irritating or disruptive background sounds ...

Fitness trackers

GPS-enabled fitness tracking devices and apps can monitor children's sleep patterns. These tracking technologies use small accelerometers to measure motion, but they're often too sensitive to accurately record children's sleep habits as they are notoriously active sleepers.

These devices may however be helpful for concerned parents who think there may be a sleep issue, who perhaps want to validate their intuition before seeking medical help.

White noise apps

White noise combines sound waves with both high and low frequencies. The constant repetitive sounds include TV static, vacuum cleaners, hair dryers or fans. The brain has trouble distinguishing one sound from another so white noise can help induce sleep or counteract irritating or disruptive background sounds, which can also help to prolong sleep.

In today's app market and online music stores there's a preponderance of white noise apps and music files. Parents can easily emulate womb-like sounds or the hum of the fan to comfort newborn babies, or they can have a vacuum cleaner humming along to induce or prolong sleep.

However, be mindful that white noise apps are a form of sleep association. This is where our child *needs* particular objects or situations to induce sleep. So if, for example, we forget to take our smart phone (or need to use it while baby is sleeping or if the device goes flat) it could cause sleep problems.

TECH TIP ✄

Switch smart phone devices to airplane mode before using them near a baby's sleep areas. This helps to minimise electromagnetic-radiation (EMR) exposure that is potentially harmful to little ones. See Chapter 11 for further details about possible health effects of EMR.

Baby monitors and apps

Baby monitors, some with video capabilities, make it easy for parents to hear and see their babies without having to constantly hover over the cot (and run the risk of waking the baby). There are also baby monitors that can send parents – or babysitters! – an SMS when the baby has been crying for a certain number of minutes. And baby jumpsuits with sensors to help reassure parents about baby's health. (The sensors send data to an app that monitors the baby's temperature, movements, respiration and heart rate.)

There are also portable options that are much like a traditional baby monitor. A smart phone's camera can observe our baby and the device can call us when the baby wakes or cries (if another phone is handy). It's important to note that none of these technologies are substitutes for parental supervision.

We do need to be careful that we're not over-complicating things, especially for new parents. Even though many of these products have been designed and marketed to give parents peace of mind, they may sometimes cause more anxiety about our child's health and sleep than need be.

Personally, I'd be reluctant to use these devices without a health professional recommending them. An upset baby is usually more than capable of informing parents of their distress through loud cries (at least that's been my experience with my two loud criers)! In addition, there are possible health concerns associated with babies and EMR exposure from baby monitors, so we need to use these devices carefully and sparingly with infants. See Chapter 11 for further details.

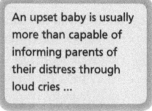

An upset baby is usually more than capable of informing parents of their distress through loud cries ...

Screen dimmers

There are more and more apps that we can use on computer monitors to automatically adjust the brightness of the screen. For example, f.lux lowers the tint of the monitor toward the end of the day. There are also physical filters that we can place over screens to minimise the emission of blue light. By reducing the blue light emanating from screens, children's circadian rhythms aren't adversely affected (read more about the adverse impacts of blue light in the following section).

Screen dimmers and physical filters can be helpful every now and then if we really need to use screens before bedtime, but in an ideal world we want children to form healthy technology habits where they can switch off from technology 90 minutes before sleep time. (This is explained further in the next section).

Responsive night-lights

There are now night-lights and lamps that can gradually brighten (much like the sun rising), allowing our children's body to wake up naturally. The can also dim to help little ones fall asleep. Such a product is obviously only applicable if you're one of the lucky parents whose child doesn't wake up at the crack of dawn!

There are also lights that have detachable globes. They can be placed anywhere in a room for a peaceful glow that lasts for approximately 30 minutes, which is usually sufficient time for children to fall asleep. These are also great for alleviating children's concerns about monsters in their bedrooms (and a cheap alternative to night-lights).

While all of these devices can help children's sleep patterns, we have to be careful not to rely on these devices and make sure that they're not exacerbating sleep problems. We want children to develop healthy and sustainable sleep habits and this primarily involves switching off technology, not using more of it or relying on it to sleep.

How technology can hamper our children's sleeping patterns

Our children's sleep patterns and habits are under threat from a range of digital technologies. The use of screens and digital devices before bedtime has serious adverse impactions for children's sleep habits and patterns.

Various studies published in journals such as *Pediatrics*, *The Journal of School Nursing* and *Sleep* confirmed that young children (and teenagers) who spend time on screens – watching television, playing video games or using the computer – in the pre-sleep window are more likely to take longer to fall asleep than those who watch less or no digital media.

Two separate studies in 2013 also showed that screen time in the 90 minutes before children's bedtime can cause sleep delays. Over time this sleep loss accumulates and can cause an overall sleep deficit, which impacts children's intellectual capabilities, behaviour and development.

An extensive literature review completed in 2014 revealed an association between screen time and sleep outcomes among school-aged children and adolescents. Even modest sleep debts can have a long-term effect. For example, 30 minutes less sleep each night adds up to a sleep deficit of over 3.5 hours in a one-week period alone.

Sleep debts accumulate over time, which can have a substantial impact on children's overall health and their capacity to learn. Poor sleep can have significant implications on a child's development, health and wellbeing.

Technology can adversely affect children's sleep patterns in the following ways:

- screens displace sleep
- over-stimulated brains
- blue light hampers melatonin production
- sleep hygiene is poor
- scary content
- electromagnetic radiation emissions.

Using screens can arouse children, making the onset of sleep more difficult.

Screens displace sleep
The use of digital devices can delay children's bedtimes, which simply results in less time available for sleep. This is something that we can control by enforcing bedtimes for digital devices too.

Over-stimulated brains
Using screens can arouse children, making the onset of sleep more difficult. Rapid-fire TV or video games can overstimulate young children and activate areas of the brain that require more passive activities before

the onset of sleep. Some, but not all, screen activities are too stimulating for developing brains and bodies, which need the exact opposite. Interactive screen use can be more stimulating than just watching TV. Children need time to unwind and calm down and predictable patterns. Technology does not provide these pre-sleep conditions.

Blue light hampers melatonin production

The blue light that radiates from devices can affect circadian rhythms and adversely affect a child's ability to fall asleep. Direct short wavelength blue light, emitted from tablets and other screens, interferes with the production of melatonin (the body's hormone that aids with sleep), which the body produces in darkness. Without sufficient levels of melatonin it is more difficult for children to fall asleep or achieve good quality sleep. This can result in sleep delays and over time, these delays can accumulate into a sleep deficit.

TECHNO MYTH-BUSTER

MYTH: Avoid eBooks and book apps before bedtime.

FACT: Make careful choices about the types of eBooks and book apps used before bedtime (especially if it's within the 90-minute window before they go to sleep). Some devices are specifically designed to be read at night without blue light.

While there's no need to completely ban devices before bed for reading purposes, use them sparingly and in conjunction with more traditional books.

Avoid book apps that contain too many bells and whistles like animations and sound effects, as they are likely to arouse children. Use basic eBooks and book apps with minimal distracting elements and limited interactive features (like matching games or puzzles within the book).

Look for eBooks and book apps with a very simple design and remember to dim the brightness of the screen to reduce blue light exposure.

Case STUDY

When Melanie's family bought a touch-screen device, she thought that watching videos before bedtime would be a great way to calm her two daughters down before they went to sleep. In the past, they'd watched TV for about 20 minutes before bed and it seemed to relax them. So Melanie assumed the same would be true for the touch-screen device.

Over the course of a week or so, Melanie noticed that both her daughters took much longer to fall asleep than what they'd previously taken. At first, Melanie thought this was a coincidence, but after a few more weeks the sleeping situation was not resolved. Melanie was bewildered because her children were watching the same TV shows on the tablet as they were on the TV. Melanie recalled hearing me speak about screen time before bedtime at a parent seminar and connected the dots.

The next night, Melanie switched around her routine so that her daughters still got to watch things on the iPad, but they did this *before* dinner (not bedtime). She also dimmed the brightness of the touch-screen device and insisted that her daughters distance themselves from the screen. Melanie was astounded when over the next three nights their sleep habits improved dramatically (and have stayed this way). She was thrilled that such a simple change could yield such drastic results.

TECH TIP ✂

Reduce the brightness of the screen if children are using it before sleep time. Also, increase the distance between the child and the device to reduce the absorption of blue light. (This is why TV is sometimes a better option before bed than a tablet or smart phone as it emits less blue light and children sit much further away from it and so the blue light effects aren't as detrimental as they are for a mobile device.)

Sleep hygiene is poor

As technology has become increasingly portable, children often bring (or sneak) tablets and gaming consoles into their bedroom. (It was much harder when we were young to sneak the TV into our bedroom!) As parents, we're often oblivious to children's screen habits in their bedrooms. We sometimes assume our children are sleeping or at least relaxing, when in fact they're plugged in. Using technology and screens in the bedroom does not create healthy sleep associations. The bedroom needs to be associated as a sacred space for rest and relaxation. Nothing else.

... boys were more vulnerable to the effect of TV on their sleep than girls.

Some children are forming poor sleep associations with technology. In 2005 Thompson and Christakis conducted a study that linked TV to irregular nap times in children less than 3 years of age.

Two different studies published in *Pediatrics* in 2005 and 2014 have also showed that TV viewing and the presence of a TV in children's bedroom has been associated with shorter sleep periods and more irregular sleep patterns from infancy to mid-childhood. An interesting anecdote from the studies is that boys were more vulnerable to the effect of TV on their sleep than girls.

In other instances, children are relying on technology to fall asleep. Many parents report that allowing their child to watch TV or a DVD helps their child to fall asleep, and it has become part of the bedtime routine. This is not a healthy or sustainable habit that we want children to develop (as screens in bedrooms can also disrupt sleep cycles).

TECHNO MYTH-BUSTER

MYTH: It's okay for children to fall asleep with the TV switched on.

FACT: Falling asleep with the TV (or other devices) can impact on the quality of children's sleep.

Children are forming attachments to gadgets to help them fall asleep, much like they do with their dummy or snuggly toy. It might be the TV that's switched on in a bedroom to help little ones fall asleep or the DVD they watch while they fall asleep. Other children literally crave using technology before they sleep. For example, playing a video game or using a tablet may have become so habitualised that they can't fall asleep without the aid of the device.

While using technology to help children fall asleep may appear to work, it's strongly discouraged. TV might help children fall asleep, but it comes at a cost: children who've fallen asleep with TV have increased rates of sleep disturbances and irregular sleeping patterns. Using screens as a sleep aid for children, regardless of their age, is strongly discouraged.

MYTH: It's okay to use screens around sleeping babies.

FACT: Screen use around infants can have potential negative effects and no known positive effects, especially for children younger than two.

Children form strong sleep associations. If screens and other technologies are *always* used to pacify babies or encourage them to sleep, they can quickly become accustomed to this type of stimulation in order to fall asleep. It is not healthy for infants to form such attachments.

We also know that TV can also disrupt infants' sleep, as the audio and/or visual stimulus can awaken them prematurely or between sleep cycles, making it difficult to transition back to sleep. This is also why it's sometimes impossible to settle a baby in front of the TV.

Babies don't have well-developed circadian rhythms. This is why they often confuse day and night and why they require darkness to establish good sleeping habits. When TVs and other brightly lit digital devices are used around babies, it can hamper their ability to develop their circadian rhythms. The rhythms begin to develop at about six weeks and by 3–6 months most infants have a regular sleep/wake cycle.

This isn't to suggest that we should never watch TV or use a screen around our baby or toddler. This is not feasible, nor necessary. My iPhone was my sanity-saver during the early morning feeds when I was worried about falling asleep with my babies. I certainly didn't do it all the time, but there were times when watching a bit of TV while I fed the baby or scrolling through my Facebook feed was helpful for me and I don't believe that it hampered my ability to care for or connect to my babies.

So don't fret. I'm not suggesting that bit of background TV while we feed or settle is harmful to our infants. We just have to be mindful about switching on the TV or illuminating a dark room with our tablet device or having devices switched on when we're trying to help our little one sleep. It's can be counter-productive.

Case STUDY

Jessica's parents ensured she went to sleep each night by 8:30 pm and she woke up between 6.30 and 7 am most days. They had resisted Instagram for a long time, but they eventually gave in when Jessica explained that she would legally be able to join in 3 months' time when she turned 13. But after she started using it, her parents noticed that Jessica was waking up very lethargic. Her teacher also noticed a change in Jessica's attention at school.

Jessica was naturally waking up in the middle of the night to use the bathroom, then quickly checked her Instagram account to see how many likes or comments her last post had received. This made Jessica alert and interrupted her sleep cycles. While she was getting an adequate number of hours of sleep (quantity), she wasn't getting adequate *quality* of sleep as her sleep cycles were being disrupted.

A typical cycle takes approximately 90–110 minutes to complete – four stages of non-rapid eye movement (NREM) and one stage of rapid eye movement (REM). Jessica was waking between cycles and having to start each cycle again so her body didn't get a sufficient number of sleep cycles to perform the necessary roles and hence she felt exhausted (children Jessica's age should be having between four and six sleep cycles per night). This is the exact reason why you would have felt very tired with a newborn baby, even if you were lucky enough to get close to your normal number of hours of sleep each night – you weren't having a sufficient number of sleep cycles because of the sleep interruptions that comes with a newborn baby.

Scary content

Many children experience night terrors from time to time and their screen habits can be to blame. Night terrors are distinct from nightmares. Night terrors happen in the first 2–3 hours of sleep while nightmares occur during the second half of their sleep. Both are considered a normal part of a child's development, especially as children learn to distinguish between fantasy and reality (see below).

> Night terrors happen in the first 2–3 hours of sleep while nightmares occur during the second half of their sleep.

Many children report more frequent night terrors *after* they've watched inappropriate content and they can also become more severe if children are worried about a situation they've seen in a movie or video game. Violent or inappropriate programming can also increase the chances of children having problems falling asleep and/or staying asleep or having nightmares, according to Garrison and Christakis.

It's not just scary movies and games that we need to be wary of, it's also the prevalence of scary images and events that are featured on the news and in movie trailers and promotions. Much promotional content is unpredictable and can contain intense or disturbing material that is not suitable for young children who don't typically learn to distinguish fantasy from reality until they're approximately 3–5 years of age. Children under 10 are still particularly susceptible to experiencing intense fear as a result of viewing images out of context or intense violence or devastation. This is another reason why co-viewing is essential and why we must be careful about *what* children watch on-screens – or what they're absorbing via background media.

TECH TIP ✂

Avoid watching movie promotions at the cinema or on DVDs with children under 10 years. Arrive at the cinema just before the movie starts and skip the trailers when watching DVDs.

Case STUDY

Tom was 8 years old when the Sydney Siege took place in late 2014. Christine, his mum, didn't typically watch the morning news, but when she'd read about the terrible situation on social media she decided to switch the TV on that morning so she could find out more about the events unfolding. Tom didn't appear to be very interested in what was taking place on the TV and continued his normal morning routine.

A couple of weeks later, one night before Tom went to sleep he started to ask Christine questions about the siege. She encouraged him to do so. Through her questioning she realised that Tom had been quite distressed by some of the footage he'd seen, second hand, being played repeatedly on the TV that one morning. Images of the victims running from the café and the bright flashes when gunfire had been exchanged had been firmly imprinted on Tom.

Christine was alarmed. She didn't think Tom had absorbed much of the footage and was oblivious that he was so upset by it. In fact, he'd been so upset that he'd been having night terrors since watching the footage, but Christine had simply dismissed these as a typical developmental milestone.

When news of emergencies and disasters break on TV, there's often limited footage. Broadcasters replay the same footage over and over. For young children, who may not have the skills to rationalise this, they can sometimes misconstrue this as the event occurring repeatedly. Young children often can't contextualise events they see on TV and may worry about their safety if the threat seems looming.

Electromagnetic radiation emissions

It's postulated, although unproven at this stage, that electromagnetic radiation (EMR) emitted from smartphones, tablets and other digital devices *may* compromise children's sleep. There's a lack of research at this stage about the impact of EMR on children's sleep. While there's some preliminary evidence that EMR can moderately impair adults' sleep patterns and brain physiology whilst they sleep there are inconsistent findings in the literature at this stage. We don't yet have a clear picture about the health consequences of EMR on our sleep, especially as it relates to children's sleep patterns. So I advise parents to be cautious about their children's EMR exposure – better to be safe than sorry! (More details about EMR are available in Chapter 11.)

TECHNO MYTH-BUSTER

MYTH: Baby monitors emit dangerous levels of EMR.

FACT: Typical use of baby monitors is usually well below the limits of the Australian standard.

Digital baby monitors emit EMR as do other common household wireless devices like wi-fi routers and cordless phones.

Scientists agree that radiation is dangerous at high levels, but the long-term health effects of low levels are largely untested and the possibility of small risks cannot be eliminated. As such many countries, including Australia, are recommending precautionary approaches when it comes to EMR exposure, especially around children.

Using baby monitors according to the user's manual is unlikely to cause ill health for infants, but if parents place the antennas very close to the body, babies can be exposed to levels that are closer to the standard. Again, there's no conclusive scientific evidence at this stage to show that EMR from common household devices causes any detrimental health effects, but precautionary approaches are advised, especially around infants.

TECH TIP ✂

Err on the side of caution. Reduce infants' exposure from baby monitors by increasing the distance between the monitor and the baby's cot and switching them off when not in use.

MYTH: Baby monitors can cause Sudden Infant Death Syndrome (SIDs) and autism.

FACT: There's no research evidence to show that SIDs or autism are linked to wireless baby monitors.

Medical experts have dismissed some media claims that baby monitors are in any way connected to SIDs or autism. Some manufacturers of baby monitors suggest that their devices can prevent SIDs, but these claims haven't been supported by research.

Taking technology out of children's sleep routine

If technology is a regular part of our child's sleep routine, it may be time for us to rethink our approach. Children are unlikely to embrace drastic change so it's important to gradually and incrementally remove TV (or other devices) from sleep and nap routines.

Here are some tips for changing screen habits before bedtime or naps:

1 **Gradually reduce the amount of screen time before bed** – rather than going cold turkey. It will save everyone tears and tantrums.
2 **Move screen time away from nap and sleep time** – again, do this gradually and give children ample warning that changes will be implemented.

3 **Introduce alternative, non-screen activities into children's sleep routines** – find an alternative, calm activity your child likes to fill the space of the TV (or iPad). You could try reading a book or making time for a massage, puzzle or block time. This will help children calm down before sleep.

4 **Make bedrooms tech-free zones** – and remove all digital devices. Don't dangle the carrot.

At a glance

To minimise the impact of technology on children's sleep habits try the following suggestions:

- **Make bedrooms tech-free zones** – this is the hardest but most effective solution. This means no smart phones, tablets, gaming consoles or TVs in bedrooms for children. This works wonders for adults too! Children form strong sleep associations so it's important to establish bedrooms as a place of rest.

- **Implement technology curfews** – minimise children's exposure to screens in the 90 minutes before sleep (including nap time) and establish and enforce clear cut-off times for digital devices. Remember to also dim the brightness on the screen, increase the distance between the child and their screens and provide some screen-free time. Psychologist Jocelyn Brewer calls this a 'digital sunset'.

- **Specify tech landing-zones** – where digital devices are stored overnight for charging or storage. This makes it much easier to do a quick head count and ensure all devices are out of bedrooms!

- **Avoid screens in the 90-minute period before bed or reduce blue light exposure** – and encourage children to hold mobile devices at least 40 cm away from their face. Increasing children's light exposure in the morning fosters healthy sleep patterns and develops their circadian rhythms).

- **Reduce children's exposure** – if the 90-minute screen-free period is too difficult to implement start slow and for shorter periods of time. Reducing screen time (for any amount of time) in the pre-sleep window is an effective strategy to ensure healthy sleep habits.

- **Avoid apps before naps** – and afterwards too. Toddlers' sleeping patterns are often more vulnerable than older children's and adults'.
- **Monitor content** – avoid violent or age-inappropriate programs (even news programs contain graphic and violent content) as this can cause night terrors and nightmares for children.
- **Avoid rapid-fire, fast-paced screen action before sleep** – this can excite children and delay the onset of sleep. Do a technology swap. Instead of playing a video game before bedtime, allow children to watch a slow-paced TV show or perhaps listen to some music.
- **Establish and maintaining screen-free bedtime rituals** – be consistent with the rituals enforced each night, especially when it comes to using devices. Encourage children to engage in some winding down activities to calm them down and help them prepare for sleep. Over time these rituals become habitualised and will last our children a lifetime.
- **Model healthy sleep habits** – and positive attitudes toward sleep. Don't wear sleep-deprivation like a badge of honour. Sleep is a basic need which we need to teach our children.

Sleep is an essential building block in a children's overall development. The prevalence and seduction of digital devices can significantly impact our children's sleep habits. This doesn't mean that we need to ban digital devices, but we do need to teach our children how to form healthy technology habits, especially when it comes to sleep. This isn't a difficult process, but it does require conscious choices and consistency.

The next chapter will examine the fourth building block for children's development: play.

6

Building block #4: Play

We need to see cyberplay as another way that our children can play today. It's a valid form of play.

Most children have an innate desire to play – and it's exactly what their developing brains and bodies need. Play is an organic way for young children to learn while helping them develop many of the other building blocks addressed in this book: relationships, language, movement and executive-function skills.

Research confirms that play builds children's social, cognitive, emotional and physical skills. In one study, three cohorts of children were followed from preschool (aged 4 years) to Years 5 and 6. The study examined the influence of three different preschool models on later school success. The study found that by Grade 6, children whose preschool experiences had been academically directed scored significantly lower grades than those children who'd attended child-initiated preschool classes. The authors of the study suggested that later school success is likely to be enhanced by active, child-initiated early learning experiences.

There is universal acceptance, particularly among early childhood educators, that play is critical for a child's development. But there are increasing concerns that modern children's play patterns are changing, in part due to technology. Educators and health professional are worried that a decline in opportunities to play is having a detrimental impact on young children's learning and development.

Are our kids playing enough?

As the infographic below shows, research corroborates what many of us lament: children today have less time for unstructured and outdoor play. A 2006 study published in *The Journal of the American Medical Association* showed that there's been a gradual decline in children's free and unstructured play since the late 1970s. Today's children are venturing outside much less than previous generations.

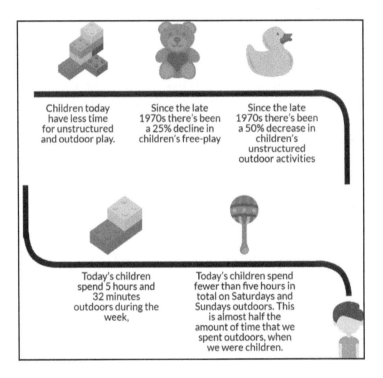

Children today have less time for unstructured and outdoor play.

Since the late 1970s there's been a 25% decline in children's free-play

Since the late 1970s there's been a 50% decrease in children's unstructured outdoor activities

Today's children spend 5 hours and 32 minutes outdoors during the week,

Today's children spend fewer than five hours in total on Saturdays and Sundays outdoors. This is almost half the amount of time that we spent outdoors, when we were children.

Why aren't our kids playing?

There are many forces combining to threaten children's play. Screen time is often solely blamed for the changes in children's play patterns, but it's not the *only* reason to account for changes in children's play activities. There are other, broader societal factors that are combining to reduce children's opportunities to play.

Hurried child phenomenon

In today's frantic world there's pressure on kids to grow up quickly. 'The hurried child phenomenon' was a term coined by psychologist Dr David Elkind in his book *The Hurried Child*. It describes how some parents attempt to accelerate their child's development by pushing them along the developmental trajectory at unnecessary speeds. This results in overscheduling children in classes and promoting academic achievement (often at very young ages) at the expense of other more developmentally appropriate activities, such as play and physical activity.

Some parents brag at what age their child learnt to walk or read a book or play a musical instrument – we all had one of *those mums* in our mothers' group! Some parents are trying to accelerate their children's development and give them a head start by overestimating their competencies and overexposing them to academic pressures at young ages.

However, we actually need to teach children how to slow down.

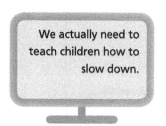

We actually need to teach children how to slow down.

We're conditioning young children to live in a frenetic world. We're raising them in a world where being constantly switched on and busy are worn like badges of honour. Our children are adopting this frantic lifestyle too and it's not ideal for their development. Childhood is a precious time. Children don't need to be in a hurry. We need to slow down and enjoy childhood. It's such a brief period of time in their lifespan.

Over-scheduled childhoods

Many children are enrolled in organised activities and lessons often from very young ages. As modern parents we're under increasing pressure to enroll our little ones in art, music or drama lessons or sport activities. These highly regimented timetables are displacing our children's opportunities for unstructured play, according to the *Active Healthy Kids Australia Report Card on Physical Activity for Children and Young People*.

TECHNO MYTH-BUSTER

MYTH: Children are spending less time in organised sport because screen time has taken over.

FACT: Studies suggest that Australian children are playing more sport than ever before, but are ironically doing less physical activity than ever.

An Australian report on children's physical activity levels confirmed that children are spending more time participating in organised sport activities than they previously did and spending more time on screens, displacing opportunities for play. Time to hang out and explore has been lost. Modern families are finding it difficult to balance time spent between structured sport activities and unstructured play time. Previously, children spent time in structured activities but used the time outside of these activities engaged in physically active tasks like chasing friends, playing at the park or in the backyard. Now, screen media has replaced this mucking around time.

Cotton wool kids

In previous generations children spent hours each week exploring backyards and local neighbourhoods *without* adult supervision or strict limits being imposed. Today this isn't the case: we're limiting children's opportunities for free play.

There's increased pressure on parents, educators and carers to restrict some of the more traditional play experiences for children because of risks of litigation associated with children's injuries. And there's a sense of hyper-vigilance when it comes to young children and opportunities to play. In extreme cases, some schools have banned or reduced play opportunities during break times to reduce playground injuries.

Children need opportunities for free play so that they can learn to take risks, build confidence and resilience, overcome failures and cope with fears and uncertainty. Children cannot develop these critical life skills if their play experiences are truncated.

This is one reason why the computer game Minecraft has been so incredibly popular with young children. They can roam and create and try out new ideas online without their parents watching on imposing limits and restrictions. They're literally roaming and testing their capabilities and problem-solving in a digital context. Today's digital kids hanker the freedom to explore and create unsupervised. Minecraft presents this opportunity for many of them.

Helicopter parents

Misguided parental fears and perceived risks relating to children's personal safety and security has resulted in some parents restricting children's free play opportunities. Some parents have climbed into the helicopter pilot's seat because of misinformation and fear relating to abduction and physical injury. In turn, some of us are confining our children's play indoors with structured, supervised activities.

Case STUDY

Julia is an early childhood educator and sees herself as a 'caterpillar' parent. She explains, 'Just like caterpillars need to make their own way out of cocoons to transform into butterflies, so too do our children. As humans, if we interfere with the process and assist the caterpillar transition, it dies. And I think we're killing off some of our kids' development if we're always interfering, hovering nearby and restricting what they can do. There's learning and growth in the struggles. Their failures and frustrations build character, resilience and coping mechanisms better than any lesson I can instil as a parent or as a teacher. I intervene but only when there's a risk to serious injury, or a child is floundering in a situation. Other than that, I leave my caterpillars to figure things out themselves.'

Academic pressure

We're also witnessing an academic creep where curriculum goals that were once typically applicable to kindergarten and even Year 1 are now being pushed down to preschoolers. Parents and educators often report feeling under increasing pressure to accelerate their child's learning.

Ironically, this isn't actually conducive to children learning. In fact, two longitudinal studies published in 1997 and 2002 examined how different preschool curriculum models impacted on children's subsequent academic outcomes. In both studies it was found that children from play-based, child-directed preschools out-performed their peers who had attended preschools with a more formal academic curriculum.

As parents we're also under pressure to buy edutainment products. As previously explored in Chapter 4, there's an entire market of baby media and educational products that are marketed to parents under the guise that they'll accelerate learning.

How much play do children need?

Children need one hour per day of unstructured, open-ended play. They need time to unwind, relax and engage in creative, unstructured play each day. Unstructured play is in addition to time required for physical activity.

Most 1–5-year-olds need 3 hours of light moderate or vigorous exercise spread throughout the day. Most 5–12-year-olds need 1 hour a day of moderate to vigorous exercise every day. Children need at least one afternoon each week without structured activities or classes.

How technology can help support children's play

Sometimes referred to as cyberplay, digital play opportunities are very new to parents and educators. When children engage in cyberplay as adults, we often have to assume the role of novice not expert. We often have to learn how to play video games or use apps alongside our children and we can't necessarily guide their play. So our natural tendency is to fret and worry that cyberplay experiences must be detrimental to our child's development.

> We need to see cyberplay as *another* way that our children can play today.

We often feel that we should be encouraging more traditional play experiences that we're comfortable and familiar with – playing outside, climbing trees and riding bikes. These important components of our analogue childhoods are still vital experiences for our children.

But we need to see cyberplay as *another* way that our children can play today. It's a valid form of play. Of course it's critical that we don't let cyberplay interfere with opportunities for more traditional play experiences, but carefully designed technologies can support and facilitate young children's play opportunities.

Positive technology-based play experiences include:

- using techno-toys
- playing video games
- expanding opportunities to explore
- engaging in interactive play
- expanding children's social skills
- extending play beyond the screen.

Using techno-toys

Flicking through the latest toy catalogues reveals just how many techno-toys (battery-operated, digital toys) there are available. There are teddy bears with mobile phones attached to their paws, tablet and smart phone devices designed for babies and voice-activated dolls for preschoolers.

Techno-toys can offer a range of benefits to children if they're carefully selected. For example, some toys have voice recording capabilities and can encourage children to speak. Other techno-toys can respond to children's input which, in turn, can encourage them to critically think (such as interactive atlas toys). Some techno-toys can provide new opportunities for play (such as interactive apps that explore the human body).

We need to ensure that digital toys don't replace other valuable analogue toys. There needs to be room in the toy box for traditional and technological tools. Children need a variety of toys for optimal development.

What should parents look for in quality toys for young children?

Regardless of whether children are using traditional or digital toys we need to find toys that encourage children to think, explore, manipulate and use language. Techno-toys, because they're pre-programmed, can sometimes limit play experiences (see the section in this chapter about the potential harmful effects of techno-toys).

Susan Linn suggests applying this simple formula when selecting toys for young children:

Ideal toy = 90 per cent child-directed + 10 per cent toy-directed

We want children thinking and interacting with toys. We don't want the toy doing all the hard work *for* our child. Look for toys that promote thinking skills, problem solving or interaction.

Playing video games

There's a growing body of research to support the educational use of video games. Educational researchers and educators are seeing video games as viable learning tools, so much so that researchers are examining gamification in education.

Research published by Adachi and Willoughby and Gentile and others has shown that gaming is positively associated with cognitive, motivational, social and emotional benefits. Video games have been shown to improve children's visual processing skills, spatial reasoning, attention, visual perception, problem solving and planning skills.

Parents are often relieved to learn that the hours that their children spend gaming are not necessarily wasted. So long as children are playing age-appropriate games and for suitable durations, they can actually benefit from the experience.

> There's a growing body of research to support the educational use of video games.

However, there are also negative effects associated with gaming including addiction, depression and aggression. Boys in particular are much more susceptible to some of the adverse effects of gaming, especially in relation to violence and aggression. Sophisticated and realistic graphics and easy access to sexualised or violent content means that parents have to be extremely vigilant about the content of children's video games. This is another reason why digital devices need to be played in visible places in the family home and why co-viewing is important.

Tips on the positive effects of Minecraft if it is carefully managed

Minecraft is a popular digital block world with universal appeal to millions of children worldwide. It's a captivating online world where users build (craft) 3D blocks within a digital world with various habitats and terrains. As an immersive experience, users have to gather materials and use tools to survive. Unlike many other video games, Minecraft has relatively simple graphics and there are no levels. It's literally a game that never ends.

While many children become obsessed by Minecraft, there are also educational benefits according to work published by Dezuanni, O'Mara, and Beavis. As parents we're relieved to learn that Minecraft can be beneficial if it's carefully managed. Children apply sophisticated problem-solving skills, use advanced numeracy concepts and develop a range of other academic skills when playing Minecraft. Educators and researchers are currently exploring the educational potential of Minecraft and have seen positive effects for learning.

Expanding opportunities to explore

Kids are increasingly using digital devices in their playtime, which can help them explore and learn more about their world. They can explore distant countries on interactive globes, learn and use a foreign language, travel to outer space, step inside the human body and travel the seven seas and to Antarctica – all while sitting in their lounge room on a touch-screen device. Technology can open up completely new opportunities for play.

In fact some of these opportunities were previously inconceivable *without* technology. For example, traditional books about the human body are no comparison to interactive apps that allow children to explore and learn in engaging, informative and dynamic ways. These experiences are now part of children's everyday play.

We need to look for apps, websites and games that provide unique opportunities for young children to explore more about themselves and the world in which they live. We need to avoid (or make minimal use) of technologies that are simply a digital replica of an existing toy, book or game. Instead, look for digital play experiences that add value or provide a unique way of learning or playing. Technology becomes truly exciting when it presents new opportunities for play.

Here are some prime examples of innovative technology experiences that expand children's play opportunities.

- **The Human Body** is a wonderful app that enables children to explore inside the various systems in the human body.
- **Toca Hair Salon** is a brilliant augmented reality app that enables children to play hairdressers without risking the permanence of a bad haircut. Children insert a photograph of themselves (or their parents or siblings) and then use a range of tools to create elaborate haircuts and designs.
- **Happi Full Throttle** is an app that turns a tablet device into the dashboard of a vehicle, including a fire truck and submarine. The app uses the tablet device's built-in camera to allow the child to pretend to be inside the vehicle operating the dashboard.
- **Portable North Pole** website and app allows parents to create personalised messages from Santa to be sent to their child with photos of the child and important events embedded in the message.

Tips on finding apps

It's often difficult to find a specific app in the popular app stores, especially if the developer has utilised unusual capitalisation or spacing in the app's name – they aren't typically very good databases. To find a specific app I recommend doing a Google search with the name of the app and the phrase 'and app'. Do not go directly to the app store. The first few Google search results will usually provide you with a direct link to the app store where you can then download the app.

TECHNO MYTH-BUSTER

MYTH: Apps are killing children's creativity.

FACT: Some apps foster creativity while other apps can hamper children's creativity. It really is determined by how the app is designed and how children use it.

Parents and educators often worry that touch-screen technologies are stifling young children's creativity. The design of an app shapes *what* and *how* a child learns.

There are two broad types of apps:

Consumption apps	Creativity apps
▪ include handwriting, spelling, times tables, phonics apps, YouTube ▪ fosters lower-order thinking skills ▪ click and tap until the correct, pre-determined answer is selected ▪ children *consume* pre-made content ▪ children assume a *passive* role.	▪ include drawing, art, music, movie-making, animation, digital book creation apps ▪ fosters higher-order thinking skills ▪ allows children to *create* their own digital content ▪ children assume an *active* role.

Ideally, we want children to spend more time with *creativity* apps and less time with *consumption* apps. (We don't have to completely avoid them, but we should use them sparingly.)

If we provide opportunities for children to use creativity apps (and occasionally use consumption apps), it's more likely that their imagination skills will be fostered.

Engaging in interactive play

It's now possible for children to have truly interactive technology experiences (more than just tapping on a screen or selecting a correct answer from a menu of responses). Some examples of innovative, interactive play experiences include:

- **Osmo** – children manipulate real 3D tangram objects in front of the tablet and the attached mirror sends data to the app and feedback is provided. For example, in Tangram for Osmo the app will flash and signal to the child where an incorrect tangram piece is located and then model how to correctly place the tangram tile. It also gives the user feedback if they've correctly positioned a tangram piece.
- **Make it Kids app** – children can create and share their own interactive games and activities. The app has interactive menus, drawing, memory, relationships and quizzes and a range of content libraries (sounds and images) to access or children can select their own content.

To source quality reviews of apps and keep abreast of the latest innovations in terms of children's technology, these are essential parent resources:

- **Common Sense Media** (website and app): https://www.commonsensemedia.org/
- **Children's Technology Review** (website): http://childrenstech.com/
- **Kapi Awards** (website): http://kapiawards.com/

Of course we need to be mindful that technology doesn't dominate play situations. We still want the child, not the gadget, to be in control of the play (remember the 90 per cent and 10 per cent rule). And we want the children to think, engage and learn when using these technologies.

We don't want children's play to be determined solely by the design of the technology and limited to simply observing the toy or superficially interacting by tapping every now and then as the toy demands.

Expanding children's social skills

Many cyberplay activities require multiple users. While screen time is often criticised as promoting social isolation, cyberplay experiences can have the opposite effect. Even devices like tablets that are thought to promote solitary play are rarely used by children on their own. This co-play is brilliant for their language and social skills so, where possible, encourage cyberplay *with* someone else.

Extending play beyond the screen

Technology can be a wonderful way to stimulate children's play. For years we've seen children re-enact scenes from popular TV shows and movies and emulate cartoon characters in their play experiences. These familiar contexts and characters give children the language skills they need to engage in socio-dramatic and pretend play. Studies published in 2007, 2009 and 2012 all confirm that children's modern play patterns are being *shaped*, not necessarily *displaced* by the screen media that surrounds them. Children can creatively use media as a springboard for play.

How technology hampers children's play

If technology isn't carefully selected and/or if it's used inappropriately or excessively, it can in fact impede children's play experiences. Technology can inhibit play by:

- techno-toy fears
- restricting play
- displacing unstructured play
- commercialising childhood
- creating nature deficit disorder
- privacy fears.

Children can creatively use media as a springboard for play.

Techno-toy fears

There's an assumption that techno-toys, with their sophisticated and pre-programmed responses, are superior to more traditional toys. The marketing claims surrounding many techno-toys suggests they provide educational benefits and a head start.

However, research suggests that infants don't necessarily benefit from techno-toys. A study published in 2015 found that play with electronic toys is associated with decreased quantity and quality of language input, as compared to play with traditional toys or books. As outlined in Chapter 4, language development is critical for young children's overall development so play with electronic toys should be discouraged with babies.

Case STUDY

Monica's 10-month-old daughter Isla was constantly grabbing her smart phone. In most instances Isla simply wanted to chew on the device or swipe at photos. Monica didn't want Isla to damage her smart phone (she was a big dribbler). She didn't want her being exposed to the nickel either so she decided to buy Isla a plastic smart phone (which ironically also poses potential health risks associated with digesting chemicals from plastics).

Monica was surprised to read the packaging. The product claimed that the plastic smart phone device, designed for 6–36-month-olds, would teach numbers, counting and greetings. These claims actually made Monica feel anxious. Did her 10-month-old daughter *really* need to start learning academic concepts like numbers? (No, that's not a developmentally appropriate expectation for a 10-month-old.) On the flipside, Monica worried that Isla might fall behind her peers if she wasn't using techno-toys as a tot. This is the modern parents' dilemma.

Restricting play

The design of children's technology determines the type of play that it supports. Consider what a child does with a video game or drill-and-practice app compared to a set of blocks, a doll or some trucks. Children use their imagination with traditional toys and this requires our child's input.

When playing a very regimented drill-and-practice app or video game (again it depends on the design of the app or video game), the technology can potentially limit what a child can do. It can place a ceiling on what they can learn or play.

It is also often pre-programmed so the flow of play is determined by the programmer, *not* the child. With some technology (not all) there are pre-determined answers and input required. This isn't the case with more traditional toys where children exert the greatest influence over the toy and direct the play experience.

There are also concerns that battery-powered toys and commercial characters can limit children's play opportunities. There are concerns that commercial characters can shape *what* and *how* children play with them by placing a ceiling on their play experiences as they tend to emulate episodes and on-screen actions. However, popular media characters can also feature in and initiate children's creative play.

Displacing unstructured play

If media or screens *always* dominate children's play experiences, then this can potentially stifle children's creativity and imagination. There are concerns that screens and the hurried child phenomenon are eroding unstructured play. When digital devices are frequently used as the digital pacifier or always used to alleviate boredom, it's little surprise that children today don't know what to do to with unstructured time.

Case STUDY

Maryanne has been a teacher for 32 years. She's seen a dramatic shift in children's play patterns over the last five years in particular. Maryanne explains, 'I dread wet weather day supervision at school. Previously, kids knew how to entertain themselves when it was wet. They'd make up a game. They'd use cardboard boxes and turn them into something. These days the kids whine and complain. They have no idea what to do if I give them cardboard boxes and a blanket. They don't know how to entertain themselves. They plead desperately to watch a movie on the interactive whiteboard or request to play on the computers or iPads. Kids just don't know how to entertain themselves without a screen. It's really quite sad.'

Maryanne's story is reverberated by educators throughout Australia. Teachers are increasingly worried about young children's over-reliance on digital devices for their entertainment and leisure needs.

It's vital that we preserve opportunities for unstructured play. Kids need to experience boredom. It's actually one of the greatest gifts we can give our children. It's through moments of empty space that children discover how rewarding their own company and thoughts can be.

Despite what they may tell us, children don't need to be constantly plugged in to devices and entertained. It's okay for them to switch off (in fact it's essential for their brain development). It's okay for them to be bored. It's okay if we're not filling every moment for them. We don't want our children to be a slave to a digital master.

Commercialisation of childhood

There are also concerns that technology-based play can:

- **promote unhealthy stereotypes** – such as princesses and superheroes
- **increase commercialisation** – through pressure to buy the purchasable toys and paraphernalia that accompany popular movies, video games and apps
- **come at an opportunity cost** – what other play experiences are children missing out on if their play is *always* dominated by media characters?

Again, this is why a balanced approach is necessary and why we need to assume an active role when children are using technology.

Nature deficit disorder

Many children would prefer to stay inside rather than play outdoors because they've become accustomed to indoor play, according to Richard Louv the author of *Last Child in the Woods*. He coined the term 'nature deficit disorder' to explain the impact of children being disconnected from nature. Louv draws on research to show that today's digitally saturated children need direct exposure to nature for healthy development.

In his film *Project Wild Thing*, filmmaker David Bond also explains how children's digital dependence has shaped their childhood at the expense of time in nature. In a quest to remedy the situation, Bond appoints himself as the Marketing Expert for Nature and with the help of a marketing and outdoor expert launches a national campaign to get British children outside using the free wonder product: nature.

Outdoor play is vital for physical and emotional development. It's also vital for promoting sleep, as time in natural light, especially first thing in the morning, helps the body regulate the production of seratonin, which boosts mood and helps children feel calm and focussed. We need to ensure that young children's digital habits aren't encroaching on opportunities to engage and play in nature.

How to balance children's green time with screen time

Time outdoors in nature is vital for optimal brain function, but many children spend their idle time staring at screens, *not* the sky. If children are constantly tethered to devices their brains don't get down time. They don't get to switch off. Children need white space for their minds to wander and process information and the opportunity for creative expression. But they can't do this if they're constantly processing information on screens. We need to teach children how to unplug from technology and plug back into real life (and the slower pace of life that nature organically offers).

Digital kids also need tech breaks by immersing themselves in nature. We need to encourage our children to have green time *after* they've used technology at home or school. Time in nature allows the brain to recalibrate and calm down after it's been stimulated by screen action.

Time in nature also switches off the prefrontal cortex of the brain where executive function or higher order thinking takes place (see Chapter 9 for more details). When the prefrontal cortex rests, it allows the subconscious to work. This is called mind wandering and it allows new ideas to flourish.

Time in nature also helps the brain to release dopamine, the feel-good neurotransmitter. Taking a walk, running or jumping on the trampoline can be a great incubation period for thinking and creativity – and this is why as adults we often have our best ideas in the shower or when listening to music or exercising (our prefrontal cortex is switched off and our brains are releasing dopamine.)

Privacy fears

Advances in voice-recognition software have seen new digital toys introduced to children's toy shelves. For example, children's toy manufacturers Mattel have released a smart doll, Hello Barbie, that can have conversations *with* children through voice recognition technology (and record and save the conversations that your child has in their own bedroom too!). The doll works in a similar way to that used by Apple's Siri. By simply pressing a button, the doll can understand what a child says and then respond. Privacy advocates are concerned about the risks this poses in terms of the potential for recording private conversations, and confidential data being used by third parties to target their advertising towards children.

> Major security breaches involving children's toy and technology companies are becoming more widespread.

Using techno-toys with internet-enabled capabilities, children can divulge sensitive or private information and there's no guarantee that this data is secure (even with the best security systems in place). So always be mindful about what data you share when setting up these toys.

Major security breaches involving children's toy and technology companies are becoming more widespread. They can have potentially damaging effects as personal accounts can be compromised and children's chat logs, photos, names, birth dates and security question data can be leaked online.

In addition to the data security risks associated with internet-enabled toys, there are also concerns about marketers' access to children's data. The increase in different mobile technologies combined with sophisticated technological advancements makes it easier for marketers to have direct access to our children and capture a comprehensive picture of their interests. Data aggregated from children's on-screen activities are sometimes sent to third-party advertisers, which is used to target advertising campaigns geared towards children.

There are concerns that exploitive child-targeted marketing tactics are undermining our parental values and our children's privacy.

Moreover, agencies and policies designed to protect children from harmful marketing have been unable to keep up with the avalanche of technologies that young children are now using, especially mobile devices and gaming consoles.

At a glance

How to encourage children's play in a digital age:

- **Encourage balanced play** – children need to play with both traditional and technological toys. They need a full range of play experiences that includes a balance between time spent indoors in virtual worlds with gadgets and time spent in the real world, interacting and playing with real people.
- **Evaluate marketing and advertising claims** – especially about products or programs that claim to be educational.
- **Make unstructured play a priority every day** – unstructured play is not wasted time. It's critical to our child's development.
- **Focus on the child, not the toy** – whether it's a digital or a traditional toy, the child needs to dominate and control the play experience. Remember the 90 per cent and 10 per cent rule when purchasing toys.
- **Provide a variety of play experiences** – children need opportunities for imaginative and physical play.
- **Prioritise green hours (even on wet days)** – provide and timetable opportunities for outdoor play.
- **Let children experience boredom** – it's one of the greatest experiences we can give them. Empty spaces in time enable children to explore and learn in creative ways.
- **Be careful about what information you (and your child) disclose online** – internet-enabled toys pose serious risks to children's privacy. Think carefully about using these toys with children and about what personal information you disclose online.

As busy parents, we're often afraid to slow our pace of life and provide opportunities for our children to engage in unstructured, outdoor play. There's a misplaced fear that our children will fall behind if they're not introduced to academics early on, or enrolled in structured activities, or using gadgets.

This isn't what young children necessarily need to thrive. They need opportunities for play. Unstructured, outdoor play is vital. It's imperative that we value play and teach our children to do so too, even in this digital age.

Closely related to play is physical movement. The next chapter explores why physical movement, the fifth building block in children's development, is critical for children and the ways in which technology is shaping children's physical activity levels.

7

Building block #5: Physical movement

In an increasingly sedentary world, we need to encourage our children to value and engage in physical activity.

Children's screen habits are encroaching on their physical activity levels. This chapter will highlight some of the critical physical movement skills that children need to master for optimal development and how their screen time can impede this process. This chapter will also highlight possible ways that technology can be used in healthy and helpful ways to support and promote children's physical activity.

Physical movement and the development of the brain

It is well known that physical movement is absolutely vital to children's brain development as well as their overall wellbeing. Indeed, brain architecture starts with the sensory and motor regions, which are located in the posterior part of the brain.

The posterior, more primal part of the brain was developed earlier in the history of evolution and is the part of the brain that controls the body's responses essential to survival. The next part of brain development involves the prefrontal cortex. Found at the front of the brain, this is where executive-function skills, like impulse control, are developed (see Chapter 9 for more details).

Physical movement actually sets up neural pathways (brain connections). Simple things like crawling, rolling, rocking, swinging and skipping all develop the brain architecture that's needed for subsequent, formal academic learning.

Indeed, a child's early physical and sensory experiences literally shape their brain. It's amazing how physical and cognitive development are intricately connected. The earlier example in Chapter 2 explained that a child who hasn't spent sufficient time rolling, swinging and tumbling often hasn't developed a good sense of balance (under-developed vestibular system) which makes it difficult to sit on the floor and on chairs in the classroom.

When children engage in physical experiences, their senses are recruited and their brain encodes and records information. Over time, these accumulated experiences allow the brain cells to connect and make associations (synaptic connections), helping children understand the world and how they can operate in it. This is the genesis of learning.

Once these basic movement skills and sensory information become automated, it frees up the brain to engage in higher-order thinking tasks.

Sedentary childhoods

Sadly, today many children lead sedentary lifestyles which can cause health problems. There's no denying that excessive amounts of screen time are to blame, at least in part. When children use screens there's a *displacement effect*. Playing video games, watching TV, or using the iPad, displaces physical activities like running, climbing, crawling or rolling, which leads to a less active lifestyle.

Increased screen time is certainly a contributing factor to children's declining physical movement patterns, but it's not the *only* culprit. There are other reasons for children's declining physical activity levels.

Children's opportunities to move and explore are being restricted and limited in a number of ways:

- **From a young age we place babies in containers** – rockers, slings, prams, high-chairs, seat-props all restrict movement. Physical containers may inhibit children's development according to baby expert Pinky McKay.

- **There's a culture of surplus safety** – parents, educators and carers are expected to police, restrict and minimise any element of perceived danger in our children's lives. The designs of playgrounds are being modified because of fears of litigation due to accidents (it's so hard to find a merry-go-round anymore). To further compound this problem, time restrictions are also being placed on their play activities (as outlined in the previous chapter).

The designs of playgrounds are being modified because of fears of litigation due to accidents.

- **Increasing pressure on families and early childhood educators to introduce formal academic learning earlier and earlier in childhood** – has resulted in physical activity and play being undermined and undervalued. (Chapter 6 explored the academic creep and other socio-cultural factors that account for why children are spending less time playing.)

- **Changing family structures and life** – many families now have dual income-earners and this has reduced time available for physical movement and incidental exercise.

- **Schools are changing too** – some have even reduced playtime because of fears of injuries while others have restricted play spaces and implemented rules that reduce opportunities for creative and active play (e.g. banning cartwheels, chasing games).

Obviously, a multitude of factors are combining to diminish children's physical activity levels, including the explosion in screens.

How technology can hamper children's movement skills

Children's passive lifestyles impacts on their physical development in two ways:

- poorer cardiovascular health, increasing the risk of obesity and other health conditions
- waning motor skills.

One of the greatest threats to young children's health and wellbeing is excessive screen time. The health implications associated with a sedentary lifestyle are significant and in addition, can cause physical developmental delays. This is a serious issue that we must address (and quickly) so our children's health isn't jeopardised. The solution isn't to ban screens altogether (we all know this would be near impossible), but we must find healthy and balanced ways to incorporate technology into children's lives.

Obesity and health risks

Active Healthy Kids Australia estimates that one in three Australian children will be obese by 2025. Inactive lifestyles and unhealthy food habits are contributing factors. An Australian study has found that 80 per cent of Australian children aged five to 17 are not getting daily exercise.

There's a very distinct correlation between the number of hours spent with screens and the rates of childhood obesity. It's a simple cause-and-effect relationship: the more time children spend with screens, the less time they have being physically active and the increased risk of obesity and other health ailments.

Overuse of digital media is associated with negative health consequences for children, with screen time in excess of recommended limits (see Physical activity and screen time recommendations on p 137) associated with obesity, increased risk of the precursors to cardiovascular disease and negative effects on academic performance and social skills.

TECH TIP ✂

Keep TVs out of bedrooms. Children with TVs in bedrooms are more likely to be overweight. Dennison and Jenkins found that on average, children who have a TV set in their bedroom view over 4.5 hours more TV per week than children without one in their bedroom.

It's imperative that children's bedrooms are TV-free (and tech-free) spaces.

Lack of physical activity

Most health guidelines suggest young children accumulate 60 minutes of moderate-to-vigorous physical activity each day *and* spend no more than 2 hours engaging with screen media each day (see infographic and table below). Failure to adhere to the physical activity guidelines results in a three to four times greater chances of obesity. Importantly, the adverse health consequences persist even among children who meet physical activity guidelines, but not screen time recommendations.

The impacts of children's physical inactivity are further compounded by the food habits that they often adopt when using screens. Children tend to eat more calorie-laden, nutrient-poor foods when using technology and are exposed to advertisements for unhealthy foods too. (See Chapter 8 for more details about how children's nutritional patterns can change because of technology.)

Physical activity guidelines

Young children need to accumulate 60 min of moderate-to-vigorous physical activity each day.

Young children shouldn't spend more than 2 hours engaging with screen media each day.

Children are 3 to 4 times greater of suffering from obesity if they don't adhere to the physical activity guidelines.

Children who meet physical activity guidelines, but not screen-time recommendations are more likely to have adverse health.

Children tend to eat more calorie-laden, nutrient-poor foods when using technology

Children are exposed to up to 40 000 advertisements each year, many of which are for unhealthy foods.

Case study

Eight-year-old Max loved playing in his cubby house, riding his bike and jumping on his trampoline, but this changed very dramatically when he received a video-game console for his birthday.

'Max was mesmerised with playing his video game and he didn't want to play outside. When he wasn't playing the game he was either sulking about it or talking about it. My happy-go-lucky boy no longer got excited about the little things. He was immersed in his digital world and totally disinterested in the real world. I was petrified that a video-game had stolen my son!'

Max became very agitated if his parents he suggested he turn off the video game and he started having trouble sleeping at night. Max's friendship circle diminished. Within a couple of months Max's parents noticed that he'd gained a significant amount of weight.

When his teacher reported that his school performance had declined too, Max's parents decided to enforce some strict screen time limits and curtail his video-game time. Over the period of three months, Max eventually found a more balanced approach to using his video game console.

Physical activity and screen time recommendations

Physical activity and sedentary guidelines*		
Age	Recommended physical activity levels and suggested activities	Sedentary guidelines
0–1 year (babies)	**Floor-based play** is recommended for this age range. It's difficult to specify an exact amount of time as their waking hours vary so much.	**No screen time** for 0–2 year olds.**

0–1 year (babies) continued	**Suggested activities:** • provide toys for floor-time play that encourage them to reach, roll and explore • play music to encourage movement • encourage physical movement in the bath.	Children aged 0–5 years should be restrained or inactive for **no more than one hour** at a time (excluding time for sleep).
1–5 years (toddlers and preschoolers)	**Three hours** per day of **physical activity** (light, moderate or vigorous) spread throughout the day. **Suggested activities:** • ball and balloon play • movement games • running, walking, skipping, rolling, climbing, crawling, jumping.	**No screen time** for 0–2 year olds**
		No more than **one hour per day** of screen time for 2–5 year olds.
		Children aged 0–5 years should be restrained or inactive for **no more than one hour** at a time (excluding time for sleep).
5–12 years	At least **one hour** of moderate to vigorous intensity physical activity every day. Additional benefits will result from more physical activity (i.e. greater than an hour). **Suggested activities:** • aerobic activities requiring vigorous intensity such as running, climbing, surfing, bike riding, obstacle courses. Visit playgrounds, parks, beaches/ lakes. Enjoy gardening, games and structured classes (e.g. tennis, soccer, martial arts, netball).	No more than **two hours per day** of screen time.** To minimise the time spent being sedentary each day, break up long periods of inactivity with one of the suggested activities.

*These guidelines are based on the Australian Department of Health Guidelines. These are very closely related to the American Academy of Pediatrics' guidelines that were proposed until late 2015.

** Screen time is referred to as TV viewing, touch-screen devices, watching DVDs, computers and electronic games.

Virtually impossible guidelines?

Before we worry that we've failed as a parent because our children have exceeded these recommendations for screen time or we've not met the physical activity requirements, rest assured that many parents find these guidelines, especially the screen time guidelines, unrealistic in a digital age where screens are ubiquitous.

Consider:

- In 2006, Rideout and Hame's study revealed that 61 per cent of children under 2 years of age use screens on a daily basis – and this was before the introduction of touch-screen devices!
- Findings from the 2014 Australian Physical Activity Report Card showed that only 26 per cent of Australians aged 2–4 years met the recommended Australian screen time guidelines of accumulating no more than 1 hour per day. Further, only 29 per cent of Australians aged 5–17 years met the recommended Australian screen time guidelines of accumulating no more than two hours per day.
- Other studies have found that 45 per cent of 8-year-olds and 80 per cent of Australians aged 12–17 use screens more than the recommended limit of two hours per day.

Children certainly need screen time limits, but I don't think we can prescribe universal, safe amounts of screen time based on a child's chronological age. This isn't an exact science and we don't have empirical research that confirms that there are 'safe' amounts of screen time.

In fact, screen time recommendations can potentially lull parents into a false sense of security. If we focus exclusively on quantifying how much a child is consuming at the expense of considering *what* or *when* they're using the technology, it can be detrimental. (See Chapter 10 for more details about screen time guidelines and a formula for determining healthy screen time limits.)

In 2015 the American Academy of Pediatrics (AAP) announced that it will be reviewing its existing screen time recommendations in 2016 due to fears that the current recommendations (zero screen time for under 2 and no more than 2 hours/day for children aged over 2 years) were considered to be outdated. Put simply, the existing recommendations don't fit with the modern reality and need to be adjusted so they don't become obsolete.

The following health and safety tips from the AAP suggest:

- **Treat media as you would any other environment in your child's life.** The same parenting guidelines apply in both real and virtual environments. Set limits; children need and expect them. Know your children's friends, both online and off. Know what platforms, software, and apps your children are using, where they are going on the web, and what they are doing online.

> The same parenting guidelines apply in both real and virtual environments.

- **Set limits and encourage playtime.** Tech use, like all other activities, should have reasonable limits. Unstructured and offline play stimulates creativity. Make unplugged playtime a daily priority, especially for very young children. And don't forget to join your children in unplugged play whenever you're able.
- **Families who play together, learn together.** Family participation is also great for media activities – it encourages social interactions, bonding, and learning. Play a video game with your kids. It's a good way to demonstrate good sportsmanship and gaming etiquette. You can also introduce and share your own life experiences and perspectives – and guidance – as you play the game.
- **Be a good role model.** Teach and model kindness and good manners online. And, because children are great mimics, limit your own media use. In fact, you'll be more available for and connected with your children if you're interacting, hugging and playing with them, rather than simply staring at a screen.
- **Know the value of face-to-face communication.** Very young children learn best through two-way communication. Engaging in back-and-forth 'talk time' is critical for language development. Conversations can be face-to-face or, if necessary, by video chat, with a traveling parent or far-away grandparent. Research has shown that it's that 'back-and-forth conversation' that improves

language skills – much more so than 'passive' listening or one-way interaction with a screen.

- **Create tech-free zones.** Keep family mealtimes and other family and social gatherings tech-free. Recharge devices overnight – outside your child's bedroom to help children avoid the temptation to use them when they should be sleeping. These changes encourage more family time, healthier eating habits, and better sleep, all critical for children's wellness.

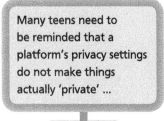

Many teens need to be reminded that a platform's privacy settings do not make things actually 'private' ...

- **Don't use technology as an emotional pacifier.** Media can be very effective in keeping kids calm and quiet, but it should not be the only way they learn to calm down. Children need to be taught how to identify and handle strong emotions, come up with activities to manage boredom, or calm down through breathing, talking about ways to solve the problem, and finding other strategies for channelling emotions.

- **Apps for kids – do your homework.** More than 80,000 apps are labeled as educational, but little research has demonstrated their actual quality. Products pitched as 'interactive' should require more than pushing and swiping. Look to organisations like Common Sense Media for reviews about age-appropriate apps, games and programs to guide you in making the best choices for your children.

- **It's OK for your teen to be online.** Online relationships are part of typical adolescent development. Social media can support teens as they explore and discover more about themselves and their place in the grown-up world. Just be sure your teen is behaving appropriately in both the real and online worlds. Many teens need to be reminded that a platform's privacy settings do not make things actually 'private' and that images, thoughts, and behaviours teens share online will instantly become a part of their digital footprint indefinitely. Keep lines of communication open and let them know you're there if they have questions or concerns.

- **Remember that kids will be kids.** Kids will make mistakes using media. Try to handle errors with empathy and turn a mistake into a teachable moment. But some indiscretions, such as sexting, bullying, or posting self-harm images, may be a red flag that hints at trouble ahead. Parents should take a closer look at your child's behaviours and, if needed, enlist supportive professional help, including from your pediatrician.

Despite the changes being made to the AAP screen time guidelines, the Australian Department of Health confirmed in 2015 that there are no immediate plans to revise the current Australian guidelines because they're not prescriptive screen time limits, but are instead recommended guidelines. In Chapter 10 a simple formula is provided for determining healthy screen time limits for children of various ages, without prescribing a universal amount of time based on children's chronological age.

Waning physical skills: the displacement effect

Studies are showing that increasing numbers of children are entering primary school with movement skill deficits. Under-developed gross and fine motor skills can hamper children's capacity to learn and result in increased injuries.

Physical skills are essential to learning

Movement literally wires the brain for learning. But poor physical development and motor skills can be a bottleneck for later learning. If a child's cognitive energy is directed towards performing basic motor skills or processing sensory information, they are unable to direct their attention to higher order thinking processes like impulse control and working memory.

Over time – and with a variety of physical experiences – children's brains and bodies can work together to learn about the physical environment they're in and automate these movement skills and sensory information.

It's therefore critical that children's basic movement skills are adequately developed in the early years and not hampered by excessive screen time. If they're not well developed, it can have a cascading effect on their subsequent learning and wellbeing.

There are some rudimentary physical skills that young children must develop and master to ensure that their future learning and development are supported. Important skills include:

1 **Crawling** – this is a vital skill for a child's neurological development. Not only is it a new form of moving for the infant, it also develops a host of other skills that are critical for later learning and development (e.g. shoulder and hip girdles, upper body strength, visual tracking skills that are essential for reading later on, the tonic neck reflex that is required for sitting at a desk and then staring straight ahead as we may do in a classroom and the creation of connections between the two cerebral hemispheres in the brain). It's imperative that children aren't propped in front of screens or other devices that prevent them from crawling.

SCREEN-FREE TIP ✂

This is a critical stage so don't be in a hurry to bypass it. Provide lots of opportunities for infants to crawl and creep. Provide objects for them to chase and use tunnels and ladders to crawl along.

2 **Vestibular development** – the vestibular system gives children a sense of balance and helps to keep them upright. This is one sense that children aren't born with, but is developed

over time through the process of movement. It's located deep within the inner ear. When children move, the fluid in the inner ear shifts and provides sensory input about the position of their body in space, allowing them to maintain balance.

Children's bodies literally crave this type of sensory input. This is why children love merry-go-rounds and rolling down hills (and why we hate it as adults as our vestibular system is well developed). So the child in the classroom who finds it virtually impossible to sit still on the carpet, constantly fidgets or wants to rock continually on their chair may, in many instances, have poorly developed vestibular skills. This can greatly impact on their ability to learn as their cognitive resources are directed towards the sensory region of the brain (not the prefrontal cortex where higher-order thinking occurs).

SCREEN-FREE TIP ✂

Provide lots of opportunities for children to roll, spin, rock and hang. Playgrounds and outdoor play in general provide natural opportunities for children to explore many of these movements.

3 **Proprioception skills** – these skills are developed when children know where their physical body is in space. For most adults it's intuitive and automatic, but children are still learning to figure out where their physical body is and what it can do. This is why we can walk up a flight of stairs without looking directly at them and why our children need to do it very carefully. This is also why children have more accidents as they're often unaware of what their body is capable of doing.

SCREEN-FREE TIP ✂

Provide lots of opportunities for children to find out what their bodies can do via pushing, pulling, playing, climbing, lifting, jumping, bouncing, squeezing, sucking, chewing, blowing. Again, physical and unstructured play is the best way to develop such skills.

4 **Fine-motor skills** – involve the use of the small muscles in the fingers, hands and arms to control, manipulate and use materials and tools. These skills are a foundation for the attainment of other essential academic and life skills: e.g. writing, cutting with scissors, independent dressing and toileting.

SCREEN-FREE TIP ✂

Provide lots of opportunities for children to manipulate, explore and create with playdough, pegs, tweezers and tongs, squeeze fruit and enjoy messy play with slime, sand, clay and mud as well as use construction materials and toys.

Children should have a dominant hand between 4–6 years. This means that they should consistently favour one hand over the other for fine motor activities.

5 **Rough and tumble play** – is a crucial part of childhood. Children test and rehearse their physical skills, develop important social skills, learn about their physical strengths and what their bodies can do via rough and tumble play. One of the key skills they develop is impulse control, which is a higher order thinking skill (see Chapter 9 for more details on executive-function skills).

SCREEN-FREE TIP ✂

Encourage opportunities for children to engage in rough and tumble play. For babies and infants this can involve bouncing and being lifted into the air, but never shaken as this can be very dangerous. For toddlers and preschoolers it can mean chasing and spinning, for primary school children it often means chasing and wrestling. Boys in the primary school years in particular need lots of opportunities for rough and tumble play as their hormones surge.

Case STUDY

Jenny has been a kindergarten teacher for 23 years. She's noticed a rapid decline in children's fine motor skills.

Jenny explains, 'Ever since touch screens became popular for little ones and they started spending more time playing video games than hanging in trees and roaming backyards, I've noticed how their fine-motor skills have changed. I'm worried that their screen time is also impacting on the development of a dominant hand. Kids today enter kindergarten without a hand preference – they simply don't have the opportunity to practice these skills.'

TECHNO MYTH-BUSTER

MYTH: Children should use a stylus when using a touch-screen device.

FACT: A stylus doesn't replicate the natural pencil grip and isn't necessary.

Holding a stylus requires a slightly different pencil grip to what's required to hold a pencil/pen. The hand doesn't rest on the screen and styluses are often a different weight to a pencil/pen. So holding a stylus doesn't necessarily equate to holding a pen/pencil. Styluses are fine to use, especially if more precise actions are required on the screen, but they don't necessarily develop handwriting skills.

Increasing injury rates

The Australian Centre for Research into Injury in Sport and its Prevention has reported that children's sports injury rates are increasing. It has been suggested that their declining motor skills may be one reason to account for these increased injury rates and that their diminishing physical skills may also be a result of excessive screen time.

Hospital emergency departments and paediatricians are reporting increasing numbers of children presenting with playground injuries. While there's no conclusive research evidence to account for the increase as yet, there are two broad speculations as to why this may be occurring:

1 parents who are absorbed in their own screens and smart phones may not be adequately supervising children in playgrounds (i.e. techno-glect)
2 children don't have the motor skills required to navigate some playground equipment because they're not spending enough time playing outdoors required to develop these necessary skills.

This is compelling evidence that we need to ensure kids are getting opportunities to be physically active. Outdoor playgrounds are ideal tools to develop children's physical skills and competencies.

How technology can help children's physical movement

Technology and screens can certainly inhibit physical activity, but there are also some potential positives to consider too. The following technologies encourage physical activity:

- exergames
- interactive TV
- kids' exercise trackers.

Exergames

The use of exergames – video games that require gross motor activity – can encourage children to be physically active. Products like the PlayStation Move, Wii Fit and X-Box games are promoted as healthier alternatives to more sedentary push-button video games.

A 2013 study found that playing active video games uses more energy than playing sedentary games, but often not as much energy as playing the actual physical game itself. (Often exergames aren't as beneficial as other forms of physical activity because the energy expended is often not of sufficient intensity or duration to contribute toward the daily recommendations for physical activity.)

However, in a 2011 comparison study the energy expenditure associated with six different types of interactive digital exercise games was measured among children of various body masses. The researchers found that all exergames helped to elevate energy expenditure levels among children in the normal and overweight ranges. They also found that five of the six exergames studied elevated the children's heart rates more than walking at a pace of 4 kilometres per hour.

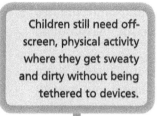

Children still need off-screen, physical activity where they get sweaty and dirty without being tethered to devices.

(It's important to note, however, that expenditure levels in this study were only measured for 10 minutes.)

Exergames may be a better choice than other less active games and screen activities – and might be a possible form of therapeutic exercise for obese children – but we shouldn't be duped into thinking that these games are beneficial in terms of exercise. Children still need off-screen, physical activity where they get sweaty and dirty without being tethered to devices.

Other recent technology-movement initiatives that are yet to be researched include exercise bikes that have video-game screens attached. The bikes literally power the video game console. There are also digital playgrounds with interactive walls and floor tiles that encourage children to run, jump, tap and swipe, using motion-sensing technologies.

While these products may boost children's physical activity in the short term (and be a viable option for very inactive or overweight children), they are unlikely to have the comprehensive or lasting results that can be achieved by outdoor, vigorous activity.

Interactive TV

Thanks to significant technological advancements, interactive children's TV is now a reality. Video game consoles with motion- and voice-sensing controllers connect to TVs and allow young children to interact with TV characters and scenes.

For example with Kinect Sesame Street TV, on-screen characters can catch a talking ball if children throw it to them. Children can pick carrots from a garden, clap a certain number of times or perform physical movements such as jumping, skipping, waving, throwing or standing stationary, according to the on-screen character's instructions.

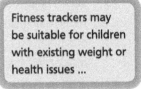

Fitness trackers may be suitable for children with existing weight or health issues ...

This is a significant evolution in children's TV as it promotes more interactive learning and reduces sedentary behaviour. As with exergames, however, interactive TV will not necessarily yield wonderful results for children's physical activity levels, but it's a superior option to traditional, sedentary TV viewing.

Kids' exercise trackers

Fitness trackers designed for children have been marketed as a tool to help combat childhood obesity. Trackers can provide data on children's sleep patterns, accumulated physical and sedentary activity. Few studies have examined the benefits of trackers for children but studies with adults have shown that there's typically a novelty factor associated with them.

Fitness trackers may be suitable for children with existing weight or health issues, but it's unlikely that these gadgets will become popular for otherwise healthy children. In addition, trackers are a costly device to give children and many require frequent charging.

Most trackers also need to be physically connected to another device (a computer, smart phone or tablet) to extract data. Children (and their time-poor parents) are unlikely to continue these habits over time.

At a glance

How to encourage movement in a technology-fuelled world:

- **Limit screen time** – children's general health risks can be reduced by minimising their sedentary time, especially excessive screen time. Establish and enforce clear expectations about how much screen time children can have each day. (See Chapter 10 for more details about health digital habits.)

- **Avoid using screen time as a reward (or punishment)** – in desperation, our children may promise to walk the dog, set the dinner table and make their bed every day in order to watch screens. But using screen time as a reward can be counter-productive as it makes screen time even more important to children. It is preferable for children to see screens as part of their everyday lives and most importantly, learn how to use them appropriately. Children need to see technology as a tool, not a toy.

- **Encourage physical activity** – in previous generations children were naturally more physically active. As we lead more sedentary lives today, we need to actively encourage our children to be physically active.

- **Minimise sedentary time** – look for incidental ways to exercise. Standing desks can be a great alternative. Encourage children to take regular tech-breaks and do something active. (See the 20-20-20-20 Rule detailed in Chapter 11.)

- **Discourage binge TV** – long periods of sedentary activity are not recommended for young children (unless there are extenuating circumstances like illness).

- **Model healthy habits** – it's no coincidence that children with active parents tend to be more active themselves. Talk and model healthy habits by maintaining a healthy lifestyle. Implement incidental exercise like walking to the shops or parking the car further from the destination and walking. It's during childhood that physical activity habits are ingrained.

▪ **Keep media out of bedrooms** – children with digital devices in their bedrooms are much more likely to be more sedentary than their peers whose bedrooms are tech-free.

▪ **Understand that there is no substitute for real physical activity** – there's something magical about running around huffing and puffing. Exergames, interactive games/TV and exercise trackers can be beneficial, but they're no substitute for untethered, physical activity.

If it's not carefully managed, technology can significantly encroach on children's physical activity levels. While there are some positives to exergames, interactive games/TV and exercise trackers, these digital tools are no substitute for real physical activity. In an increasingly sedentary world, we need to encourage our children to value and engage in physical activity.

The next chapter will explore the sixth building block for children's development, nutrition, and consider how technology is shaping this building block.

8

Building block #6: Nutrition

Technology can hamper children's nutrition through the advertising of unhealthy foods, snacking patterns, screen-dinners and the promotion of disordered eating habits.

This chapter isn't intended to provide a comprehensive overview of children's nutrition. Instead, it will present an overview of the current research about the dietary needs for young children's optimal development. It will also focus on how technology is changing children's eating habits and food preferences.

Quality foods build brains

The early years are a time of rapid brain development. Developing brains, from 24 weeks of gestation, right through to about five years of age, are particularly vulnerable to nutrient insufficiencies. So we need to carefully consider *what* we're feeding our children. Quality nutrition builds brains. There's increasing evidence to confirm that children's diets need to be rich in certain foods (and to minimise other foods) to facilitate optimal development.

Science is pinpointing *exactly* what developing brains and bodies need for optimal health and nutrition. Like many of the other building blocks explored in this book, research is now confirming what our grandparents knew – whole, unprocessed foods are best for children (and adults too). Recently updated Australian guidelines now recommend 'choosing whole foods or minimally-processed foods'.

The brain also requires a lot of energy. It uses 20 per cent of our daily food intake. Brains are comprised primarily of fat and water. Neurons, which drive our thinking, learning and states of being require:

- good fats
- protein
- complex carbohydrates
- micronutrients
- water.

These neuro-developmental needs are also consistent with the updated *Australian Dietary Guidelines* released in 2013.

Good fats

One of the key findings from the paeditric nutrition research is that babies and young children need good fats. Given that the brain is 60 per cent fatty tissue, essential fatty acids (EFAs) are required for optimal health and nutrition as well as brain development in infants and young children. Good quality fats include avocado, coconut oil, oily fish, nuts, butter and full-fat dairy.

Hydrogenated or trans fats (often found in long-life packaged foods such as biscuits, cheap margarines and fried foods), should be consumed sparingly.

Children don't need low-fat diets. They need EFAs, as well as quality protein, complex carbohydrates, micronutrients and water.

Young children need a diet high in EFAs

EFAs are vital for an important neurological process to occur – myelination. Neurons (brain cells) send signals to one another along an axon. Early in life, axons are like uninsulated wires. The process of myelination involves the axons being coated with a myelin sheath, a fatty-white substance that helps make the transmission of neural signals smooth and efficient (they're like an insulated wire). This process begins in week 14 of foetal development, peaks during the early years of life and continues until adolescence.

EFAs are critical for myelination to occur as they're a key component in the myelin sheath. EFAs can be consumed through diet or with purified supplements, as the body cannot produce them. Nuts, unprocessed oils, avocado, cold-water fish and dark leafy greens are the most abundant sources of EFAs.

Protein

Protein is critical for children's brain function, their overall emotional wellbeing and assists with their concentration and learning.

Proteins provide amino acids which neurons need for optimal function. Amino acids make up the brain's neurotransmitters which are biochemical messengers that carry signals from one brain cell to another. The brain cells in turn transmit signals to different parts of the body so that they can perform their individual tasks. Basically, if these messengers are fed quality proteins, they can perform more efficiently and deliver the goods.

> Proteins are also essential for children's emotional wellbeing, in particular their happiness.

Proteins are also essential for children's emotional wellbeing, in particular their happiness. Insufficient protein means that the brain cannot produce enough of the neurotransmitters such as serotonin (mood and sleep regulator) and dopamine (aids in keeping children alert, focused, managing stress and assists with memory). These neurotransmitters are required in the correct balance for children to feel good.

Great sources of protein for young children include meat (beef, poultry, lamb, pork), fish, beans, nuts, legumes and dairy.

Micronutrients

Vitamins and minerals are essential for building and rebuilding the brain. They come from fruits, vegetables and whole foods. For example, B vitamins aid in the production of energy for the brain cells and help to produce neurotransmitters such as serotonin which gives a sense of wellbeing, and GABA which assists in concentration and focus.

Now before you rush off to your health food store and buy supplements to boost your child's brain functioning, first consider their diet. These food sources can help:

- *leafy greens* – are a great source of B vitamins, as are the hulls of grains
- *seeds, nuts and red meats* – are great for the production of zinc, which is needed by the hippocampus (the area of the brain that processes short- and long-term memories)
- *calcium* – is a mineral used to maintain the electrical environment of the brain and displace harmful substances.

Some food sources can actually counteract the beneficial effects of other nutrients. These foods can diminish the valuable nutrients in the body. Refined sugars, hydrogenated and trans fats, chemical additives such as food colouring, artificial sweeteners and high-fructose corn syrup, and preservatives should be avoided, where possible.

Complex carbohydrates

Carbohydrates, also referred to as sugars, act as fuel for the developing brain. So children do need carbohydrates for brain function. However, not all carbohydrates are created equal. We have to ensure that children consume the *right types*, the *right amount* and carbohydrates at the *right time* to be beneficial.

Too many simple carbohydrates can result in blood sugar spikes and this can sometimes translate into hyperactivity and poorer concentration and attention spans in children. Similarly, too little carbohydrate consumption can make children feel tired, irritated and unable to concentrate. Excessive amounts of carbohydrates, particularly simple carbohydrates, can be stored as fats.

Children today are consuming more sugar than ever before. On average children aged 1–3-years-old are consuming 12 teaspoons of sugar each day and on average 4–8-years-olds consume 21 teaspoons according to the American Heart Association. This exceeds the limit of 3 to 4 teaspoons for preschoolers and early primary years and between 5 to 8 teaspoons for older children.

> On average children aged 1-3-years-old are consuming 12 teaspoons of sugar each day ...

Children need to consume complex carbohydrates for healthy brain development. When considering your child's complex carbohydrate needs:

- look for foods with slow-releasing sugars. For example, rolled oats, brown rice, rye bread, vegetables (excluding potatoes and parsnips).
- combine proteins with carbohydrates. For example, sourdough toast with eggs, fruit with yogurt and seeds.
- encourage children to eat smaller meals, more often, to keep energy levels consistent. This aids with concentration too.

Hydration

It's critical that children are adequately hydrated for optimal brain and body function. Brains depend on proper hydration to function optimally. Our brain cells typically require twice as much energy as other cells in our body. Water best meets children's fluid needs and not juices, cordials and soft drinks.

When children don't consume enough liquids, the brain cells lose efficiency and children find it harder to maintain their focus.

Dehydration can also impair short-term memory function and recall long-term memories. Basic thinking is impaired when we're dehydrated.

Dehydration can lead to dizziness, fatigue, lethargy, decline in concentration and reduced cognitive ability. By the time a child feels thirsty there could already be up to a 10 per cent decline in their cognitive function.

Recommended daily amount of fluids is:

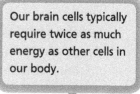

Our brain cells typically require twice as much energy as other cells in our body.

- 5 glasses (1 litre) for 5 to 8 year olds
- 7 glasses (1.5 litres) for 9 to 12 year olds
- 8 to 10 glasses (2 litres) for 13+ years.

How technology can help children's nutrition

Sadly, this is one building block where technology has few advantages to offer. Fortunately, there is an increasing focus and interest on healthy eating for children. As parents we're spoilt for choice when it comes to finding blogs, apps and websites dedicated to healthy eating for children. We can quickly google a recipe or have tips and tricks about preparing healthy family food at our fingertips.

The trick is to find credible sources whose work is supported by research. Unfortunately there are many bloggers who have gained immense popularity in online spaces whose methods, practices and philosophies are not grounded in research. In some instances, their suggestions have proven to be dangerous and very unhealthy for young children, so make sure you're sourcing nutritional information from reliable online sources.

How technology can hinder children's nutrition

As outlined in Chapter 7 there's a direct cause-and-effect relationship between screen time and obesity. Researchers have hypothesised that children's media habits increase the chances of obesity in several ways:

- food advertising promotes unhealthy foods
- unhealthy snacks
- screen dinners
- disordered eating.

Food advertising

Media advertising has a powerful effect on children's food choices as children learn from what they observe on screens. Research by Kunkel and Strasburger has found that children under 8 are cognitively and psychologically defenseless against advertising. Children haven't yet learnt to understand the notion of selling and typically accept claims, without questioning them.

> Research has found that children under 8 are cognitively and psychologically defenseless against advertising.

Given that young children are consuming vast amounts of screen media, it's easy to see how food advertising – be it overt or covert – is affecting children's food habits. A 2006 position statement from the American Academy of Pediatrics claims that children are exposed to over 40 000 advertisements each year and that this exposure contributes to obesity, poor nutrition and cigarette and alcohol use.

Most of the research in this area is on children's exposure to food advertising via TV advertising, but children now have access to many screens and are likely to be exposed to even more food advertising today. Food advertisers can now reach children through websites, social media and even advergames (branded games and apps with advertising).

Studies published in 2007 and 2001 provide evidence to suggest that fast-food branding influences children's taste perceptions. In a 2010 study published in the *Pediatrics* journal, young children tasted identical foods side-by-side such as chips, nuggets, juice and baby carrots. One was on a popular fast-food wrapper and the other one was on a plain wrapper of the same colour and texture.

When asked which foods tasted the same or better, the majority of children overwhelmingly selected the foods on the fast food wrappers. The study also found that branding had a significantly greater effect among children with more television sets in their homes and with children who ate at the fast-food restaurant more frequently – evidence that advertising exerts a strong influence on children's taste perceptions.

As parents we also have to contend with the nag factor or pester power – our children's repeated requests for particular products associated with popular TV or movie characters (if you've ever taken your little ones grocery shopping you'll know exactly what I'm talking about.) A team of researchers from the John Hopkins Bloomberg School of Public Health examined the nag factor. They interviewed 64 mothers of children aged 3–5 and they found

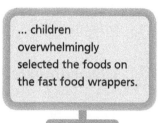

... children overwhelmingly selected the foods on the fast food wrappers.

that a child's familiarity with commercial television characters was significantly associated with overall, as well as specific, types of nagging. Packaging, commercials and characters were seen to be compelling factors that prompted children's nagging.

While its affects have not yet been researched, there's also subliminal advertising in popular media. For example, brands carefully ensure favourable product placements in popular movies and TV programs. Social media is also gaining popularity with children and there are targeted advertisements that users consume that are typically for unhealthy food and drink products.

While large food and drink companies have agreed to implement some self-imposed restrictions in terms of food and beverage advertising in children's media targeting children under 12, there are no formal checks in place to ensure companies are complying with these guidelines. In Australia there's a stringent self-regulatory system and voluntary codes for food and beverage advertising directed towards children but there's insufficient evidence to determine whether the codes have affected the rate of food and beverage advertising on commercial, free-to-air TV.

Unhealthy snacks

Children, like us, often eat more of the wrong types of snacks when using technology. They are also unaware of how much they're eating when they're watching screens, which can cause them to overeat.

> Children also tend to eat unhealthier foods when using technology.

Children also tend to eat unhealthier foods when using technology. Harris, Bargh and Brownell found that children who watched cartoons with food commercials ate 45 per cent more snack foods than those children watched cartoons without food advertising.

Screen dinners

Eating meals while in front of the TV or touch-screen device is common practice for many families. In a 2015 poll conducted by the American Speech-Language-Hearing Association, 24 per cent of 2-year-old children use technology at the dinner table and by the age of eight, it was nearly 45 per cent. However, this is a prime time for interaction and language development.

Now I'm not suggesting that occasional screen dinners are bad. We often enjoy Mexican with a movie on a Saturday night (when I'm too exhausted to cook). It's a lovely ritual. But we need to be careful that screen dinners don't become the norm *every* night.

When children regularly eat in front on the TV or with other media devices like tablets, there are opportunity costs. For example, they are not getting the language interaction they require for optimal development (see Chapter 4 for more details).

There are also concerns that this encourages mindless eating. Some paediatric nutritionists have even raised concerns that children's food preferences and taste palettes may be changing because they're not focusing on really tasting food when in front of a screen.

Obviously this mindless eating isn't conducive to healthy food habits. We need to put a lid on children's screen time at meal times. There really should be no tablets at the table and we should try to switch off the TV during meal times. We need to keep the dinner table as a sacred place for conversation.

Case study

Mia was a fussy eater. This is common for many 2-year-olds whose once-ravenous appetite seems to disappear in an instant. One night in a desperate attempt to get Mia to eat her dinner, her mum Kylie offered to turn on an episode of *Peppa Pig* on the iPad during Mia's meal time.

Kylie was shocked when Mia not only ate all her dinner, but there was no negotiating or pleading with Mia to try what was on her plate or persuading her to eat more, as was often the case. She was amazed.

So the following night Mia insisted – and we all know how 2-year-olds can insist – that the iPad was turned on during her dinner. Kylie was reluctant at first but then the techno tantrum ensued. Coupled with the usual witching hour tantrum, Kylie turned on the iPad. Mia was elated and once again ate all of her dinner without complaint.

Over the course of the next few weeks, Kylie started to turn on the iPad before meal times and Mia continued to eat her dinner. But Kylie noticed that she and Mia weren't interacting, except for when Kylie had to try and pry the iPad out of Mia's hands so that she could tidy the table and start the bath routine.

Finally after a huge meltdown when *Peppa Pig* was turned off, Kylie decided that she no longer wanted the iPad at the dinner table. She explained the new rules to Mia and the first new nights were horrendous.

Still, Kylie persisted and started to do something special with Mia before mealtime instead. Even if it was just some one-on-one play time, a fun activity or a quick walk around the block, it was enough for Mia to disassociate the positive rewards she'd associated with watching *Peppa Pig* at mealtimes and transition positively to dinner time. Over a couple of weeks Kylie was able to have Mia eating at the dinner table – *without* the iPad.

Disordered eating

Not only is obesity a health risk associated with children's screen habits, but so too is disordered eating. Described as behaviours that reflect many, but not all of the symptoms associated with feeding and eating disorders such as anorexia nervosa, bulimia nervosa and/or binge eating. Disordered eating can cause significant health issues for some tweens and teenagers.

Between 1995 and 2005 the prevalence of disordered eating doubled amongst both males and females. Research by Becker and others suggests that media consumption is associated with dangerous methods of weight reduction. The study examined the impact of the introduction of television on Fijian adolescent girls' disordered eating attitudes and behaviours. The study found that 15 per cent of girls had induced vomiting to reduce weight a few years after TV was introduced and many no longer wanted to emulate their more rotund mothers and aunts (as they had previously done), but instead wanted to look like popular TV show characters.

> Between 1995 and 2005 the prevalence of disordered eating doubled amongst both males and females.

Sadly disordered eating is sometimes glamorised by popular media and on social media sites. To further compound this problem, children can easily gain access to websites promoting unhealthy eating practices.

As parents, we have to acknowledge and discuss the incidence of unhealthy eating habits when children see this in the media and constantly highlight healthy eating examples depicted in the media. Another reason why co-viewing is essential, where possible.

At a glance

How to encourage good nutrition in a digital age:

- **Eat EFAs** – encourage young children to eat EFAs and minimise consumption of unhealthy fats.
- **Provide healthy snacks for children when watching TV or movies** – so that children are less likely to want nutrient-poor, calorie-laden food choices.
- **Teach children to recognise advertising** – so that they're not passive consumers. Advertising can seem obvious to us as adults, but children are often unable to distinguish between advertisements and programs. Advertising can also be covert and subliminal with product placements and endorsements in TV shows and on websites.
- **Eat meals without media** – while there's nothing wrong with the occasional TV dinner, doing it every night isn't recommended. The benefits of talking around the table cannot be underestimated from a health and wellbeing perspective.
- **Discuss unhealthy eating habits** – talk about disordered eating habits that are shared or glamorised online.

While there are many apps and websites that promote healthy eating, we need to ensure that they're grounded in the latest research and from reliable sources. We also need to be mindful of how technology can hamper children's nutrition through the advertising of unhealthy foods, snacking patterns, screen-dinners and the promotion of disordered eating habits.

The next chapter looks at the seventh building block for optimal development in a digital age: executive-function skills. This chapter will explore how technology is shaping the part of the brain that's responsible for controlling impulses, memory and decision-making.

9

Building block #7:
Executive-function skills

There are mounting concerns that the development of executive-function skills is changing in the digital age as we're bombarded with sensory stimulus and information which activates the more primal part of the brain.

Just behind our child's forehead is the CEO of the brain: the prefrontal cortex. This is where executive-function skills are developed. These skills provide children with cognitive control, allowing them to resist impulses, stay on task, ignore distractions, make connections and decisions and solve problems.

Increasingly, researchers are discovering that a child's capacity to develop executive-function skills is a reliable predictor of not only their academic performance, but also their lifelong outcomes.

Being an effective learner is so much more than reciting numbers and recognising shapes, letters and colours. To be effective learners (and lead productive lives), children need to be able to work with others, work with distractions (and these are many in a digital world), retain and retrieve information, think flexibly and cope with multiple demands (again, lots of digital disruptions nowadays). These are examples of the multitude of skills that constitute executive-function skills.

Like all the building blocks explored in this book, technology can support or stifle the development of executive-function skills depending on how it's used with young children.

What are executive-function skills?

Executive-function skills are a suite of basic, generic skills that children need to *thrive* (not just *survive*) at school and beyond. Just like an air traffic control system, a child has to process multiple streams of information, know what to focus on, adjust tasks based on observations and new information, recall and apply details and evaluate their actions. It's basically the ability to simultaneously focus on multiple streams of information and then revise and adjust plans as necessary.

There are three broad components to executive function. They include:

1 **inhibitory control** – this is often referred to as self-control or impulse control, and is the ability to keep feelings and attention in check
2 **working memory** – is a child's capacity to retain, manipulate and recall pieces of information over short periods of time
3 **mental flexibility** – involves a child being able to adjust their thinking to meet different situations.

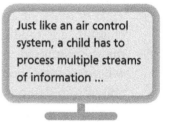

Just like an air control system, a child has to process multiple streams of information ...

Children need to be able to focus, retain, and process information. They also need to filter distractions and superfluous information and switch gears in the process. These are sophisticated skills and there are mounting concerns that the development of these skills is changing in the digital age as we're bombarded with sensory stimulus and information which activates the more primal part of the brain (see Chapter 2 for more details).

Executive-function skills in action

In a kindergarten classroom, Tom was assigned a group problem–solving activity with three of his peers on the iPad. Tom needed to:

- **recall** his teacher's instructions and the parameters of the activity (working memory)
- **adjust** his contribution to the activity according to what other group members say and do with the iPad (mental flexibility)
- **use** the app that his teacher asked him to use and not look at others if he becomes disinterested in the one he was assigned (impulse control)
- **learn** to effectively function in a group (self-control).

When are executive-function skills developed?

Children aren't born with executive-function skills, but they can be explicitly taught. It's our job as parents and educators to develop these skills in children. We can do this by establishing and reinforcing routines, modelling social behaviour and creating supportive and predictable relationships.

The roots of executive-function skills are established when children are toddlers and preschoolers. There's a sharp peak in the development of executive-function skills between the ages of 4–6 years (preschool years). This is when we're often encouraging children to demonstrate self-control (inhibitory control) and focus on following multi-step instructions (working memory).

Executive-function skills improve throughout adolescence, but it's not until early adulthood that they're fully developed. This is because the prefrontal cortex, which is responsible for the vast majority of executive function, doesn't fully develop until early adulthood (it's the last part of the brain to be myelinated – which is the fatty white sheath that coats the axons). It also tends to develop earlier in females than males. (This is why males are disproportionately represented in fatal car accidents – their impulse control isn't fully developed.)

How technology can help children's executive-function skills

Intentional use of technology can actually enhance children's executive-function skills. In particular, technology can be used to support children's working memory, impulse control and mental flexibility.

> Students can access information more quickly and efficiently with technology, which in turn sustains their attention.

Working memory

Specifically designed computer games can teach children how to pay attention. A study conducted by Ashman-East sought to determine whether low-achieving primary school students would significantly improve their mathematics achievement (on standardised tests) and working memory through computerised cognitive training addressing working memory. Ashman-East found that there were significant differences between the group receiving progressive computerised working-memory training compared to the group receiving basic computerised working-memory training.

Impulse control

Technology can help children improve their impulse control by teaching them to manage their attention. Educators and researchers are looking to harness the positive potential of gaming as an educational tool, especially for those subject areas like mathematics and science that are often perceived as difficult or dull. The gamification of education is one way that educators are looking to leverage the positive potential of digital tools to engage learners in these subject areas.

Teachers have also acknowledged the positive potential technology offers children's learning. In a 2012 study, 2500 teachers were surveyed and they acknowledged that the ability to instantly access information and move nimbly between tasks can improve students' learning. Students can access information more quickly and efficiently with technology, which in turn sustains their attention.

Teaching mindfulness

Mindfulness practices have become increasingly popular in Western cultures. There are compelling arguments and a growing body of research in different journals including *Science, American Psychological Association, Clinical Psychology Review* and *Psychiatry Research* that provides evidence to justify the use of mindfulness practices with young children.

As Weare proposes, while the research on the effectiveness of mindfulness for children is still in its infancy, the tentative findings from neuroscience and brain imaging is that mindfulness training reliably and profoundly alters the brain architecture and improves the quality of thoughts and feelings. In particular it helps children to manage their impulses and direct their attention. The weight of evidence concludes that mindfulness training:

- improves emotional, social and physical health and wellbeing of children
- helps children manage their behaviour and emotions
- reduces stress, anxiety and sleep issues
- improves cognitive performance and executive-function skills.

Research has shown that mindfulness training helps children stay in touch with their experiences and live in the present moment. Cultivating such awareness and the ability to sit in stillness and silence will be critical for today's children who have inherited a busy digital world. Through mindfulness training, children learn about personal insight and clarity and are more likely to experience emotional stability, have greater attention and resilience.

> Mindfulness ... improves emotional, social and physical health and wellbeing of children.

Ironically there are some brilliant apps that teach children meditations and mindfulness. Smiling Mind and Super Stretch Yoga are two popular examples for kids. There is also a wealth of free YouTube videos and websites dedicated to this area and this is likely to continue to expand, given the increased awareness of the importance of mindfulness training. These online mindfulness meditation trainings are a great way to utilise technology to teach mindfulness.

Mental flexibility

Mental flexibility involves adjusting to the unexpected. Children need to learn to roll with the punches or think about things from another perspective. Like the other components of executive-function, technologies can be used to strengthen this skill.

Research published by Davis and others has shown that physical activities, computerised games and specially modified school curricula can improve cognitive control skills in 4–12-year-olds. Video games develop children's ability to rapidly switch between tasks with competing demands, without errors. Three studies published between 2002 and 2014 have found that video games can improve older students' mental flexibility and it's possible that similar results would be replicated with young learners.

> Children need to learn to roll with the punches or think about things from another perspective.

How technology can hamper children's executive-function skills

Each of the three aspects of executive function – impulse control, working memory and mental flexibility – can be hampered by technology if it's not used appropriately. This section will outline simple ways that we can ensure that we preserve and promote children's executive-function skills in a digital age. In particular, it will examine how technology is shaping children's impulse control and working memory.

Managing impulses

It's critical that our children learn to manage their impulses. They need to filter their thoughts and impulses so that they can resist temptations and distractions. In classrooms, children rely on this skill to wait to be called upon for the answer as opposed to calling out, and it's used to refrain from hitting or yelling at peers who have hurt or frustrated them.

Paying attention in the digital age

As humans our brains have finite capacities, yet they're operating in a world with infinite technological distractions. We're bombarded with alerts, notifications and flashes that divert our attention from the task at hand and have the potential to incessantly distract children.

Think for a moment about the apps on our smart phone's home screen. I have a camera, calendar, internet browser, eBook reader, music player, weather app, email and photo gallery. That's a lot vying for my attention. Then add the vibration that occurs when I get a message or phone call, the red icon that tells me I have 39 unread emails, or the ping I get when a tweet is re-tweeted or I'm mentioned on other social media. I'm living in a perpetual state of distraction.

> ... attention is a limited, non-renewable resource in the digital age.

Now think about the many digital devices, screens and technologies clamouring for our children's attention. There are mounting concerns that children's attention spans may be declining because of the intrusive digital technologies that are surrounding them. Children can be perpetually distracted if the sensory region of their brain is constantly activated before they develop their impulse control in the prefrontal cortex.

If our children are to thrive in a digital world they need to learn how to manage their attention. This is the most vital 21st century skill for both children and adults. Jason Silva suggests that attention is a limited, non-renewable resource in the digital age. Children have to learn how to avoid external distractions (like social media alerts, the background sound effects or animations in a book app). They also need how to manage internal, self-generated distractions (thoughts that are unrelated to the task at hand).

How to set restrictions on tablets and help children stay focused

When using a tablet with children, set up Guided Access (on iOS devices) or Kids Corner (on Android devices) in settings. This function allows parents or educators to lock children into an app. This prevents them from starting an app and jumping into something else that's more appealing after a couple of minutes. This function teaches children that they need to focus on one thing at a time and see a task through to completion (not jump between apps as their attention wanes.)

Given that the technology evolves so quickly, it's best to search for an up-to-date video tutorial that shows users how to set up Guided Access or Kids Corner on specific devices.

Are children's attention spans changing?

Everything seems quicker in this digital age. Speed is rewarded and revered and we crave faster internet connections, better download speeds and instant access.

Even TV shows appear to be mimicking the fast-paced digital world as scene changes occur more quickly to sustain our attention. Research by Bordwell revealed that TV programs made in the 1930s to 1960s had scene changes every two to four minutes, while today's TV shows transition every 45 seconds if not quicker.

While there's no long-term research on the impact of technology on children's attention spans, there's sufficient anecdotal evidence from educators that this is a serious issue that warrants further investigation. Two separate studies, both published in 2012 by Pew internet & American Life Project and Common Sense Media, showed that teachers and parents were concerned that children's attention skills were waning in a digital age. Of the 2500 teachers surveyed 87 per cent believed that new technologies were creating an 'easily distracted generation with short attention spans'. In addition, 64 per cent believed that today's digital technologies 'do more to distract students than help them academically.' In another study published by Common Sense Media, nearly three-quarters of the teacher survey respondents believed that technology 'has hurt student's attention spans a lot or somewhat.'

There are collective concerns that children's concentration now drifts after a couple of minutes on a task. (I think, as adults, many of us are noticing this too as we forage the internet, scan emails while listening to videos and watching TV.)

Multi-tasking

Humans cannot multi-task. We're so much more efficient when we focus on one task. It's a physical impossibility for our brains to simultaneously perform two tasks. A 2009 study presented by Ophir, Nass, and Wagner found that multi-tasking overloaded children's working memory, caused fatigue, divided students' attention, forced them to process information at shallow and superficial levels and was a predictor of depression and social anxiety symptoms.

Case STUDY

Peter has his headphones plugged in listening to music, is playing Minecraft on his gaming console and the TV is playing in the background. He vehemently assures his parents and teachers that he *can* perform all of these tasks simultaneously and do them all equally well. He genuinely believes he can do more, faster.

This is what's referred to as task-switching, but Peter cannot multi-task. Instead, he's engaging in continuous partial attention where he quickly shifts his focus from task to task.

TECHNO MYTH-BUSTER

MYTH: Today's digital children can multi-task with technology.

FACT: Media multi-tasking compromises children's learning and attention.

A 2010 study found that children aged 8–18 were spending an average of 7.5 hours a day with media, but this figure increased to over 10 hours per day when media multi-tasking was factored in.

Even though children think they're capable of multi-tasking (a study by Rosen, Carrier and Cheever revealed that teenagers believed they were capable of performing six to seven tasks simultaneously), they're actually task switching – mentally and rapidly moving between tasks – not simultaneously performing the tasks.

Multi-tasking impairs performance, especially for heavy multi-taskers. Multi-tasking has cognitive costs – it disrupts attention, results in increased error rates and decreases academic performance. Multi-tasking also results in fatigue as it depletes glucose stores in the prefrontal cortex and increases the production of the stress hormone, cortisol. So children often feel exhausted or scrambled after multi-tasking (and so do we as adults – this explains your mental fog after a busy day multi-tasking).

When children are task-switching, their hippocampus (the part of the brain responsible for memory) is not working optimally and is compromising learning (especially in relation to consolidating information from short to long-term memory). For example, when learning new information while also multi-tasking, information goes to children's striatum (part of the brain that stores procedures and skills, not ideas and factual information). However, when children avoid multi-tasking, information goes to their hippocampus (where it's organised and categorised for later recall).

Multi-tasking also appears to overload our working memory and divide attention – it can also be a predictor of depression and social anxiety. It can also cause fatigue and shallow, superficial processing of information. When multi-tasking children skim the material preventing them from making intelligent and lasting associations with the content, resulting in a shallow understanding.

Nicholas Carr likens this shallow processing to being a jet-ski rider. In his book *The Shallows: What the Internet is Doing to our Brains* Carr suggests that we read and process online information in different ways to reading books or on paper (static media). He writes, 'Once I was a scuba diver in the sea of words. Now I zip along the surface like a guy on a jet ski.'

TECH TIP ✂

Encourage mono-tasking (and teach children that multi-tasking is a misnomer). Given that the brain can't multi-task we should encourage children to use one source of technology at a time and devote their attentional resources to that technology.

Continuous partial attention

When children attempt to multi-task they're actually engaging in rapid task switching that results in continuous partial attention (CPA). CPA involves paying attention to multiple streams of information, but only at a superficial level. Children split their attention between multiple tasks, scanning for opportunities from the surrounding stimulus that seduces their attention.

In a digital world, the seductions are ongoing and multimodal (images, sounds, animations). Children skim the surface, extrapolate the most important information and then move onto the next source of information, after their attention has been aroused. This obviously compromises children's ability to reflect, think critically and deeply engage with new ideas.

Our human brains simply aren't optimised to switch between multiple streams of information. In fact, research confirms that CPA compromises students' learning. When students' attention spans are depleted and they face information overload, their learning suffers according to work published in 2009 and 2012.

A 2009 Stanford University study also provided definitive evidence of the perils of multi-tasking on students' performance.[130] When multitasking, students are prevented from making intelligent and lasting associations with the material and have a superficial understanding of what they've been processing.

In small doses this scanning isn't necessarily harmful but over time it can lead to feelings of overwhelm, over-stimulation and a sense of feeling unfulfilled. Students are often left looking for another high and are therefore perennially distracted.

Tips for developing deep-thinking skills

Children process online information in different ways to traditional media (books and printed forms). They scan short chunks of text, look for headlines and gravitate towards graphics before text. This is sometimes referred to as the staccato quality of thinking. If we want children to engage in scuba-diving type of thinking, it's best that we print the information for them to read, as opposed to reading it on-screen.

How to develop children's attention skills in the digital age

- **Schedule green time** – time in nature calms children's brains. Time in nature, green time, has been shown to restore children's attention and improve their information processing. The attention restoration theory suggests that time in nature also increases the release of the neurotransmitter dopamine and lowers stress. Children need time away from screens and gadgets to effectively learn. Without downtime, children don't get the processing time required for memory consolidation. This is a crucial process for committing things to short-term memory.

- **Mono-task, don't multi-task** – train children to focus on one task at a time (whether that's with or without a screen). Teach children the mantra, 'Mono-tasking is best.'

- **Teach children to use technology intentionally** – have dedicated and specific times when they use technology as opposed to constantly dipping in and out of it, which is easy to do.

- **Turn off alerts** – switch off the alerts and notifications on the devices that they use in the device's settings. Also be mindful that our mobile phone alerts can also disrupt our child's attention.

- **Have tech-free zones** – specify areas in homes (or classrooms) where technology will *not* go. Children need to be able to retreat to areas without technology interfering.

- **Minimise stress** – stress can meddle with children's attention spans. Provide outlets for children's stress by exploring mindfulness practices and meditation. Regular physical activity is also encouraged.

- **Use technology aids** – if children can't refrain from using a website on a computer or laptop (for example, they open Minecraft instead of Mathletics), download an app that allows you to specify websites that can't be accessed at certain times. (It's also great for adults who find that instead of responding to emails they end up on Facebook or eBay!) Try Self-Control (Mac) or Freedom (Mac or PC). When using tablets, encourage children to do one thing at a time or set up Guided Access (iOS devices)or Kids Corner (Android devices) to teach children to complete one app before jumping to another.

- **Walk the talk** – if *our* attention is scattered, we can't bring ourselves back to the present moment and meaningfully engage with our children. So switch off phones when watching a movie and don't try and check emails while replying to an SMS. Just do one thing at a time and have ample screen-free time too.

Working memory

Just like impulse control, our children's digital immersion is changing their memory skills too.

Infobesity and the Google effect

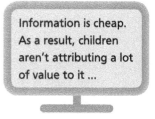

Information is cheap. As a result, children aren't attributing a lot of value to it ...

Can you recall more than three phone numbers? Can you recall five-step directions without relying on a map app? Our memory capacity as adults is changing because of technology and so too are our children's memory skills.

Information is cheap. As a result, children aren't attributing a lot of value to it because answers can be easily retrieved online. 'Just google it...' is a phrase that has become part of today's vernacular.

Children are living in an age of infobesity. They're digesting a colossal amount of information each and every day. Levitin claims that in 2011 we were consuming five times more information on a daily basis (about 174 newspapers worth of data each day) than we were in 1986 – and this figure is growing exponentially as technology develops. We're literally drowning in information and sadly this is the reality for our children too. When children are constantly bombarded with new information this can place them in 'cognitive overload'.

As a result, children aren't committing things to memory. Instead they're engaging in cognitive offloading – handing things over to technology that they'd otherwise memorise. They're often unable to recall information but can remember the key terms they entered into Google to retrieve the same information.

The Google Effect was first coined in 2011 after a study conducted by Harvard psychologists Daniel Wegner and Adrian Ward.

It's a phenomenon that explains why we're less likely to remember certain details if we believe that they're accessible online. Instead of recalling facts and details, we're recalling keywords and search terms used on Google (or other search engines) to later retrieve facts and information. The researchers explained that we're using the internet like a memory partner by offloading memories and trivial details to technology.

Case study

Judy has been a teacher for 28 years. She's recently noticed a decline in her students' recall of the times tables. 'Kids today just can't seem to recall their multiplication and basic maths facts like they used to be able to do. Their memory skills are so much poorer. I tell them that they need to practice their times tables, but they tell me that they can just use their calculator app if they need to.'

Digital dementia

Children are handing over more and more of their mental tasks to technology. There are concerns that some children are suffering from digital dementia. This was a term coined by German neuroscientist Manfred Spitzer in 2012. It describes how our overuse of technology is causing a breakdown in cognitive abilities in ways that resemble patients who've suffered head injuries or psychiatric illness.

Children's cognitive off-loading may result in under-developed reasoning and memory skills. Children are simply offloading so many things to their devices that they're not developing their memory muscle.

On one hand it appears that our children's brains are being more resourceful and selective about what they commit to memory – their brains are being efficient about what they store. This cognitive off-loading means they can free up their cognitive resources for other more important, higher-order thinking skills.

On the flipside, it may mean that children simply aren't developing their memory muscles. There are some details that do require rote learning and memorisation but like any muscle, our memory has to be regularly exercised for peak condition.

Practical tips for developing children's working memory skills in the digital age

There are lots of things we can do to ensure that our children's working memory skills are used and extended. Encourage children to:

- **Respond to information** – for example by asking them questions after they've watched a TV show. Or you might ask them to write down three facts after they've watched a YouTube clip. Children need to process the information they've consuming and not just simply absorb it. When we ask children to respond after (or even while) they're using technology, it means they're actively involved. And this can stop the technology zombie effect.
- **Enjoy music, singing and dance** – teach children fun songs and rhymes to build their working memory.
- **Play puzzles** – good old-fashioned puzzles (and also computer puzzles and apps) can build working memory skills in a playful context. Strategy and logic games are great for older children too.
- **Play physical, board, card or video games** – whereby children have to establish and abide by a set of rules. This requires working memory and impulse control skills.
- **Tell stories** – children love hearing and telling stories and it develops their working memory skills too. Audiobooks are a great digital resource too.
- **Read real books** – to help memory recall.
- **Play in an unstructured way, especially outdoors** – it's certainly children's most natural way to learn. They acquire a host of cognitive, social and physical skills and develop all their executive-function skills too.
- **Make a mental list** – challenge children to go to the shops and purchase five items on a mental list. Gradually increase this list over time. We can also introduce other lists for children to recall.

- **Do organic searches** – don't always rely on Google. Try and commit some things to memory.
- **Engage in physical activity** – exercise stimulates the brain and body.
- **Learn a new language or an instrument** – to develop children's working memory skills.
- **Teach and practice mindfulness and/or meditation** – to quieten the outside world and truly experience moments firsthand, not always via a screen.

At a glance

How to support executive-function skills in a digital age:

- **Use technology intentionally** – have a purpose in mind and use it for set periods of time.
- **Discourage multi-tasking and teach children how to mono-task** – model it too. Try where possible to do one thing at time.
- **Teach mindfulness** – start to cultivate ways to be present and experience the moment. Do some mindfulness training with children. Switch off devices (or at least turn them to silent) when interacting with children. Avoid documenting every experience digitally.
- **Allow children time to play** – it's the most natural and effective way for young children to develop executive-function skills.

There's a general sense that life is speeding up. This is one reason why children's attention spans and memory skills are changing. We need to teach children – and model ourselves – to slow down and manage our attention and memory. Constantly leading a frantic pace of life is not sustainable, nor is it desirable or to be revered. (Do we *really* need 20 browsers open simultaneously on our computer?)

Mindfulness training is a simple, yet highly effective way to do this and will be a vital skill for our children who'll inherit a busy digital world.

Children's technology habits are affecting the ways in which their impulse control skills are developed and how their attention is managed. Developing children's executive-function skills is critical to their learning and development and can be taught explicitly. This is the most important skill we can teach our children in the digital age.

The next chapter will look at practical ways in which we can help children form healthy and sustainable relationships with technology through the establishment and enforcement of healthy media habits.

10

Developing healthy digital habits

As parents, we need to set strong boundaries when it comes to screen time so children can form healthy relationships.

Children need moderation not abstinence when it comes to technology. They need a digital diet where they learn to carefully manage their daily digital dose. It's imperative that as parents we guide our children's digital choices in terms of what Australian Registered Psychologist Jocelyn Brewer calls 'nutritious technology' and limit their intake of junk.

Just like there are consequences associated with excessive food, a digital overload can also impair our children's social, physical, emotional and intellectual development.

This chapter will explore what healthy digital habits look like in young children and will provide tips and ideas about simple things parents and educators can do to establish healthy habits at home or school. It will also explore unhealthy digital habits such as addiction and techno tantrums and will arm parents with simple strategies to minimise the likelihood of these occurring. It will also explore how to establish a family media plan so that we can make sure that our child's screen time isn't detrimental to their development.

What are digital habits?

Digital habits are the patterns that children form around technology. It's what, when, with whom, where and why children use technology. Parents and educators play a pivotal role in shaping young child's digital habits. We must get this right early on in life or children may form toxic relationships with technology, which can lead to problematic or psychological issues later on.

Technology addiction

Parents frequently lament, 'My child's addicted to technology.' Children's intense reluctance to disengage from technology has left many parents worried that their child's addicted. There's no denying that some children have a digital dependence. Asking them to switch off a device or asking them to play outside is often met with reluctance or a techno tantrum. But this doesn't mean that children are *necessarily* addicted to technology.

Before we delve into addiction, consider if we would be so concerned if our child was spending a lot of time reading books. Would we automatically consider them addicted to books? Often we fret about screen time because it's new and our children's digitalised childhoods are very different to our analog childhoods. Our nostalgic accounts of our childhood can cause us to panic about our child's tech habits.

TECHNO MYTH-BUSTER

MYTH: Toddlers are addicted to technology.

FACT: Toddlers aren't addicted to technology. They've simply formed unhealthy attachments to technology and in some instances a dependence on technology.

I don't believe that children 8 and under are addicted to technology. They can certainly form obsessive or compulsive relationships with technology – the techno tantrums that result from asking for our smart phone to be returned are intense; I've weathered the storm too! But this doesn't necessarily mean they're addicted. Addiction is a behavioural disorder and young children are still developing their behaviours.

Young children can certainly become dependent on technology though. Much like substance dependence, children can develop a tolerance to technology and need more and more of it to reach the same level of pleasure. They can also experience withdrawal symptoms (neurobiological changes in the brain) if they suddenly have to stop or are unable to use the technology. This is dependence, not necessarily an addiction.

For technology use to be considered an addiction, children need to be able to make a conscious choice to keep using technology even when they understand that prolonged use will have adverse consequences. Young children don't yet know or fully comprehend what the adverse consequences may be to their prolonged or excessive technology use. (Older children, teenagers and adults on the other hand, typically *do* understand the ramifications of their actions and can make a conscious choice when using technology.)

Children under 8 years of age haven't typically yet mastered self-regulation skills because the prefrontal cortex (where executive-function skills like impulse control, decision making and memory reside) is still developing. These critical executive-function skills are required to manage technology habits. Most young children are still learning how to make choices and regulate their emotions and manage their impulses.

As parents, it's our responsibility to make sure young children understand how to manage technology.

Why are children so attached to technology?

The parts of the brain associated with pleasure are often activated when using technology. As with anything pleasurable that we experience in life (such as eating chocolate), the amygdala releases dopamine, the feel-good neurotransmitter, and we naturally want more and more of it.

Emotionally charged technology experiences like watching a funny TV show or playing a video game or app where we're rewarded for achieving a higher level release dopamine. So children quickly associate screens with pleasure – and why young infants and toddlers very quickly get accustomed to using parents' smart phones.

The brain craves novelty and technology offers constant novelty. The prefrontal cortex has a novelty bias, meaning it's easy for our focus and attention to be hijacked (see Chapter 9 for more details). The prefrontal cortex is one of the main parts of the brain that's required to manage our attention, but it's being constantly bombarded by a sensory smorgasbord offered by the digital world.

TECHNO MYTH-BUSTER

MYTH: My child's addicted to watching unboxing videos on YouTube.

FACT: Your child's unlikely to be addicted to these videos, but their brain is having a strong neurobiological response that's driving their behaviour.

Unboxing videos, where children literally watch other children unwrap toys on YouTube, have become increasingly popular. Kids are mesmerised by manicured or tiny hands that hover over toy boxes and slowly unwrap packages and gifts. Unboxing videos have attracted thousands, even millions of viewers and are a lucrative business for some video creators.

The anticipation associated with unwrapping a gift actually releases adrenaline and endorphins in the brain. So when they're viewing these types of videos they're having a neurobiological response, which makes it difficult for them to switch off these videos.

In essence, these are lengthy advertorials. They're very different to traditional 15-second TV commercials. As parents we need to be wary of this indirect form of advertising and consumerism. The pleasure associated with buying can also release dopamine, the feel-good neurotransmitter and kids naturally want more and more of that feeling! So children can become very dependent on these videos.

Try to limit your child's viewing of unboxing videos. Have strict limits on what they can watch and the exact number of episodes and try to co-view or ask them questions about what they were viewing and discuss the subliminal ways the toys is being advertised.

Are older children addicted?

It's possible that children over 8 may be addicted to technology if they meet diagnostic criteria (although these aren't yet universally accepted) *and* are assessed by a medical expert. Technology addicts continue to use technology despite attempts to distract them, even if they no longer experience the same levels of original pleasure and they're aware of the negative consequences. There are also often behaviour patterns that often occur to avoid feelings of withdrawal.

Many parents share stories of their children's technology addictions and this is often fuelled by media reports. However, it's important to note that it's not yet medically recognised as a psychological condition in children.

Internet Gaming Disorder (IGD)

IGD, also referred to as pathological internet use, is a condition that's currently being further investigated and researched to ascertain if it is in fact a formal mental disorder. It is currently under consideration for the *Diagnostic and Statistical Manual of Mental Disorders (DSM)* as a mental disorder and preliminary evidence suggests that in some instances, IGD is a legitimate mental illness.

Technology addiction is still considered an invisible phenomenon. Gaming or internet addicts don't often present with overt symptoms and there are few social implications associated with their addiction – they don't usually get into trouble with the police and they aren't intoxicated. However, there are usually significant personal costs. The absence of standard diagnostic criteria makes a formal diagnosis difficult at this stage. However, technological addiction is becoming increasingly recognised as a problematic and psychological issue that warrants further investigation and medical treatment in some cases.

In their 2010 descriptive review of the existing research evidence, Chakraborty, Basu and Kumar highlight that there's inconsistent evidence about the rates of IGD (varying between 0.3 per cent and 38 per cent) because there's no standard diagnostic criteria at this point in time to medically diagnose IGD.

However, in many countries IGD is now considered a significant public health threat and specific treatment facilities and programs are being developed. Paediatric psychologists and psychiatrists are acknowledging that pathological internet use is becoming problematic, particularly with children aged 11–18 when gaming and social media become more dominant leisure pursuits and when more and more children are using tablet and laptop computers at school.

Gaming addicts often report that gaming environments are the only place where they feel powerful, respected and valued by others. This can be a very powerful lure and a reason why young children can sometimes experience addiction problems. This also suggests that perhaps, in some instances, IGD may also be associated with other psychological and emotional issues and not an isolated mental disorder on its own.

Case STUDY

Dr Jones is a Melbourne-based paediatrician. He's seeing increasing numbers of children aged 5–9 present with urinary incontinence (UI), the loss of bladder control resulting in the release of urine. Daytime UI is common in children until around three and night-time UI can persist until seven.

Dr Jones has noted that he's treating increasing numbers of older children for daytime UI. Initial anecdotal observations suggest that some, though not all, of these children are also presenting with symptoms of gaming addiction. It appears that many of these children are so obsessed with playing video games and apps that they're not able to effectively control their bladders and in some instances, their bowels too.

These cases alone are not sufficient to prove that technology is causing these problems, but there's enough anecdotal evidence to warrant further study and for parents to be vigilant.

So while young children may not be *clinically* addicted to technology, there's no denying that they may be obsessed, engaged or entranced with it. Many children do form very strong and sometimes unhealthy attachments to technology. Over time these patterns can become entrenched and the child can form poor media habits. To remedy this, their behaviour patterns need some refining. The good news is that the brain is very malleable so these attachments and habits can be changed. (That doesn't mean it's easy to do though!)

Unhealthy digital habits

We need to reframe our thinking as parents. Instead of considering our child's technology obsession as an addiction, we need think of it as an unhealthy attachment to technology and overuse. As parents we need to set strong boundaries when it comes to screen time so children can form healthy relationships.

Case STUDY

Ben was a 10-year-old boy who liked playing Minecraft. Initially he was only allowed to play it on the desktop computer in the lounge room but he started playing it in his bedroom when he received a laptop from school. Ben would stay in his room all afternoon after school and would only emerge when he needed help with his homework or when dinner was ready. (Even then it was a struggle to get him to leave his bedroom.)

Ben started using multi-player mode where he'd play Minecraft with children all over the world. Getting him to stop playing and go to sleep became increasingly more difficult. Ben's parents became particularly worried when they discovered that Ben was waking at 3 am every day so that he could play with his American friends online.

Under treatment from a psychologist, Ben was eventually able to modify his addiction and develop healthier digital habits. Like most internet addicts (unlike drug or alcohol addicts), the aim for Ben's treatment was moderation, not complete abstinence from using technology.

If we think in terms of children forming digital habits, that gives us – as parents and educators – a sense of control over shaping and modifying their behaviour (as opposed to simply labelling them as addicted to technology). It's more empowering to think in terms of changing and shaping their digital habits.

Red flags

Following are some signs that children may be forming unhealthy media habits, based on the work of Cash, Rae, Steel and Winkler. It's important to note that this checklist doesn't provide a medical diagnosis, but may indicate some possible red flags for technology addiction. If parents are in any way concerned, it's best to seek the help of a medical professional.

Be on the lookout for a child who displays the following behaviour:

- **Spends vast amounts of time engaged with technology** – there's no specific number of hours that's safe or healthy for young children to use technology. Digital devices shouldn't dominate their entire leisure time.
- **Is constantly preoccupied by technology** – if a child cannot sit anywhere and be idle without using a gadget of some description, then this may indicate that they have a technology addiction.
- **Withdraws from social situations** – in preference to using digital devices. Can your child sustain friendships away from screens? Do screens dominate their play activities?
- **Tired and irritable because of inadequate sleep due to overuse of technology** – poor sleep habits are a key sign of poor technology habits.
- **Withdraws or no longer enjoys traditional activities that they previously enjoyed** – to pursue activities only on digital devices. Has there been a sudden change in a child's leisure pursuits? (This one is tricky because it's a natural part of child development to change and alter.)
- **Is restless, moody, depressed or irritable when attempting to reduce or stop technology activities.**
- **Has lied or tried to conceal the extent of their technology use to parents, teachers or therapists** – perhaps by waking up in the middle of the night to play a game, or hiding devices in bedrooms.
- **Needs to use technology for increased amounts of time in order to achieve the same level of satisfaction.**
- **Uses technology as a way of coping with or avoiding psychological problems.**
- **Has had their technology use infringe on their school performance** – many teachers report that children clock-watch towards the end of the school day as they are anxious to get home and continue playing a social online game such as Club Penguin or Minecraft.

Concerned parents are advised to keep a diary and monitor exactly how much media children are consuming over a weekly period.

Dealing with techno tantrums

Managing children's screen time often becomes scream time. Many parents are pulling their hair out trying to manage their child's screen time. In fact a 2016 study by the Action for Children organisation found that 23 per cent of parents surveyed struggled to get their children to unplug from television, phones and computer screens. This is a universal parenting digital dilemma that's becoming more difficult as screens become more prevalent.

Why does our otherwise well-behaved and well-adjusted child turn into screen-agers when we ask them to switch off the TV or pass back our smart phone?

As previously explained, children are often receiving squirts of the neurotransmitter dopamine when they're using technology. So naturally they want more and more of whatever is eliciting a positive response.

For many children who've grown up in a digital world, technology is akin to oxygen. It's become their norm and they expect it and see it as a toy (not a tool). So many children also feel that it's a right – they're entitled to use technology whenever they'd like.

But with any privilege comes responsibility. Part of our role as modern parents and educators is to teach children about how to use technology in responsible ways and that involves being able to switch if off and recognise that technology is a tool, not a toy.

Tantrums are a normal part of a child's development

Firstly, it can help to understand why children have tantrums. While it pains me to write it, tantrums really are an essential part of a child's developmental trajectory. They help children deal with a surge in their emotions and find appropriate and effective ways to communicate their feelings. They often occur as a result of a mismatch between the child's emotional feelings and their language. (They may not have the verbal skills to explain the new or unusual feelings they're having.)

So here are some possible explanations for techno tantrums:

- **Interrupted state of flow** – when children are immersed in a game or deep in creation mode in an app they often enter the psychological state of flow. This is where time seems to stand still and they are completely immersed in what they're doing. This state of flow is disrupted when they're asked to switch off and they're frustrated as a result.

- **Dopamine withdrawals** – when children are playing a video game or using an app they're often rewarded or praised, which spikes their dopamine levels. They become conditioned to the praise and rewards and want more and more dopamine. So for some young children, being asked to switch off the game or tablet results in a withdrawal of dopamine.

- **Language skill deficits** – younger children haven't developed the language skills to articulate their feelings when they're asked to switch off devices. Instead they have a tantrum to release their pent-up emotions as they don't have the words to convey this emotional state.

Tips for avoiding techno tantrums

Whilst techno tantrums are often inevitable (and a normal part of development), there are some simple strategies that parents can implement to minimise their likelihood, severity and/or intensity:

1 **Establish and enforce firm guidelines** – about how much screen time they can have each day. Be explicit about this *before* they switch on the device – it's too late once the device is turned on.

2 **Focus on quantity not duration** – time is an abstract concept that many young children simply don't understand. Rather than enforcing time limits, quantify the number of episodes a child can watch or the level in the game that they can reach. This is much more understandable, especially for young children.

3 **Use a timer** – our child is much less likely to argue with a smart phone timer or an egg timer than with us! For older children,

media tokens and media contracts are effective and explicit ways to monitor screen time.

4   **Provide cues that they need to transition away from the screen** – give children ample warning that they need to switch off the device. They can become engrossed in what they are doing so make sure they make eye contact and acknowledge what has been said.

5   **Encourage young children to switch the device off themselves** – this seems trivial but it's very different to us quickly or angrily flicking off the TV or prying the tablet from their hands. They're more likely to feel like they've had some control over switching it off while giving us something positive to reinforce and encourage.

4   **Have a succession plan** – find an activity our child will enjoy doing when they've switched off the device. Alternatively have a Bored Board (a list of screen-free ideas) from which they can pick an activity to undertake after they've switched off the device.

7   **Play bad cop** – when we experience a techno tantrum after using the tips above, have a direct consequence such as not allowing the same privilege the next day. This is very effective as our child's desire to use the device is a very strong motivator for them, especially when they realise that these limits are enforceable. (This is different to using technology as a general form of punishment.)

How can I cope with techno tantrums?

Techno tantrums are often a normal part of development – an emotional storm children aren't yet equipped to handle. That's why our job as parents is so critical – we have to show them how to deal with emotions without combusting into fits of tears.

Remember, young children don't yet have the hindsight or catastrophe scale to deal with this situation because of limited life experiences. Don't take the situation personally. Deal with it rationally and help them through it with the following suggestions:

1 **Listen respectfully to their demands** – try to see the situation from our child's perspective. This doesn't mean we need to give in to their demands but we all like to be heard. Sometimes the tantrum actually has nothing to do with having to switch the screen off at all.

2 **Offer reassurance and comfort** – this is where we can actually use the tantrum as a learning experience and help our child develop self-regulation skills. Try to label their feelings and in so doing, build their emotional vocabulary. For example, perhaps we could say, 'I understand you're feeling frustrated that Mummy's asked you to turn off the TV.'

3 **Don't give in to their demands out of embarrassment** – I know firsthand how tempting it's to cave into their (often completely irrational) demands, especially in public. While this may alleviate the situation at hand, it doesn't solve the problem long-term. In fact, it can only serve to exacerbate it. Be firm and our child will soon learn that a tantrum is not a negotiating tool.

4 **Express our feelings** – this strategy is often best used after the tantrum has subsided.

5 **Avoid saying 'yes' or 'maybe'** – it's important to stand firm with our decision about screen time.

6 **Discuss how to better handle future situations once the tantrum has subsided** – let the storm pass. Then talk about what happened and how future episodes can be avoided. This is a really important part of the process. Try to encourage children to use their language. This builds their emotional vocabulary, which equips them to deal with similar situations in the future.

What can I do if my child has already formed unhealthy media habits?

It's not too late to start to implement healthy media habits. Even if our child has formed some unhealthy attachments, we can still intervene. It will be more difficult, but it's achievable and very worthwhile.

Simply imposing new media rules and habits is probably the *least* effective way to improve a child's unhealthy media habits. Instead we can try the following:

1 **Openly discuss the changes we want to implement and explain why they're important** – children are much more likely to agree to our changes if they understand our reasoning.
2 **Involve them in the process** – if they feel like they have some control over the situation or the outcome they're much more likely to be involved.
3 **Activity swap** – children love being given choice so give them some options. from which to select an alternative activity. The trick with this strategy is in the choice of activity: it has to be something that really appeals to our children.
4 **Gradually implement change** – so our child has time to adjust to their new media habits. If children feel that the changes are too drastic or too quick, they're likely to resist them.

A simple way to work out healthy amounts of screen time

In 2015 the American Academy of Pediatrics updated their screen time guidelines after mounting concerns that their existing time-based guidelines were unrealistic and driven by science and would risk becoming obsolete.

Rather than quantifying screen time limits, I propose that parents and educators think of screen time as part of a child's overall development, as do the latest APA guidelines. It's not a discrete entity or add-on. It's not a toy or something we use as a punishment. It needs to be viewed as part of their overall development.

We need to think of a child's life as a glass jar. Each of the different aspects of their life – the seven building blocks outlined in this book (language, relationships, play, movement, sleep, nutrition and executive-function skills) – are represented by blocks.

If all of the blocks are in the glass jar on most days, then there's room for screen time to fill up the extra space in the jar. In this instance, screen time would be like water that we could tip into the jar – it would take up any extra space that's available *after* the seven blocks have been added.

With this approach all the essential building blocks for a child's development are in the jar first – and we can rest assured that our children's screen time isn't hampering their development. Screen time is then determined by the amount of available spaces in between the blocks.

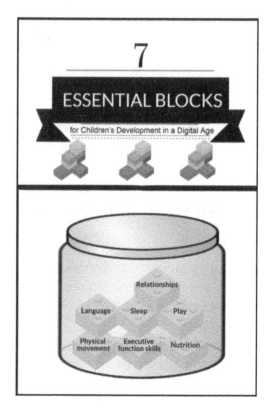

Content is really important

As parents we play a critical role in helping our children form healthy media habits, much as we do when helping our little ones develop healthy food choices. We have to help them consume (and create) healthy forms of media in healthy doses.

Psychologist Jocelyn Brewer suggests that parents and educators need to help children consume the digital kale and minimise the consumption of digital candy. There are high-calorie, nutrient-poor food choices (think junk food like crisps) and the same goes for technology choices. Think mindless TV episodes or YouTube clips or gaming apps with no educational merit for example.

In this instance a bit of digital candy every now and then is unlikely to harm our children. They certainly shouldn't be the only thing that our children consume or create, but we can use them sparingly.

In some instances young children should never consume digital candy at all as it's really unhealthy for them. For example violent video games and TV programs with adult content. This is much like children consuming alcohol – it just shouldn't happen. On the whole though, every now and then a little bit of digital candy is okay.

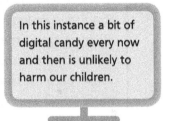

In this instance a bit of digital candy every now and then is unlikely to harm our children.

Obviously we want children consuming more nutrient-dense technology – the digital kale. In terms of technology this might be educational TV and educational apps or communicating via Skype or creating a digital book with an app or recording and editing a video. We need to teach our children how to distinguish between digital kale and technological crisps.

Talk early and often about technology

The minute we hand over our smart phone, switch on the TV or allow our little one to use a tablet is the moment we need to start having discussions about digital habits. It doesn't have to be anything formal, just simple conversations will do.

Ongoing, conversational approaches tend to work best. Incidental conversations about switching off devices after periods of time, discussing and showing children how to use devices in appropriate and safe ways (for example switching mobile devices to airplane mode and not placing them in laps) are great ways to start to introduce the concept of healthy digital habits.

Children are never too young to start learning about healthy digital habits. In fact the earlier we start the easier it typically is. We need to have ongoing and age-appropriate conversations about technology. These obviously will evolve over time and it's the type of thing we constantly need to be revisiting as the technology changes (and so do our child's tech preferences). These patterns and rules become habitualised over time and we're less likely to meet with reluctance.

As children become more independent their screen exposure often broadens too. This can increase the risk of cyberbullying and access to inappropriate content (such as pornography or violence). If we have open and ongoing discussions with our children about technology from an early age and take a keen interest in what they do online, it's much more likely that they'll come to us to report any unpleasant encounters or problems.

But if technology is something that's simply managed in our household or school or if it's rarely discussed, we aren't establishing the conversations that will ensure that our child forms healthy digital habits. Instead, it's likely that technology becomes something that is taboo or feared.

Helping children develop healthy digital habits

There are three things that parents can do to develop healthy digital habits with young children:

1   model healthy habits
2   establish a family media plan
3   enforce the plan.

Model healthy habits

As parents we exert a powerful influence on our children's digital habits. Children imitate our media habits because of their mirror neurons (see Introduction for more information) and because of the availability of digital media in the home.

A 2014 study by Jago and others found strong associations between children's screen time and parents' screen time. We have to be really mindful that if we're glued to our devices, it may confuse our children if we ask them to do something different.

The most effective way to develop healthy media habits in our children is to model healthy media habits ourselves. I've experienced this firsthand and declare that I'm still working on this one.

This doesn't mean that we avoid technology around young children. It doesn't mean that we never take a phone call or scroll through our phones when our children are nearby. That's not realistic and it's not teaching our children how to use technology in healthy ways. (It's also not what our parents did – they pulled out magazines and read them when were growing up, they just didn't have the same captivating pull on our parents' attention that smart phones do.)

This doesn't mean that we avoid technology around young children.

We need to be mindful that our time with digital devices doesn't encroach on our time with our children. When our smart phone constantly illuminates our face and we ignore their attempts to engage us, are we subtly teaching them that technology is more important than relationships?

When we're mesmerised by our device, we're not devoting our full attention to our children and we're parenting without presence. This can potentially compromise our children's development. It is vital that our two greatest resources, time and attention, aren't constantly absorbed by screens.

Establish a family media plan

Some of us are planners. We like to download and print out planners and templates. Some of us are more carefree and like to go with flow. Either way, it's imperative that we at least give some thought to how our children manage technology. We can determine if we want to formally document the plan or just have a discussion about how technology will be used in our home.

So what does a family media plan look like?

A family media plan addresses many issues, from how much time our children can spend on technology to where, when, what and with whom they can use it. Ideally it is in written form, perhaps on a whiteboard, or for older children you could use a contract that they keep.

The basic components of a family media plan address:

1 how much technology can be used
2 where technology can be used
3 when technology can be used
4 what technologies can be used
5 with whom technologies can be used.

The following is a guide to some of the more important issues to consider.

How much time will our child spend on technology during the day or week?

I'm going to (controversially) say that this is probably the *least* important question. Quality trumps quantity when it comes to screens. This isn't to suggest that we don't need to consider how much time kids are spending with devices, but we shouldn't focus solely on quantifying and enforcing specific time limits – remember this isn't an exact science.

By focusing narrowly on how much screen time children consume, we overlook other really critical considerations such as *what* children are watching or creating and *when* they're using screens.

Ideally, I suggest we find an amount of time that works best for our child. All children are different. For some, a little bit of technology goes a long way. Others can cope with more. The trick is knowing what works for your child.

As previously discussed, if we ensure that each of the seven essential building blocks are addressed and not being hampered by our child's screen time, then that's a fairly good indication that their screen time habits are healthy and pose no risk to their health and development.

Another approach I recommend parents employ to determine safe amounts of screen time for children is to ask:

- **what content** – what is your child doing with a screen? Is their screen time supporting or stifling their development? (See below for more details.) This helps parents to determine if their time online is worthwhile.
- **what's the opportunity cost** – what is your child missing out on doing if they're using a screen? If it's one of the seven essential building blocks then we need to carefully assess the time they're spending with screens.

A screen time formula

Parents often want to know a specific amount of screen time so that they can rest assured that their child's screen time is not damaging their child's development (as parents we love checklists and specific details). As I've outlined throughout the book it's not advisable to adhere to universal time limits, that are based simply on a child's chronological age (remember, this isn't an exact science).

Instead I suggest parents calculate healthy amounts of daily screen time by applying this formula:

24 hours – sleep hours (including naps) – school/care time (if applicable) – time for play (relationships + language + exectutive function) – time for movement – time for eating

For example, my 5-year-old's healthy level of screen time is calculated by:

24 – 11 (sleep) – 6 (school) – 2 (play) – 2 (movement) – 1 (eating) = 2 hours

Now he certainly doesn't have 2 hours of screen time every day (although he'd probably love it). But this gives me an idea of a healthy amount of time with technology that's unlikely to cause developmental or health problems.

How will we manage tech-free times and zones?

Children need opportunities to play and interact *without* the interference of technology. This is essential for developing brains and allows for creativity and inspiration to arise.

So as part of our media plan it's important to specify exactly when and where our child can use technology. Please do not think that you need to implement all of these tech-free times and zones. Some suggestions are listed below:

- **Before sleeping** – screen time in the 90 minutes before sleep delays the onset of sleep and should be avoided. (See Chapter 5 for more details.)
- **Before school** – avoid rapid-fire, fast-paced screen action before school as it overstimulates the brain.
- **Schedule screen-free Sundays or digital sabbaticals** – or perhaps an ad hoc fashion is more our style. It really doesn't

matter how we go about it as long as our children have some time to switch off.

- **While playing** – background media can be detrimental to a child's language development, as discussed in Chapter 4.
- **When not being used** – switch off devices.
- **Play zones** – keep playrooms and spaces tech-free so that children can focus on playing without being distracted.
- **Bedrooms** – try to keep bedrooms as tech-free zones for sleep hygiene purposes as well as for visibility and transparency.
- **Meal areas** – we need to preserve our dinner conversations and allow children to focus on tasting and eating. (See Chapter 8 for more details).
- **Cars** – can be a great opportunity for some one-on-one or uninterrupted time with our children, so try to make cars a screen-free time (at least every now and then).

What technology can our child use?

This is probably the most important area to focus on. Content is king! As parents we need to carefully regulate the content that our children encounter. The revised AAP guidelines advise parents to carefully select content.

Children respond well to parameters. So have open conversations about exactly what apps, websites, video games and TV programs they can watch/use. Children often get into strife when there are ambiguous or few guidelines about what they can watch or use on screens so be very explicit.

TECH TIP ✂

1 **Get smart** – Create a folder on touch-screen devices with the apps that are suitable for our childrenn to use. Create YouTube playlists of appropriate content. Pre-record TV shows or specify channels that we're happy for our child to watch.

2 **Keep up-to-date** – Stay abreast of the newest apps, websites and gadgets that are geared towards young children. Common Sense Media is one of the most comprehensive sites (and apps) available for parents of 0–18-year-olds trying to navigate the digital world. They provide independent reviews, age ratings and other essential information about a range of media. In fact, their mobile app is an essential must-have for all modern parents.

Where and when can technology be used?

Identify specific places in your family home where technology can be used. Ideally, it should be in public, high-traffic areas like the kitchen or living room.

A technology landing zone where digital devices like smart phones, tablets and gaming consoles are parked at night (and perhaps recharged) is a great idea. It might be the kitchen bench or the dining table, it doesn't matter. It just needs to be a designated place for gadgets to be placed at a certain time (so that they don't end up in pyjama pockets).

With whom can our child use technology?

Specify the TV programs, apps or websites that we don't want younger siblings watching or using. There are increasing numbers of social media apps, games and websites dedicated to children like Club Penguin and Moshi Monsters. These sites often allow children to interact and chat in real time and often with minimal supervision.

In addition, specify and know exactly who our children are communicating with and playing with online. We need to have explicit conversations with our children about stranger danger online and who it is – and isn't – appropriate to chat with online.

If you wish, make note of special games and apps and the people you play them with, for example, scrabble with Mum or Skype with grandparents.

Final tips about family media plans

It's important that our family's media plan is communicated with carers, babysitters and grandparents. This is sometimes why a written plan is better as there are no ambiguities, especially if it is on the fridge!

It's also important to remember to review the plan regularly. Technology evolves, children develop and their needs and preferences change too. The plans also need to evolve and adjust according to our child's schedule.

Enforce the plan

Establishing a family media plan is the easy part. Actually enforcing the agreed parameters is when it becomes difficult. But this really is the most critical part in developing healthy media habits with kids.

We need to remember (and muster all our will and strength) to be able to impose the limits we've established. Sometimes we just need to say, 'No, it's time to turn it off and pass over Mummy's smart phone.'

> Establishing a family media plan is the easy part.

It may feel like an agonising battle at first but if we're firm with our technology parameters, over time they will become easier to enforce.

Practical tips for monitoring and managing children's screen time

Even though there isn't necessarily a specific amount of screen time that's healthy or recommended, we still need to be mindful about *how much* time children are spending with technology.

Here are some practical ideas for monitoring and managing children's screen habits:

- media tokens
- screen time printables
- timers
- screen time management products
- technology contracts
- bored boards.

Media tokens

Media tokens are a simple yet highly effective way for children to keep track of their media time (it also helps busy parents too). They typically work best for children aged 4–10 years and are an easy visual representation of time spent on technology.

Media tokens are a simple yet highly effective way for children to keep track of their media time.

Old milk bottle lids, plastic counters, plastic money or even paddle pop sticks work well. The tokens are placed in a transparent jar or bowl as a visual reminder of time spent.

Depending on the age of our child, we could have different tokens worth different amounts of media time. For example, yellow milk bottle lids might represent 30 minutes of media time and the blue lids might represent 60 minutes. This is suitable for children aged 6–10 years.

For children under six who are still developing an understanding of time, they can simply use tokens to quantify the number of TV episodes they have watched or the number of apps that they have used.

For example, we found it really helpful with our (then) 3-year-old to put paddle pop sticks in a glass jar so that we could both keep track of the number of TV episodes he had watched.

We can either pre-specify the amount of screen time that our child can have each day and they can then use the tokens to manage this daily quota (for example, children might have 60 minutes each day, Monday to Friday and 120 minutes on weekends).

Some families prefer using a daily quota, whereas other families are a little more fluid and allow unused screen time to be transferred to other days (for example, I only had 15 minutes on Monday, so on Tuesday I can have 45 minutes).

Alternatively, some families prefer to give children a total allocated amount of media time for the week and then the children can use the tokens to keep a tally of the cumulative total.

Screen time printables
Download a free printable screen time weekly calendar. These can be filled in by hand or laminated and the tokens can be stuck on with sticky velcro.

A printable which has been designed to keep track of the amount of screen time that children consume over a weekly period (which can be downloaded here at drkristygoodwin.com/book_resources/. It makes it very easy to quickly calculate how much screen time children have accumulated in a week and is a great tool to plan children's screen use in advance.

Timers
For children who have mastered the concept of time, timers can be a great way to monitor screen time.

For younger children, a good old-fashioned egg timer can be great way to remind little ones that their screen time will soon be ending. They tend to argue less with objects than they do with us!

For older children a countdown timer on the microwave, stopwatch, smart phone or tablet can be a great way to monitor elapsed or accumulated time.

Many tablets and gaming devices also have an additional feature where we can specify screen limits and the device literally locks itself after the elapsed time period. Magic!

Screen time management products

There are also increasing numbers of apps and web-based software that can also monitor and manage time. I recommend:

- **Our Pact app** (available for both iOS and Android devices) – it 's a parental control app for mobile devices that allows parents to set limits on how much time children can spend with mobile devices. Parents can create and enforce schedules, block the internet and apps instantly.
- **Koala Safe** – allows parents to specify time limits, provides access to parental data and insights and facilitates app and site blocking. It works across all devices, in and out of the family home.

Technology contracts

For older children, a formal written contract is a helpful and very explicit way to manage children's media use. It's important that the contract is constructed by both the parents and children together. By not simply enforcing a contract, it's much more likely that our child will adhere to the policy. The contract can address the questions outlined above in the family media plan.

If we're really honest, technology is sometimes used as a boredom buster for our kids.

Bored boards

If we're really honest, technology is sometimes used as a boredom buster for our kids. (I've certainly done this from time to time, especially after long periods of wet weather or illness). And that's okay. We do that as adults when we flick on the TV or scroll through our newsfeed.

But we need to be really careful that technology isn't used constantly as the digital pacifier. We also need to be armed with a list of ideas that our children can use in lieu of a screen. That way we're armed with a host of practical ideas to entertain children, instead of simply reaching for the screen.

Prepare a selection of ideas for children's activities and display them on a pin board. When children declare, 'I'm bored', they can choose any activity from the board.

At a glance _____

Supporting healthy tech habits can involve:

- **Being mindful about how we use technology with or around our children** – they're watching and absorbing everything, including our digital habits!
- **Teaching our children how to manage their media use.**
- **Establishing a family media plan** – this can be a formal, written document or simply a conversation about how technology will (and won't) be used with our children.
- **Having a family media plan that looks at more than just how much screen time young children consume** – it must also consider what, when, where, with whom and why children are using technology.
- **Keeping up-to-date with strategies to manage our child's screen time** – this will be different for each child and their stage of development.

It's imperative that we teach our children effective strategies to help them manage their screen habits. As parents we must not only establish screen habits (as soon as we pass over our smart phone for the first time), but also enforce them with our children. Just as important is adopting them ourselves, which isn't always easy when we're perpetually distracted by our devices.

The next chapter will explore how to protect our children's health and wellbeing when using technology and the simple strategies we can employ to minimise potential dangers.

11

Protecting children's health

*Parents and educators need to be aware of some of the
developmental and health risks we are flirting with if children
don't use technology in healthy ways.*

There are potential risks to our children's physical and emotional
health and development if devices are used excessively or
inappropriately. We need to make careful decisions about how young
children use digital devices and show them sustainable and healthy
ways to use them.

The five major health considerations associated with young
children using technology are:

- electromagnetic radiation risks
- body image
- vision
- musculoskeletal problems
- hearing.

Electromagnetic radiation risks

Everywhere we look there are signs announcing free wi-fi. In cafes,
restaurants, hotels, airports and even department stores we have
access to wi-fi.

There's an assumption that wi-fi must be safe if it's omnipresent,
but we don't yet have conclusive scientific evidence that confirms
that long-term exposure is in fact safe, especially for young children.

Scientific opinion is split on this issue. Remember this is a relatively new technology so long-term health implications have not yet been adequately researched.

What we need to know about EMR

Electromagnetic radiation (EMR) refers to invisible electrical and magnetic forces. They're a type of radiation that takes the form of waves. Internet routers and wi-fi modems use electromagnetic radiation to send their signals to computers, tablets or mobile devices. Mobile phones also emit EMR, even when on standby mode as they're constantly searching for data.

There are three key things that parents and educators need to know about EMR:

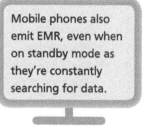

Mobile phones also emit EMR, even when on standby mode as they're constantly searching for data.

- there are *possible* harmful effects
- children are more susceptible to the possible harmful effects of EMR
- we need to reduce our family's EMR exposure.

Possible harmful effects associated with EMR

There's some preliminary research from a range of scientific disciplines indicating that EMR exposure could potentially have harmful effects on our health. In 2011 the World Health Organization (WHO) and the International Agency for Research on Cancer (IARC) classified radiofrequency electromagnetic fields as a 'type 2B possible carcinogen' (i.e. they pose a possible cancer risk to humans). This is the same category as lead, dichlorodiphenyltrichloroethane (DDT) and car exhausts.

In terms of human evidence for health risks associated with EMR, there are increasing numbers of studies that show possible health risks. A 2009 study published in the *Journal of Clinical Oncology* linked mobile phone use to an increased risk of tumors. Other studies have shown possible types of cancer, low sperm count, sleep and/or behavioural problems, physical discomfort and possible learning difficulties as some of the health implications associated with EMR exposure. It's important to reiterate that these are only possible effects – we don't yet know for sure.

While it's important to note that the WHO classification was based on research that indicated *possible* adverse health effects from EMR exposure, it's too premature to identify any long-term health implications. There's a paucity of evidence at this point in time, especially involving humans, to categorically confirm that EMR causes adverse health outcomes. However, there are indicators that we should be cautious about EMR exposure.

The WHO report acknowledged that further study is required, but did suggest we take 'pragmatic measures to reduce exposure' especially for children in regards to mobile phone radiation and wi-fi. The WHO also acknowledges that the reviews of research conducted thus far have indicated that exposure below the EMR guidelines don't produce any adverse health affects, but there are still gaps in knowledge that need to be filled. At this stage, we can't say for certain that there's an effect, but we also can't say for certain that there's no effect.

> Interestingly, many manufacturers of wireless devices ... include safety warnings in their fine print.

There's are also other difficulties when it comes to EMR exposure research: there's no worldwide consensus as to what is a safe level/ standard. This varies significantly from country to country making it difficult to extrapolate consistent research findings. In addition, the current exposure EMR standards were developed in 1993 when wireless technologies were not as prevalent as they are today.

I don't believe that we should wait for significant proof of harm to be established before we take action. By that point, it may be too late. My friends and family call me 'cautious Kristy', but one of my biggest fears is that wi-fi could potentially be the asbestos, benzene or tobacco of the 21st century. I certainly don't want this to be the case so I suggest that we adopt the precautionary principle, as suggested by WHO, especially when it comes to young children's exposure to EMR.

Interestingly many manufacturers of wireless devices like smart phones, gaming consoles and wireless printers include safety warnings in their manuals and fine print. Generally these guidelines advise that devices should be used and stored away from the physical body (various distances are suggested by the different manufacturers). However, many of us fail to read these documents so are unaware of potential dangers and warnings.

Susceptible children

Children absorb more microwave radiation because their bodies are relatively smaller than adults, their skulls are thinner and their brain tissue is more absorbent. A 2012 study published in *Electromagnetic Biology and Medicine* estimated that 5-year-olds absorb almost 60 per cent more radiation than adults. Children's heads are physically smaller than adults' and they've more fluid in their brain, which in turn increases their absorbency of EMR. As a result they may be more prone to the adverse effects of EMR.

Children absorb more microwave radiation because their bodies are relatively smaller than adults ...

It is also possible that there is a cumulative effect with children's EMR exposure. We know that children are using tablets (many of which have multiple antennae) and smart phones from earlier ages so their EMR exposure is increasing accordingly. They're also growing up in physical environments that are saturated with EMR – the internet router at home (and sometimes school or childcare), the cordless phone and even the baby monitor.

Again there's no longitudinal data at this point in time to prove that there are harmful effects associated with device use. We also don't have experimental studies with humans that show safe levels of exposure. There's a possible risk of harm associated with children being exposed to wi-fi (in fact any EMR). Another reason why we need to adopt a precautionary approach.

Reduce our children's EMR exposure

There's no denying that there's still scientific uncertainty about the effects of EMR. As parents we need to pay attention to any possible risk of harm when it comes to our children's health and development.

We need to implement the precautionary principle when it comes to wi-fi and our families by putting into practice simple strategies to help our children form healthy digital habits. We need to become wi-fi warriors (not worriers).

We need to pause and think really carefully about how we use technology with and around our little ones. I don't want us to look back in ten years, when we know more, and realise that we *should* have been more mindful about how we used technology, particularly wi-fi with and around our children.

I'd rather that we err on the side of caution and be more protective and cautionary than we actually need to be.

Simple tips for minimising our family's EMR exposure

While the scientific evidence doesn't demonstrate a causal link between EMR exposure and adverse health effects, minimising exposure is advised.

- **Limit wi-fi exposure** – minimise children's exposure to wi-fi and mobile devices. Turn off routers when not required (i.e. overnight or during the day if we're at home or school and they're not being used). Switch mobile and touch-screen devices to airplane mode when children are playing with them and keep modems away from high-traffic areas of homes (or classrooms) for example, out of bedrooms or sleeping areas. Send an SMS instead of speaking on the phone.
- **Establish tech-free zones** – don't have EMR-transmitting devices in bedrooms or other areas where children spend a high percentage of their time.
- **Increase the distance between children and the device** – use headsets or earphones when speaking on mobile phones. Keep devices at least 40 cm away from the body (remember smart phones are still emitting EMR when they're switched on

but aren't being used). Encourage children to use the speaker option when using smart phones rather than placing them to their head.

- **Wire up when possible** – find the ethernet cable (that's the blue cable we probably threw out when we got wi-fi) and hard wire devices whenever possible. Connect printers and gaming consoles using a cable (and not wi-fi).
- **Limit time on devices with poor reception** – who's done the phone dance trying to pick up a better signal? Our device has to work harder and needs to emit higher levels of EMR when it's operating with a weak signal. Send an SMS or avoid using it when there's poor reception.

Body image

As outlined in Chapter 8 the media, in part, has been blamed for increasing rates of disordered eating. Children today are bombarded with ads in TV, apps and movies as well as traditional media such as magazines, newspapers and printed advertising material (the kind that clogs our letterbox). Both forms of media exert a very powerful influence over young children's formation of ideal body image.

A 2015 Common Sense Media report found that media impacts both young girls' and boys' formation of body image. It also confirmed that children's body image now develops at a very young age. Children as young as five express body dissatisfaction and there are multiple factors that are influential including parents, some media and peers.

This doesn't mean that we need to switch off the TV or never let our little one watch a movie ever again. It means that parents need to be really careful about monitoring what children are watching (and in turn internalising and consuming). It also means that we must constantly talk to them about healthy body images from a young age too. This is why co-viewing is critical.

Tips to minimise the impact of media on children's body image

1 **Talk about body image** – openly discuss how characters and celebrities are portrayed in the media. Identify when images have been re-touched or enhanced.
2 **Find healthy examples** – talk to our children about healthy body images. Find healthy examples in books, magazines, newspapers, printed advertisements and digital media.
3 **Watch what we say** – be mindful of what we say ourselves as children absorb everything that we say (and do). Our off-the-cuff comments are internalised by children.

Vision

Children's early exposure and increasing time spent with screens may put them at increased risk of myopia, near-sightedness and computer vision syndrome.

Children's screen habits place their eyes are under many stressors at earlier ages and often for increasing periods of time. Ophthalmologists are concerned that this premature introduction and prolonged exposure to screens is potentially harmful to children's eye development.

Children are using screens for increasing amounts of time. This exposure makes their eyes much more vulnerable to complications such as myopia (near-sightedness), because they're spending disproportionate amounts of time looking at screens at a close distance.

Children are also using more and more backlit tablet and mobile devices that emit blue light. Blue light is potentially harmful because it can penetrate to the back of the eye. Children's eyes are still developing and haven't yet developed the protective pigments that enable them to filter out some of the harmful blue light.

Once damage has been inflicted, the eyes are left increasingly exposed to blue light and other harmful environment factors, which may in turn increase the risk for long-term visual impairment. It's believed that most blue light damage can occur before a child is 18 years old.

Blue light is not new as it emanates from TVs, indoor lighting, computer screens, mobile devices and the sun. A 2013 study published in the journal *Photochemistry and Photobiology* found that accumulated exposure to artificial sources can cause cellular damage.

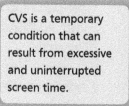

CVS is a temporary condition that can result from excessive and uninterrupted screen time.

It's proposed that over time this may cause permanent and irreversible deterioration of the macula, possibly causing conditions like macular degeneration and cataracts. Again, this isn't proven, but there are sufficient concerns that warrant limiting young children's exposure to backlit devices for long periods of time (this is another example of why we don't want to wait for the research to catch up and prove that there's harm).

Too much uninterrupted time in front of screens can also cause eyestrain, also referred to as computer vision syndrome (CVS). The symptoms of CVS include headaches, blurred vision, tiredness, dry eyes and irritable behaviour in children. CVS is a temporary condition that can result from excessive and uninterrupted screen time (usually for adults it's more than 2 hours of continual screen time).

One of the reasons it occurs is because we tend to blink a lot less (up to 66 per cent less) when we use screens and this results in dry eyes that can cause a feeling itchiness or burning. The tears coating the eye evaporate more quickly when we use screens and this can cause dryness.

Anecdotal evidence from teachers, parents and eye health professionals suggests that increasing numbers of children are presenting with symptoms of CVS.

Case study

Harry had been complaining of sore eyes every afternoon after he'd returned home from school. Harry's mum, Angie, started to observe Harry doing his homework and noticed that he appeared to be squinting a lot while he did his homework on the laptop. She then recalled information from one of my workshops where I mentioned that additional light sources could cause eyestrain when using screens.

Harry was sitting in front on a large glass door to do his homework and there was a lot of competing light streaming in the window. Harry's mum suggested that Harry try a different position to locate his laptop where he wouldn't need to squint as much. She also encouraged him to blink a lot more when using the laptop and take regular breaks.

This made all the difference and Harry's sore eyes disappeared. Just to be on the safe side, Angie took Harry to ophthalmologist for a check up and all was fine. She explained Harry's symptoms and the ophthalmologist agreed that the eyestrain from the extra light and lack of blinking would have likely caused his eye strain.

Eyesight tips

Here are some simple strategies to implement to minimise the impact of screens on children's vision:

- **20-20-20-20 rule** – children's eyes can easily fatigue when they have to focus on screens. To reduce eye-fatigue it's important that children take frequent breaks. Every 20 minutes encourage children to take (at least) 20-second break away from the computer, blink 20 times and look at something at least 20 feet (approximately 6 metres) away and do something physical for 20 seconds (star jumps, run on the spot, stretch).

Encouraging children to focus on something in the distance will minimise the development of focusing problems and eye irritation. Screen-free breaks allow the eyes to recalibrate, blink more (which we don't do when we're staring continually at a screen) and look at things in the distance, which in turn increases their lubrication and reorients the focus on long distance objects.

Screen-free breaks also have the added bonus of encouraging children to get active (so their bodies can re-adjust and find the correct posture) and also calm down their brain (so that they're not hyper-stimulated).

- **Have time in natural light** – it's imperative that young children still spend plenty of time outdoors in natural lighting to develop depth and full range of vision.
- **Minimise glare** – glare from light sources reflecting off walls and surfaces and off screens can place greater demands on the eyes and cause eye strain. Minimise external glare by closing blinds, shutters or curtains when screens are being used. Avoid using digital devices in direct sunlight, directly underneath fluorescent lights or in front of a window. Anti-glare screens can be purchased, but these aren't recommended for children as they may encourage excessive screen use.
- **Check visual ergonomics** – when using fixed screens (laptops and computers) at a close distance, the centre of the screen should be 12–22 centimetres below your horizontal line of sight. Young children may need the computer workstation modified (propping up laptops) so that they can view the screen at their eye level. The recommended distance between eyes and screens is 40–70 cm for children using computers and laptops (slightly closer for smaller screens such as smart phones and tablets).
- **Encourage children to hold mobile devices 40–50 cm away from their body** – if it's any closer, it places more stress on the eyes (and possible unhealthy EMR exposure).

- **Adjust display settings** – screen brightness should match, not compete with the surrounding brightness of the room. If the screen is too bright or too dull in the environment in which it's being used, teach children (depending on their age) how to adjust the brightness accordingly. Eyes should not have to struggle, squint or strain to read a screen. This is usually a personal choice, so it's important that we teach children how to comfortably watch a screen.
- **Blink more** – encourage children to blink more when using screens as this helps to lubricate the eyes. This is part of the 20-20-20-20 break: they slowly open and close their eyes 20 times to help lubricate them.
- **Limit screen time** – excessive amounts of time with screens are likely to have a detrimental impact on their eye health.

Hearing

Many parents joke that their child's hearing capacity has been hampered by the loud music they listen to, but this might not be too far from the truth. Noise-induced hearing loss is a serious and permanent condition. It's associated with incorrect and/or excessive headphone use or exposure to loud music.

The WHO estimates that 1.1 billion people worldwide could be affected by noise-induced hearing loss because of unsafe use of personal music devices including mp3 players and smart phones as well as exposure to noisy entertainment venues.

Our ears convert the vibrations of sound waves into signals that our brains interpret as sounds. If ears are exposed to excessive sound pressure, it can damage the hair cells in the ears that hamper their ability to transmit sound to the brain. This can result in noise-induced hearing loss, which is permanent.

The threat to children's hearing is very serious. The WHO is worried enough that they've produced guidelines for safe listening practices (the Make Listening Safe initiative) and many governments around the world are undertaking awareness campaigns (such as It's a Noisy Planet: Protect Their Hearing) as it's recognised as a growing health concern.

Symptoms of noise-induced hearing loss include muffled or distorted sound, the feeling of pressure in the ear, difficulties understanding speech and/or ringing sounds in the ear in silence (tinnitus). While it can occur as a result of exposure to one loud noise, it typically occurs because of repeated exposure to loud sounds over time.

Anecdotally, audiologists confirm that they're treating more and more young children and adolescents for tinnitus (ringing in the ears) and noise-induced hearing loss.

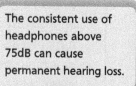

The consistent use of headphones above 75dB can cause permanent hearing loss.

The consistent use of headphones above 75dB can cause permanent hearing loss, with that damage being cumulative. What's concerning is that most commercial mp3 players can reach more than 130dB (contingent upon the model of mp3 player and brand of headphones used).

Like many aspects of children's digital health we may not yet have a comprehensive picture from the research, but we don't want to wait until it's too late and have compromised children's hearing in the process. Again, this is why precautionary measures are essential when it comes to young children using headphones.

Pedestrian risks

The use of headphones also poses a safety risk to pedestrians, especially to children who are easily distracted. A study conducted by Lichenstein and others found that the number of pedestrians that have been killed or injured whilst wearing headphones had tripled in six years. Digital distractions cause inattentive blindness that can reduce a person's mental awareness of their surroundings and can also cause sensory deprivation (so children may not hear the car horn being sounded to warn of impending danger). It's imperative that we ensure that young children don't use headphones when they're a pedestrian and talk about the possible risks so that they build healthy habits from the start.

Tips for healthy hearing

Below are some tips to ensure that your child's hearing isn't compromised in the digital age.

1 **Volume control** – show children how to adjust the volume on their headphones (ideally it would be below 75dB). While it's difficult to specify a precise decibel level on most commercially available headphones, we can teach children about relatively appropriate sound levels. With some headphones and mp3 players we can use the settings to place a limit on the maximum decibel level on the device. Check with individual manufacturers as to how to do this.

2 **Monitor time** – try, where possible, to limit children's time to less than 60 minutes/day wearing headphones.

3 **Use noise-cancelling headphones** – use ear-muff type headphones as these cancel some of the background noise, making it easier for children to listen to the music without having competing background noise.

4 **No headphones when you're a pedestrian** – warn children of the dangers associated with digital distractions.

Ergonomics

Health professionals from a range of disciplines including general medical practitioners, physiotherapists, chiropractors and occupational therapists are anecdotally reporting increasing numbers of children presenting with musculoskeletal problems. They attribute this increase to children's rising use of screens.

There are two major concerns with children and postural development in the digital age:

- **poor habits** – when incorrect body positions are used and sustained, it can result in musculoskeletal problems due to the repeated strain on the body.
- **tired muscles** – if children are spending excessive time with screens, their muscles fatigue and they're much more likely to adopt poor posture (iPosture).

iPosture describes children's poor posture that results from inappropriate amounts of screen time. This is why we see children slump over video game consoles when they're tired or sit with a leg pulled up to their chest when using the computer. Their muscles have simply fatigued.

Increasing amounts of time with digital devices can place the developing body under significant strain. Hunching over digital devices at a young age can entrench bad habits that may cause musculoskeletal issues later in life. Research from Curtin University showed that more than 30 minutes of touch-screen time per day could sow the seeds for potential neck and back issues in adulthood.

> Hunching over digital devices at a young age can entrench bad habits ...

Increasing numbers of children are also presenting with repetitive stress injuries (RSI) because of their continual and repeated use of digital technologies. Medical practitioners are colloquially calling these new physical ailments video-game thumb and text claw. These injuries can cause pain for children and can also inhibit their handwriting skills. Occupational therapists are working with more children who are presenting with fine motor difficulties because their screen habits are impacting on their fine motor skill development.

TECHNO MYTH-BUSTER

MYTH: Handwriting isn't important in the digital age.

FACT: Handwriting is still a critical skill for children to learn in the digital age as different cognitive resources are used when writing as compared to typing.

A 2014 study conducted by Mueller and Oppenheimer showed that university students could recall more from handwritten notes than from typed notes. The reasons are multiple:

- handwriting leaves a motor memory in the sensorimotor region of the brain (typing doesn't do this as typing actions are similar)
- handwriting takes longer than typing, so there's an element of time
- typing doesn't require critical thinking – students might mindlessly take notes without paraphrasing information.

While the results from Mueller and Oppenheimer's study may not be directly transferable to young children, it does suggest that there's still merit in handwriting.

Emerging research is showing that when adults use smart phones while walking they modify their gait in order to compensate for the increased distraction. Researchers from the Department for Health at Texas A&M University and from the University of Queensland have shown that smart phone users' more cautious gait shortens their step length, reduces their step frequency and increases obstacle clearance height.

If we know adults' more developed brains and bodies are changing to accommodate technology, then this raises concerns for young children's physical development. It's further evidence that we need to think carefully about how often and when young children use technology as it can impact on their physical health and development.

Practical tips for optimal iPosture:

To ensure healthy postural habits:

- **Implement the 20-20-20-20 rule** – encourage children to get up and move about for at least 20 seconds after they've been using a screen for 20 minutes and look at something 20 feet away (approximately 6 metres). Tech breaks prevent children's muscles from fatiguing and reverting to unhealthy postures. When children get up and move about, if/when they resume using a device they'll be more likely to correctly re-position their bodies.
- **Help children find the right ergonomic postures** – adjust workstations to suit children's physical needs, not the other way around. In an ideal world, children should be sitting on a chair and desk when using laptop or desktop computers. Their feet should be flat on the ground and their knees and spines should be at a 90° angle too, as the image below demonstrates.

    Select chairs with adjustable heights, tilts and lower-back support (or insert a cushion to provide extra support). Encourage children to sit with their elbows at right angles to the desk with their wrists flat. Teach them to position their backs flat against the seat, their feet flat on the ground and their knees facing forward.

For mobile devices like tablets and smart phones, encourage children to lie on their tummies as this means that they can position their eyes directly above the screen and can keep their necks in a neutral position. They also tend to lie on their tummies for much less time than they would sitting up, meaning that they're likely to naturally get up and move around after shorter periods of time.

Alternatively use tear-shaped beanbags with tablet devices if children would prefer to sit up. This allows them to easily bring the device to their eye level while maintaining their posture (just remember to switch the device to airplane mode first before popping it in their lap!). The most  important thing is that the device is brought to the child's eye level (and not their eyes that are brought to the device's level) as the image demonstrates.

- **Monitor the weight they are carrying** – given that many school-aged children are now required to bring tablets and/ or laptops to school each day, there are concerns about the increased weight of school bags. As a general rule, children shouldn't be expected to carry bags that are more than 10 per cent of their body weight. So it's important to monitor the weight of bags and make adjustments where necessary.
- **Download ErgoBreak4Kids** – this program, available via a website or app, helps children aged 5-12 years learn about healthy ergonomic practices for interacting with technology. The program allows users to set and customise their break intervals when using digital devices to relieve muscle fatigue, eyestrain and restore concentration. The break intervals are delivered via animated characters that provide stretch demonstrations and also give ergonomic tips (for tablet and computer use).

At a glance

Use the following tips to protect your child's health in the digital age.

- **Whenever possible, reduce children's wi-fi exposure** – turn off the router when not in use, use the blue ethernet cable when possible, keep mobile devices off laps and far away from the body (at least an arm's length distance), switch phones and tablets to airplane mode if wi-fi is not required.
- **Talk to children about body image** – and find healthy examples from the media and in real life.
- **Set up and enforce (that's the tricky part) healthy media habits as soon as we can** – to prevent the likelihood of them adopting unhealthy habits that can lead to addiction.
- **Implement the 20-20-20-20 rule** – to ensure that children's eyes and muscles are getting adequate rest and an opportunity to recalibrate.
- **Show children how to adjust the volume on their headphones** – so that it's at safe levels and discourage too much time with headphones (an hour a day is the recommended maximum). Use noise-cancelling headphones where possible.
- **Remind children about the correct posture** – when using devices. When they start to slump or twist their bodies in contorted positions it's usually a sign that they're fatiguing and that a change of activity is required.

Given we don't yet know the long-term implications of children's screen habits on their physical development, we must adopt some precautionary principles and ensure that screen time is part of an overall balanced approach to childhood.

Conclusion

Whether we love it or loathe it, technology is now a central part of our children's lives and ours as parents too. They are experiencing digitalised childhoods and have inherited a world where screens are increasingly ubiquitous. We have to help them navigate this digital terrain. Digital abstinence for young children is not an option.

Young children are being dunked into the digital stream at increasingly younger ages and having digital devices thrust into their hands, attached to their prams and thrown into their playpens. But we don't need to prematurely introduce technology to little ones. I certainly don't advocate the wholesale or premature introduction of screens – it's not what developing brains and bodies need.

However, we can't ignore technology and hope that it disappears. As a society *our* digital dependence is changing how we behave, sleep, socialise, interact, move and learn. Our children are not immune to this sweeping change. They're learning and developing in completely new ways.

We need to help our children to enter the digital world, bearing their safety and development in mind. We must ensure that their digital habits are not damaging their development. As parents and educators we need to guide, moderate and shape our children's digital habits so that they form healthy and helpful relationships with technology. We need to look for ways to use technology so that it enhances, not erodes children's development.

This book has translated the latest research from a range of disciplines into practical and digestible information for parents and educators trying to navigate the digital terrain with their young children (without having to ban the iPad, disconnect wi-fi or unplug the TV).

There's little doubt that a digital overload at a young age will have a negative impact on a young child's physical, social, emotional and intellectual development. Their developing brains and bodies cannot keep up with many of the demands of the digital world – and if we're really honest, neither can we as adults.

While we don't yet have a complete picture about the exact ways in which technology is shaping young children's development, this book has attempted to outline what we do know about their unchanging developmental needs and how this intersects with technology. I've outlined what the seven essential building blocks involve so that children can thrive and develop in the digital age. I've also explored how technology can stifle or support a child's development, depending on how it's used. Some of the potential harmful implications of young children's digital exposure have also been outlined in this book.

In summary, the key tips include:

- *focussing* on what our children are creating and consuming with technology (look for educational and interactive content where possible)
- *being mindful* of when our child uses technology (minimise use of screens before sleep and rapid-fire input before school)
- *keeping devices* out of bedrooms
- *monitoring* our own media habits
- *establishing* and enforcing time limits with devices
- *finding healthy* amounts of screen time
- *balancing screen* and green time
- *using technology* mindfully
- *teaching our children* how to disconnect and untether from technology.

Many parents are scrambling to keep up-to-date in this digital world and are unaware of the potential developmental dangers that we flirt with when children use technology in unhealthy or harmful ways. Chief concerns that we need to consider as parents include:

- exposure to EMR
- sleep habits
- childhood obesity
- waning social and emotional skills
- cyber safety
- addictive potential
- physical development implications (hearing, musculoskeletal and vision worries).

However, as this book has also highlighted, technology offers amazing potential for young children. It can enable children to learn, play, interact and communicate in completely new and exciting ways. Technology, when used appropriately and intentionally with young children, isn't toxic. As parents and educators we don't need to fear technology or feel guilty or concerned about using it with young children. We certainly need to minimise the potential harmful effects of technology on children's development, but we need to flip the toxic view. We need to focus on the positive potential that technology offers young children and help them to consume more digital kale.

For years there's been immense debate about the developmental appropriateness of technology with young children. It appears entrenched philosophical beliefs that technology isn't appropriate for young children are slowly being eroded. Rather than focusing on *if* young children should be using technology, discussion and research is now examining how we best use technology with young children in ways that are congruent with their developmental needs.

When used in age-appropriate and intentional ways technology *can* support and strengthen children's development. It can provide new and exciting avenues for learning and communication. These aspects are where our attention (and research) needs to go because whether we love it or loathe it, technology is here to stay.

As simple as it sounds, it's really all about a balanced approach to childhood. Today's children need both analogue and digital experiences for optimal development in the digital age. Their online and offline worlds can converge. They need to tap, swipe and pinch as well as jump, run and climb. They need green time and screen time. Their daily dose of digital shouldn't displace or supersede all the essential building blocks that are needed for optimal development. We need to make sure that their screen time doesn't rob them of the quintessential elements of a magical childhood: the joy of simple pleasures, time to play and explore and be creative with ample white space.

For most parents, raising digital kids is scary as it's completely different to our screen-free childhoods. But it doesn't have to be. If we're armed with the best ways to avoid some of the digital pitfalls and understand how we can leverage technology to support our children's development, we'll provide our children with the best start possible to thrive in the digital world they have inherited.

Tech tips

General tips

- Set parental controls on all devices, but remember that these don't completely guarantee your child's online safety. You need to actively supervise and engage with your child when they're online. This is why we need to keep gadgets in public places in the house and ban them from bedrooms.
- Establish a Media Management Plan (a plan that details what, when, where, how much and with whom children can use technology). This can be a formal written document, or a verbal plan. Remember you'll need to revisit and update this as your child grows and their digital interests change.
- Set screen limits, but don't focus exclusively on *how much* time they spend with screens. Most importantly, also consider *what* they're watching/using/playing and *when* they're using screens (minimise exposure in the 90 minutes before naps or sleep).
- Determine healthy amounts of screen time for your child by considering if they're having opportunities to meet the seven essential building blocks outlined in this book: Do they have daily opportunities for relationships, language, sleep, play, movement, nutrition and executive function skills?
- Where possible, use technology *with* your child. There's ample evidence that confirms that co-viewing is beneficial for children. Show an active interest in what they're doing online and help to transfer what they've learnt online to the offline world too.
- Minimise children's wi-fi exposure because of possible risk of harm: keep apps out of laps, turn off routers when not in use, switch mobile devices to airplane mode (when wi-fi isn't required), increase the distance between the child and the device and plug into cables when possible.
- Teach children about healthy hearing, vision and posture habits when using digital devices.
- Model healthy media habits yourself! Have clear boundaries on when you'll use your phone or gadgets around your children. Balance your green time with screen time.
- Download the Common Sense Media app to keep up to date on latest technologies for kids aged 0–18.

0–2 years

- Use screens *very* sparingly with 0–2-year-olds. Remember, there's a displacement effect when they're using a gadget (so make sure any time online is well-spent and minimal in the first two years of life). Eighty-five percent of brain architecture is formed in the first two years, so ensure that they have the best start possible and provide as much screen-free time as possible (but don't feel guilty if you do occasionally use screens).

- Co-view where possible; use technology with your infant as much as you can. Watch a TV show or DVD and talk to them about what they're watching. Help them to relate what they see on a screen to real life and their experiences. Learning from technology is greatly enhanced for little ones when an adult co-views.
- Don't be duped into thinking that products, apps and gadgets marketed as 'educational' for infants are beneficial. There's recent evidence to suggest that electronic toys reduce the quality and quantity of language that infants hear when playing, as compared to books and traditional toys.
- If you do want to use technology with your little one, limit the time to no more than 10–15 minutes/day (maximum).
- There's no rush to prematurely dunk little ones in the digital stream. Remember, it takes young children (up until about 30 months of age) twice as long to learn something from a screen than from a live demonstration. Real-life interactions and objects are best for under 2s. Use screen experiences to *complement* these real experiences (for example, taking photos whilst at the zoo, or watching videos of about animals of interest to your child).

2–5 years

- Techno tantrums are a normal part of development and are often caused by withdrawals of dopamine. Remember, set firm guidelines about 'how much' screen time your pre-schooler can have each day, give two gentle reminders before switching off, use a timer, encourage your child to switch off the device (not you) and enforce consequences for not adhering to screen rules.
- Avoid using screens as 'digital pacifier' *all the time* (but don't feel guilty if you need to do it every now and then). Allow your pre-schooler to deal with emotions and not always revert to using a screen to alleviate feelings of boredom, frustration or anger.
- Switch off the TV when no-one is watching it as background TV can impede children's language skills and alter parent-child interactions.
- Keep children's play spaces as tech-free places so that they're not digitally distracted. Soft and familiar background music is fine, but also remember to provide opportunities for silence too – we don't want our kids

always entertained. Their brains need white space!
- Keep bedrooms as tech-free zones as screens can interfere with healthy sleep habits. Avoid using screens in the 90 minutes before naps or sleep.
- When selecting apps for preschoolers, look for apps that encourage your child to create content (e.g. create a digital book) and communicate (e.g. read a book app and record your child's voice), in addition to consumption apps (e.g. watching YouTube).
- Scary content, including the daily news and current affairs programs should be avoided when preschoolers are around. They don't yet have the cognitive or emotional skills to process them and even though they may not discuss what they've observed, they're often processing it!
- Use a timer, techno-tokens or quantify the number of episodes or state a specific level in a game that your child can attain to help them manage their screen time. Healthy screen habits must be established early in life (you'll be thankful later on).

5–8 years

- There's no specific chronological age that determines a child's readiness for a smart phone. Consider their organisational skills and their social and emotional skills to determine if they're ready for a phone.
- When looking for educational apps or websites look for simple, clean designs and that use praise and rewards sparingly. Children quickly become conditioned to receiving praise and rewards and can become dependent on the external validation.
- When using apps, find apps that allow your child to create, communicate *and* consume. Try to limit their use of consumption apps (like YouTube) and encourage them to be active on a smart phone by selecting apps where they create digital content or interact on screen. A balanced approach is essential.
- Help your child relate what they see on-screen to their real life experiences. This can bolster their language skills. It also teaches your child that screen time is a fun shared experience and isn't a taboo or secretive activity.
- Avoid fast-paced, rapid-fire screens before school (and bed too). It can over-stimulate the brain and make it harder for children to focus or relax.
- Set maximum volume levels on mobile devices and music players and use earmuff-style headphones with your child. Correct poor posture and encourage the 20-20-20-20 rule when using screens.
- Teach kids at this age that technology's a tool, not a treat or a toy! Avoid using the withdrawal of screens as a form of punishment – we want them to see screens as an integral part of their life. Have firm consequences if they don't adhere to the contract.
- Use a timer or screen time printables to plan when and for how long your child can use technology each day. Be specific and stick to your plan!

8–12 years

- Don't be in a rush to prematurely introduce your child to social media. You need to ensure your child has the maturity, emotional and social skills to use social media and not because of peer pressure. Look for age-appropriate alternatives if your child isn't quite ready to enter the social media arena (like *Kuddle*). Establish firm rules and guidelines when they do start a social media account.
- Look for pro-social and educational video games. Try to play video games *with* your child where possible and avoid aggressive or violent content.
- eBooks, book apps and audiobooks are great alternatives to traditional books. But it's all about balance – these digital books can't and shouldn't replace real book experiences.
- Keep bedrooms as tech-free zones, as screen use can delay the onset of sleep (especially back-lit devices like tablets and smart phones) and can also interfere with children's sleep cycles (alerts and notifications can disturb sleep cycles).
- Keep an eye on your children's screen time. While you don't need to enforce universal, age-based screen time limits, we need to ensure that our kids' screen time is healthy not harmful. If you're concerned about how much time they're spending online you can use a

technology audit tool to monitor their usage and then use a parent control app to help you help them to manage their usage. The ultimate goal is that we want our children to have the skills and self-control to manage technology in healthy ways.

- Have regular conversations with your tween and keep actively involved in their online life to minimise the chances that they're accessing (or creating) pornographic or other inappropriate material.
- Understand that today's kids want to communicate with their friends online. It's their way of socialising (even if they've spent all day with them)!
- Teach your child to mono-task, not multi-task. Despite what they think tweens aren't capable of simultaneously performing multiple tasks (in fact no one is). Teach them from the outset that multi-tasking is a myth. Teach them to put a fortress around their focus and do one thing at a time!
- Jointly establish a written contract that clearly specifies what, when, where, with whom and for how long your child can use technology. Revise it regularly.

Author notes

Page 3 'In fact, research conducted in 2014 by AVG confirms that many children meet their digital milestones ...' AVG 2014, *Digital diaries: consumer research*, retrieved 22 March 2015 <http://www.avg.com/digitaldiaries/2014>.

Page 4 This data was yielded from studies conducted by the Kaiser Family Foundation in 2010 and Common Sense Media in 2013 ...' Common Sense Media 2013, *Zero to eight: children's media use in America*, retrieved 15 May 2014, <https://www.commonsensemedia. org/research/zero-to-eight-childrens-media-use-in-america-2013>.

Rideout VJ, Foehr UG & Roberts DF 2010, *Generation M: media in the lives of 8- to 18-year-olds*, Henry J. Kaiser Family Foundation, Menlo Park, California.

Page 6 'We do have screen-time recommendations that prescribe recommended amounts of daily screen time.' Australian Department of Health 2015, Australia's physical activity and sedentary behaviour guidelines, Retrieved January 2016, <http://www. health.gov.au/internet/ main/publishing.nsf/content /health-pubhlth-strateg-phys- act-guidelines#apa512>.

Page 8 'According to a 2015 study conducted by Miner & Co, making children watch TV (instead of playing video games ...' Miner & Co Studio 2015, *Television is now the second screen for kids with tablets*, retrieved 15 August 2015, <http://www.minerandcostudio. com/#!insights-and-ideas/c1b3v>.

Page 9 'However, research by Zimmerman and Christakis in 2007 showed that while violent and non-educational programming *is* associated with later symptoms of attention deficit ...' Zimmerman FJ & Christakis DA 2007, 'Associations between content types of early media exposure and subsequent attentional problems', *Pediatrics*, 120(5), pp 986–992.

Page 11 'This equates to spending over three hours on them a day, on average, of which 1.72 hours are spent on social media.' Meeker M & Wu L 2013, *Internet trends report*, retrieved 14 September 2014 <http://www.kpcb.com/blog/2013-internet-trends>.

Page 12 'In fact, studies have shown that babies as young as 15-minutes old are able to copy one of their parents poking out their tongue (and *not* because they're hungry).' Meltzoff AN & Moore MK 1997, 'Explaining facial imitation: a theoretical model', *Early Development & Parenting*, 6(3–4), p 179.

Page 16 'As the joint position statement from the National Association for the Education of Young Children (NAEYC) and the Fred Rogers Center for Early Learning and Children's Media at Saint Vincent College in the US reveals...' National Association for the Education of Young Children (NAEYC) & the Fred Rogers Center for Early Learning and Children's Media at Saint Vincent College 2013, *Technology and interactive media as tools in early childhood programs serving children from birth through age eight: a joint position statement of the National Association for the Education of Young Children and the Fred Rogers Center for Early Learning and Children's Media at Saint Vincent College*, NAEYC and the Fred Rogers Center for Early Learning and Children's Media at Saint Vincent College, Pittsburgh.

Page 24 'Child development researchers Fox, Levitt, and Nelson ...' Fox SE, Levitt P & Nelson III CA 2010, 'How the timing and quality of early experiences influence the development of brain architecture', *Child Development*, 81(1), pp 28-40.

Page 27 'Work by the National Scientific Council on the Developing Child suggests ...' National Scientific Council on the Developing Child 2010, 'Early experiences can alter gene expression and affect long-term development' (Working Paper), *National Scientific Council on the Developing Child*, (10).

Page 30 'A 2012 study published in the *Journal of Vision* observed that babies' serve-and-return interactions ...' Farzin F, Hou C & Norcia AM 2012, 'Piecing it together: infants' neural responses to face and object structure, *Journal of Vision*, (13) p 6.

Page 38 'Research published in 2012 revealed that infant brains respond to faces ...' Farzin F, Hou C & Norcia AM 2012, 'Piecing it together: infants' neural responses to face and object structure, *Journal of Vision*, (13) p 6.

Page 38 'Researchers from the University of California found that fragmented ...' Molet J, Heins K, Zhuo X, Mei Y T, Regev L, Baram T Z, & Stern H 2016, Fragmentation and high entropy of neonatal experience predict adolescent emotional outcome. *Translational Psychiatry*, 6(1), pp. 702-734.

Page 39 'A 2012 study found that children with responsive, warm and caring mothers ...' Luby JL, Barch DM, Belden A, Gaffrey MS, Tillman R, Babb C & Botteron KN 2012, 'Maternal support in early childhood predicts larger hippocampal volumes at school age' *Proceedings of the National Academy of Sciences*, 109(8), pp 2854–2859.

Page 41 'A 2010 study published in *Infant and Child Development* ...' Mendelsohn AL, Brockmeyer CA, Dreyer BP, Fierman AH, BerkuleSilberman SB & Tomopoulos S 2010, 'Do verbal interactions with infants during electronic media exposure mitigate adverse impacts on their language development as toddlers?' *Infant and child development*, 19(6), pp 577–593.

Page 44 'This was confirmed by a 2013 study published in *Media Psychology* ...' Howard Gola AA, Richards MN, Lauricella AR & Calvert SL 2013, 'Building meaningful parasocial relationships between toddlers and media characters to teach early mathematical skills' *Media Psychology*, 16(4), pp 390–411.

Page 45 'A large-scale global study (with over 6000 participants) by online security company AVG ...' AVG 2015, *Digital diaries: consumer research*, retrieved retrieved 22 March 2015 <http://www.avg.com/digitaldiaries/2015>.

Page 46 'The researchers believed that this was because the children felt like they were competing for attention with their parents' gadget.' Radesky JS, Kistin CJ, Zuckerman B, Nitzberg K, Gross J, Kaplan-Sanoff M & Silverstein M 2014, 'Patterns of mobile device use by caregivers and children during meals in fast food restaurants', *Pediatrics*, 133(4), pp e843-e849.

Page 49 'In a 2015 poll conducted by the *American Speech–Language–Hearing Association*, nearly 50 per cent of parents of children aged 8 years reported ...' American Speech–Language–Hearing Association 2015, *Parent Poll: Better Hearing and Speech Month* (Spring 2015), retrieved 12 July 2015 <http://www.asha.org/uploadedFiles/BHSM-Parent-Poll.pdf>.

Page 51 'A 2015 study published in the *Journal of Developmental & Behavioral Pediatrics* ...' Watt E, Fitzpatrick C, Derevensky JL & Pagani LS 2015, 'Too much television? Prospective associations between early childhood tele-viewing and later self-reports of victimization by sixth grade classmates', *Journal of Developmental & Behavioral Pediatrics*, *36*(6), pp 426–433.

Page 51 'Another study conducted in 2014 and published in *Computers in Human Behaviour* showed that just five days away from screen media …' Uhls YT, Michikyan M, Morris J, Garcia D, Small GW, Zgourou E & Greenfield PM, 2014, 'Five days at outdoor education camp without screens improves pre-teen skills with non-verbal emotion cues', *Computers in Human Behavior*, 39, pp 387–392.

Page 52 'A 2014 study from the *Social Policy Research Centre* at the University of New South Wales found that around 20 per cent of young children …' Spears B, Keeley M, Bates, S & Katz I 2014, 'Research on youth exposure to and management of cyberbullying incidents in Australia (Part A Literature review on the estimated prevalence of cyberbullying involving Australian minors),' SPRC Report 9/2014, Social Policy Research Centre, UNSW, Australia.

Page 53 'A study conducted by Emm found that young children are only three clicks away …' Emm D 2013, *Children a t high risk of accessing adult content on YouTube*, Kaspersky Lab, United Kingdom.

Page 54 'Further, in 2003 a meta-analysis by Anderson provided clear evidence that aggressive video games can be particularly problematic.' Anderson CA 2003, 'Violent video games: myths, facts, and unanswered questions', *Psychological Science Agenda*, Vol. 16(5), pp 1– 3.

Page 56 'According to research conducted by Sydney University psychologists Sitharthan and Sitharthan …' ,Sitharthan G & Sitharthan T 2011, 'Don't get worked up: you can beat your porn addiction … if you want to', The Conversation.

Page 56 'Moreover, a 2012 publication from the St. James Ethics Centre reported the worrying trend …' Arliss J 2012, 'Pornography and education', *Living Ethics: Newsletter of the St. James Ethics Centre*, Issue 88, pp 12–13.

Page 56 ' … according to a study conducted by Bobkowski, Brown and Neffa in 2012.' Bobkowski PS, Brown JD & Neffa DR 2012, 'Hit Me Up and We Can Get Down: US youths' risk behaviors and sexual self-disclosure in MySpace profiles'. *Journal of Children and Media*, 6(1), pp 119–134.

Page 57 'It was previously thought that the onset of puberty was when children started forming ideal body images …' Daraganova G 2014, 'Body image of primary school children', *Annual Statistical Report 2013*, Australian Institute of Family Studies, p 111.

Page 58 'This is supported by research published in *The British Journal of Psychiatry* that children as young as eight years of age …' Micali N, De Stavola B, Ploubidis G, Simonoff E, Treasure J & Field AE 2015, 'Adolescent eating disorder behaviours and cognitions: gender-specific effects of child, maternal and family risk factors', *The British Journal of Psychiatry*, 207 (4), p 320 – 327.

Page 63 'A study conducted by Hart and Risley …' Hart B & Risley T 2003, 'The early catastrophe', *American Educator*, *27*(4), pp 6–9.

Page 64 'Through her studies, language acquisition researcher Patricia Kuhl has shown that babies and toddlers …' Kuhl PK 2000, 'A new view of language acquisition', *Proceedings of the National Academy of Sciences*, *97*(22), pp 11850–1 Kuhl PK 2004, 'Early language acquisition: cracking the speech code', *Nature Reviews Neuroscience*, 5(11), pp 831–843.

Page 64 'A 2015 study found that it is the combination of _both_ infant-direct speech …' Lloyd-Fox S, Széplaki-Kölld B, Yin J & Csibra G 2015, 'Are you talking to me? Neural activations in 6-month-old infants in response to being addressed during natural interactions', *Cortex*, 70, pp 35–48.

Page 64 'A critical period for sound development is between 8–10 months of age, as this is when babies can recognise …' Kuhl PK 2004, 'Early language acquisition: cracking the speech code', *Nature Reviews Neuroscience*, 5(11), pp 831–843.

Page 65 'Research by Anderson and Pempek has shown that babies and infants learn half as much and recall it for much shorter …' Anderson DR & Pempek TA 2005, 'Television and very young children', *American Behavioral Scientist*, 48(5), pp 505–522.

Page 66 'Roben, Cole and Armstrong have conducted longitudinal research …' Roben CK, Cole PM & Armstrong LM 2013, 'Longitudinal relations among language skills, anger expression and regulatory strategies in early childhood' *Child development*, 84(3), pp 891–905.

Page 66 'Moreover, Hart and Risley's work found that four-year old children from language-rich environments (whose average word exposure was approximately 45 million words at age 4) …' Hart B & Risley T 2003, 'The early catastrophe', *American Educator*, 27(4), pp 6–9.

Page 66 '_Brain rules_ author John Medina claims that the …' Medina J 2010, *Brain rules for baby*, Pear Press, Seattle.

Page 67 ' A British government study found that teachers and health professionals…' Roulstone S, Wren Y, Bakopoulou I, Goodlad S, & Lindsay G 2012, Exploring interventions for children and young people with speech, language and communication needs: a study of practice. Department for Education, London.

Page 69 'Three separate studies published in the _Journal of Broadcasting and Electronic Media_ …' Livingstone S & Helsper EJ 2008, 'Parental mediation of children's internet use', *Journal of Broadcasting and Electronic Media*, 52(4), pp581–599.

Nathanson AI 2001, 'Parent and child perspectives on the presence and meaning of parental television mediation', *Journal of Broadcasting and Electronic Media*, 45(2), pp 201–220.

Valkenburg PM, Krcmar M, Peeters AL & Marseille NM 1999, 'Developing a scale to assess three styles of television mediation: "Instructive mediation", "restrictive mediation" and "social co-viewing", *Journal of Broadcasting & Electronic Media*, 43(1), pp 52–66.

Page 69 '…Over forty years of research with Sesame Street has shown greater learning benefits occur when children co-view.' Kearney MS & Levine PB 2015, *Early Childhood Education by MOOC: Lessons from Sesame Street* (No. w21229), National Bureau of Economic Research.

Leibham ME, Alexander JM, Johnson KE, Neitzel CL & Reis-Henrie FP 2005, 'Parenting behaviors associated with the maintenance of preschoolers' interests: a prospective longitudinal study', *Journal of Applied Developmental Psychology*, 26(4), pp 397–414.

Mares ML & Pan Z 2013, Effects of Sesame Street: A meta-analysis of children's learning in 15 countries, *Journal of Applied Developmental Psychology*, 34(3), 140–151.

Page 69 'There is a range of digital technologies being viewed and consumed in family homes …' Stevens R & Penuel WR 2010, Studying and fostering learning through joint media engagement, in Principal Investigators Meeting of the National Science Foundation's Science of Learning Centers, October, Arlington, VA, pp 1–75.

Page 70 'Research published in 2009 in the *International Journal of Learning and Media* showed that most ...' Barron B, Martin CK, Takeuchi L & Fithian R 2009 Parents as learning partners in the development of technological fluency, *International Journal of Learning and Media*, 1(2), 55–77.

Page 70 'Research by Leibham, Alexander, Johnson, Neitzel and Reis-Henrie found that children are more likely to engage in a sustained exploration of a topic or idea ...' Leibham ME, Alexander JM, Johnson KE, Neitzel CL & Reis-Henrie FP 2005, 'Parenting behaviors associated with the maintenance of preschoolers' interests: a prospective longitudinal study', *Journal of Applied Developmental Psychology*, 26(4), pp 397–414.

Page 73 'In 2013 Mares and Pan examined a substantial body of research that's investigated *Sesame Street* and its impact on preschoolers ...' Mares ML & Pan Z 2013, Effects of Sesame Street: A meta-analysis of children's learning in 15 countries, *Journal of Applied Developmental Psychology*, 34(3), 140–151.

Page 77 'Of the few available published studies regarding preschoolers and interactive apps is a 2012 Australian study of 109 preschoolers ...' Neumann MM 2014, 'An examination of touch screen tablets and emergent literacy in Australian pre-school children', *Australian Journal of Education*, 58 (2) pp 109-122.

Page 78 'In a 2015 study conducted by the American Speech–Language–Hearing Association, 52 per cent of parents believed ...' American Speech–Language–Hearing Association 2015, *Parent Poll: Better Hearing and Speech Month* (Spring 2015), retrieved 12 July 2015 , <http://www.asha.org/uploadedFiles/BHSM-Parent-Poll.pdf>.

Page 78 'Research conducted by Anderson and Pempek and Barr ...' Anderson DR & Pempek TA 2005, 'Television and very young children', *American Behavioral Scientist*, 48(5), pp 505–522.

Page 78 'It also means that if they're to use screens in these early years that we carefully consider what Lisa Guernsey calls the 3 Cs: child, content and context ...' Guernsey L 2012, *Screen time: how electronic media – from baby videos to educational software – affects your young child*, Basic Books, Philadelphia, PA.

Page 80 'A 2007 article published in *The Journal of Pediatrics* ...' Zimmerman FJ, Christakis DA & Meltzoff AN 2007, 'Associations between media viewing and language development in children under age two years', *The Journal of Pediatrics*, 151(4), pp 364–368.

Page 80 'Zimmerman, Christakis, and Meltzoff found that for every hour per day that babies aged 8–16 months watched baby DVDs ...' Zimmerman FJ, Christakis DA & Meltzoff AN 2007, 'Associations between media viewing and language development in children under age two years', *The Journal of Pediatrics*, 151(4), pp 364–368.

Page 81 'A 2014 study published in the *Journal of Educational Psychology* confirmed that babies don't learn to read from baby media ...' Neuman SB, Kaefer T, Pinkham A & Strouse G 2014, 'Can babies learn to read? A randomized trial of baby media', *Journal of Educational Psychology*, 106(3), p 815.

Page 82 'A 2013 study published in *The Journal of Neuroscience* suggests that immersing...' O'Muircheartaigh J, Dean DC, Dirks H, Waskiewicz N, Lehman K, Jerskey BA & Deoni, SC 2013, 'Interactions between white matter asymmetry and language during neurodevelopment', *The Journal of Neuroscience*, 33(41), pp 16170–16177.

Page 82 'However, a study by Kuhl, Tsao and Liu found that young children ...' Kuhl PK, Tsao FM & Liu HM 2003, 'Foreign-language experience in infancy: effects of short-term exposure and social interaction on phonetic learning', Proceedings of the National Academy of Sciences,100(15), pp 9096–9101.

Page 83 'Nature Play Western Australia's chief executive Griffin Longley claimed that ...' Meriles L 2014, *Mucking around takes back seat to organised sport and screen time for kids, report finds*. Retrieved 2 June 2015, <http://www.abc.net.au/news/2014-11-15/australian-kids-not-playing-enough-finds-report/5892244>.

Page 83 'In fact, a 2013 study published in the *Pediatrics* journal found that children aged 8 months to eight years were ... ' Lapierre MA, Piotrowski JT, Linebarger D.L 2013, 'Background television in the homes of US children', *Pediatrics*, 130(5), pp 839–846.

Page 84 'A 2009 study published in *Child Development* discovered that background TV impacts on the quality ...' Kirkorian HL, Pempek TA, Murphy LA, Schmidt ME & Anderson DR 2009, 'The impact of background television on parent–child interaction', *Child Development*, 80(5), pp 1350–1359.

Page 85 'The study found that fast and loud music disrupted reading comprehension ...' Thompson WF, Schellenberg EG & Letnic AK 2012, 'Fast and loud background music disrupts reading comprehension', *Psychology of Music*,40(6), pp 700–708.

Page 90 'A 2014 Australian report estimated that children's poor sleep habits costs taxpayers an extra $27 million/year in extra doctor visits ...' Quach, J., Oberklaid, F., Gold, L., Lucas, N., Mensah, F. K., & Wake, M. (2014). Primary healthcare costs associated with special health care needs up to age 7 years: Australian populationbased study. *Journal of Paediatrics and child health*, 50(10), p 768-774.

Page 90 'It negatively impacts their mood (we've all experienced a toddler emotional-tsunami from exhaustion), behavioural issues, alertness, capacity to learn ...' Sadeh A, Gruber R & Raviv A 2003, 'The effects of sleep restriction and extension on schoolage children: what a difference an hour makes', *Child Development*, 74(2), pp 444–455.

Page 91 'These guidelines are based on sleep recommendations published in *Sleep Health* in 2015.' Hirshkowitz, M, Whiton, K, Albert, S M, Alessi, C, Bruni, O, DonCarlos, L. ... & Neubauer, D N 2015, National Sleep Foundation's sleep time duration recommendations: methodology and results summary. *Sleep Health*, 1(1), 40-43.

Page 91 'A University of South Australia study showed that school children aged 10–15 years are averaging at least 30 minutes less sleep ...' Dollman J, Ridley K, Olds T & Lowe L 2007, Trends in the duration of school-day sleep among 10–15 year old South Australians 1985–2004', *Acta Paediatrica*, 96(7), pp 1011–1014.

Page 91 'This finding is also alarming given that a 2013 study published in Developmental Neuropsychology showed that even mild sleep deprivation ...' Molfese DL, Ivanenko A, Key AF, Roman A, Molfese VJ, O'Brien LM & Hudac CM 2013, 'A one-hour sleep restriction impacts brain processing in young children across tasks: evidence from event-related potentials', *Developmental Neuropsychology*, 38(5), pp 317–336.

Page 92 'A study conducted in 2000 and published in the *Journal of Developmental and Behavioral Pediatrics* showed ...' Owens JA, Spirito A, McGuinn M & Nobile C 2000, Sleep habits and sleep disturbance in elementary school-aged children, *Journal of Developmental & Behavioral Pediatrics*, 21(1), pp 27–36.

Page 92 'A 2012 study conducted at *Boston College* showed that teachers believe that their instruction is hampered by children's sleep deprivation.' Mullis IV, Martin MO, Foy P & Arora A 2012, *TIMSS 2011 International results in mathematics*, International Association for the Evaluation of Educational Achievement, Herengracht 487, Amsterdam, 1017 BT, The Netherlands.

Page 92 'It's estimated that 30 per cent of 5-year-old Australian children have a TV in their bedroom.' Cespedes EM, Gillman MW, Kleinman K, Rifas-Shiman SL, Redline S & Taveras EM 2014, Television viewing, bedroom television and sleep duration from infancy to mid-childhood, *Pediatrics*, 133, pp e 1163–71.

Page 97 Various studies published in journals such as *Pediatrics, The Journal of School Nursing* and *Sleep* confirmed ... 'Foley LS, Maddison R, Jiang Y, Marsh S, Olds T & Ridley K 2013, 'Pre-sleep activities and time of sleep onset in children', *Pediatrics*, pp 131: 276–282. Garmy P, Nyberg P & Jakobsson U 2012, 'Sleep and television and computer habits of Swedish school-age children', *The Journal of School Nursing*, 28, pp 469–476.

Hense S, Barb AG, Pohlabeln H, De Henauw S, Marild S, Molnár D et al 2011, 'Factors that influence weekday sleep duration in European children', *Sleep*, 34, p 633.

Page 97 'Two separate studies in 2013 also showed that screen time in the 90 minutes ...' Foley LS, Maddison R, Jiang Y, Marsh S, Olds T & Ridley K 2013, 'Pre-sleep activities and time of sleep onset in children', *Pediatrics*, pp 131: 276–282.

Wood B, Rea MS, Plitnick B & Figueiro MG 2013, 'Light level and duration of exposure determine the impact of self-luminous tablets on melatonin suppression', *Applied Ergonomics*, 44(2), pp 237–240.

Page 97 'An extensive literature review completed in 2014 revealed an association between screen time and sleep outcomes ...' Hale L & Guan S 2014, 'Screen time and sleep among school-aged children and adolescents: a systematic literature review', *Sleep Medicine Reviews*, 21, p 50-58.

Page 100 'In 2005 Thompson and Christakis conducted a study ...' Thompson DA & Christakis DA 2005, 'The association between television viewing and irregular sleep schedules among children less than three years of age', *Pediatrics*, 116(4), pp 851–856.

Page 100 'Two different studies published in *Pediatrics* in 2005 and 2014 have also showed ...' Cespedes EM, Gillman MW, Kleinman K, Rifas-Shiman SL, Redline S, Taveras E M 2014, 'Television viewing, bedroom television and sleep duration from infancy to mid-childhood', *Pediatrics*, 133 (5), pp 2013–3998.

Thompson DA & Christakis DA 2005, 'The association between television viewing and irregular sleep schedules among children less than three years of age', *Pediatrics*, 116(4), pp 851–856.

Page 104 'Violent or inappropriate programming can also increase the chances of children having ...' Garrison MM, Christakis DA 2011, 'The impact of a healthy media use intervention on sleep in preschool children', *Pediatrics*, 130(3), pp 1–10.

Page 104 'Much promotional content is unpredictable and can contain intense or disturbing material ...' Woolley JD & Ghossainy M 2013, 'Revisiting the fantasy–reality distinction: children as naïve skeptics', *Child Development*, 84(5), pp 1496–1510.

Page 106 'Whilst there's some preliminary evidence that EMR can moderately impair adults' sleep patterns and brain physiology whilst they sleep ...' Lowden A, Åkerstedt T,

Ingre M, Wiholm C, Hillert L, Kuster N, ... & Arnetz B 2011, Sleep after mobile phone exposure in subjects with mobile phonerelated symptoms. *Bioelectromagnetics*, 32(1), pp 4-14.

Page 110 ' In one study, three cohorts of children were followed from preschool (aged 4 years) to Years 5 and 6.' Marcon RA 2002, 'Moving up the grades: relationship between preschool model and later school success', *Early Childhood Research & Practice*, 4(1), pp 1-21.

Page 111 'A 2006 study published in *The Journal of the American Medical Association* showed that there's been a gradual decline in children's free and unstructured play ...' Ogden CL, Carroll MD, Curtin LR, McDowell MA, Tabak CJ & Flegal KM 2006, 'Prevalence of overweight and obesity in the United States, 1999–2004', *The Journal of the American Medical Association*, 295(13), pp 1549–1555.

Page 112 'These highly regimented timetables are displacing our children's opportunities for unstructured play ...' Active Healthy Kids Australia 2014, *Is Sport Enough? The 2014 Active Healthy Kids Australia Report Card on Physical Activity for Children and Young People*. Adelaide, South Australia: Active Healthy Kids Australia.

Page 113 'An Australian report on children's physical activity levels confirmed that children are spending *more* time participating in organised sport activities than they previously did ...' Active Healthy Kids Australia 2014, *Is Sport Enough? The 2014 active healthy kids Australia report card on physical activity for children and young people*, Adelaide, South Australia: Active Healthy Kids Australia.

Page 115 'In fact, two longitudinal studies published in 1997 and 2002 examined how different preschool curriculum models impacted on children's subsequent academic ...' Marcon, RA 2002, Moving up the Grades: Relationship between Preschool Model and Later School Success. *Early Childhood Research & Practice*, 4(1), p1-21.

Schweinhart LJ & Weikart DP 1997, 'The High/Scope Pre-school Curriculum Comparison Study through age 23', *Early Childhood Research Quarterly* 12, pp 117–143.

Page 118 'Research published by Adachi and Willoughby and Gentile and others ...' Adachi PJ & Willoughby T 2013, 'More than just fun and games: the longitudinal relationships between strategic video games, self-reported problem solving skills and academic grades' *Journal of Youth and Adolescence*, 42, pp 1041–1052.

Page 118 'Video games have been shown to improve children's visual processing skills ...' Gentile DA, Anderson CA, Yukawa S, Ihori N, Saleem M, Ming LK & Sakamoto A 2009, 'The effects of pro-social video games on pro-social behaviors: international evidence from correlational, longitudinal and experimental studies', *Personality and Social Psychology Bulletin*.

McCarrick K & Li X 2007, 'Buried treasure: the impact of computer use on young children's social, cognitive, language development and motivation', *Association for the Advancement of Computing in Education*, 15(1), pp 73–95.

Page 119 'While many children become obsessed by Minecraft, there are also educational benefits according to work published by Dezuanni ...' Dezuanni MO, Mara J & Beavis C 2015, 'Redstone is like electricity: children' s performative [sic] representations in and around Minecraft', *E-learning and Digital Media*, 12(2), pp 147–163.

Page 123 'Studies published in 2007, 2009 and 2012 all confirm that children's modern play patterns are being *shaped* ...' Burn A, Marsh J, Bishop JC, Willett R, Richards C &

Sheridan J 2009, *Children's playground games and songs in the new media age*, Institute of Education, University of London, 11.

Ginsburg KR 2007, 'The importance of play in promoting healthy child development and maintaining strong parent–child bonds', *Pediatrics*, 119(1), pp 182–191.

Harrison C 2012, 'Watching the children watching *Play School*: indicators of engagement, play and learning', *Australasian Journal of Early Childhoo*d, (37), p 4.

Page 123 'A study published in 2015 found that play with electronic toys is associated ...' Sosa AV 2015, 'Association of the type of toy used during play with the quantity and quality of parent-infant communication' *Journal of American Medical Association: Pediatrics*, pp 1-6.

Page 134 '*Active Healthy Kids Australia* estimates that one in three Australian children will be obese by 2025 ...' Active Healthy Kids Australia 2014, *Is Sport Enough? The 2014 active healthy kids Australia report card on physical activity for children and young people*, Adelaide, South Australia: Active Healthy Kids Australia.

Page 134 'An Australian study has found that 80 per cent of Australian children aged five to 17 are not getting daily exercise.' Active Healthy Kids Australia 2014, *Is Sport Enough? The 2014 active healthy kids Australia report card on physical activity for children and young people*, Adelaide, South Australia: Active Healthy Kids Australia.

Page 135 'Dennison and Jenkins found that on average, children who have a TV set in their bedroom view over 4.5 hours more TV per week ...' Dennison BA, Erb TA, Jenkins PL 2002, 'Television viewing and television in bedrooms associated with overweight risk among low-income pre-school children', *Pediatrics*, (109), pp 1028–35.

Page 135 'Failure to adhere to the physical activity guidelines results in a three to four times greater chances of obesity ...' Delmas C, Platat C, Schweitzer B, Wagner A, Oujaa M & Simon C 2007, 'Association between television in bedroom and adiposity throughout adolescence', *Obesity*, 15(10), pp 2495–2503.

Page 135 'Importantly, the adverse health consequences persist even among children who meet physical activity ...' Australian Council for Health, Physical Education and Recreation (ACHPER) Victorian Branch 2013, *Premier's active families challenge: school resource, sport and recreation, Victoria*, State Government of Victoria, Melbourne.

Page 138 'These guidelines are based on the Australian Department of Health Guidelines ...' Australian Department of Health 2015, Australia' s physical activity and sedentary behaviour guidelines, Retrieved 14 July 2015, <http://www.health.gov.au/internet/ main/publishing.nsf/content /health-pubhlth-strateg-phys- act-guidelines#apa512>.

Page 139 'In 2006, Rideout and Hame's study revealed that 61 per cent of children under two years of age use screens on a daily basis ...' Rideout VJ & Hame IE 2006, *The media family: electronic media in the lives of infants, toddlers, preschoolers, and their parents*, The Henry J Kaiser Family Foundation, Menlo Park, California.

Page 139 'Further, only 29 per cent of Australians aged 5–17 years met the recommended Australian screen time guidelines of accumulating no more than two hours per day.' Active Healthy Kids Australia 2014, *Is Sport Enough? The 2014 active healthy kids Australia report card on physical activity for children and young people*, Adelaide, South Australia: Active Healthy Kids Australia.

Page 139 'Other studies have found that 45 per cent of eight year olds and 80 per cent ...' Houghton S, Hunter SC, Rosenberg M, Wood L, Zadow C, Martin K & Shilton T 2015, 'Virtually impossible: limiting Australian children and adolescents daily screen based media use', *Biomedical Central Public Health*, 15(1), p 5.

Page 140 'The following health and safety tips are from the AAP suggest ...' American Academy of Pediatrics, 2015, *Children and media: Tips for parents*, Retrieved 23 October 2015, <https://www.aap.org/en-us/about-the-aap/aap-press-room/Pages/Children-And-Media-Tips-For-Parents.aspx>

Page 142 'Studies are showing that increasing numbers of children are entering primary school with movement skill ...' Barnett LM, van Beurden E, Morgan PJ, Brooks LO & Beard JR 2010, 'Gender differences in motor skill proficiency from childhood to adolescence: a longitudinal study', *Research Quarterly for Exercise and Sport*, 81(2), pp 162–170.

Barnett LM, Hardy LL, Lubans DR, Cliff DP, Okely AD, Hills AP & Morgan PJ 2013, 'Australian children lack the basic movement skills to be active and healthy', *Health Promotion Journal of Australia*, 24(2), pp 82–84.

Page 147 'The Australian Centre for Research into Injury in Sport and its Prevention has reported that children's sports injury rates are increasing ...' Pointer S 2014, *Hospitalised injury in children and young people 2011–12: Injury research and statistic Australian Centre for Research into Injury in Sport and Its Prevention*: Canberra, series 91.

Page 148 'A 2013 study found that playing active video games uses more energy than playing sedentary games ...' Staiano AE, Abraham AA & Calvert SL 2013, 'Adolescent exergame play for weight loss and psychosocial improvement: a controlled physical activity intervention', *Obesity*, 21(3), p 598-601.

Page 148 'However, in a 2011comparison study the energy expenditure associated with six different types of interactive digital exercise games was ...' Bailey BW, McInnis K 2011, 'Energy cost of exergaming: a comparison of the energy cost of six forms of exergaming', *Archives of Pediatric Adolescent Medicine*, 165, pp 597–602.

Page 153 'Recently updated Australian guidelines now recommend 'choosing whole foods ...' National Health and Medical Research Council (2013) *Australian Dietary Guidelines*, National Health and Medical Research Council, Canberra.

Page 156 'On average children aged 1 to 3 years are consuming 12 teaspoons of sugar each day ...' Johnson R K, Appel L J, Brands M, Howard B V, Lefevre, M, Lustig, R H & Wylie-Rosett J 2009, Dietary sugars intake and cardiovascular health a scientific statement from the American Heart Association. *Circulation*,120(11), pp 1011-1020.

Page 158 'Research by Kunkel and Strasburger has found that children under 8 are ...' Kunkel D 2001, 'Children and television advertising', in Singer DG & Singer JL (eds.) 2001, *Handbook of children and the media*, Sage, Thousand Oaks, CA, pp 375–393.

Strasburger VC & Wilson BJ 2002, *Children, adolescents and the media*, Sage, Thousand Oaks, CA.

Page 158 'Given that young children are consuming vast amounts of screen media ...' Strasburger VC, Jordan AB & Donnerstein E 2010, 'Health effects of media on children and adolescents', *Pediatrics*, 125(4), pp 756–767.

Page 158 'A 2006 position statement from the American Academy of Pediatrics claims ...' Strasburger VC 2006, 'Children, adolescents, and advertising', *Pediatrics*, 118(6), pp 2563–2569.

Page 158 'Studies published in 2007 and 2001 provide evidence to suggest that fast-food branding influences children's taste perceptions ...' Robinson TN, Borzekowski DL, Matheson DM & Kraemer HC 2007, 'Effects of fast food branding on young children's taste preferences', *Archives of Pediatrics & Adolescent Medicine*, 161(8), pp 792–797.

Borzekowski, D. L & Robinson, T. N 2001, The 30-second effect: an experiment revealing the impact of television commercials on food preferences of preschoolers. *Journal of the American Dietetic Association*, 101(1), 42–46.

Page 158 'In a 2010 study published in the *Pediatrics* journal, young children ...' Strasburger VC, Jordan AB & Donnerstein E 2010, 'Health effects of media on children and adolescents', *Pediatrics*, 125(4), pp 756–767.

Page 159 'A team of researchers from the John Hopkins Bloomberg School of Public Health examined the nag factor ...' Henry HK & Borzekowski DL 2011, 'The nag factor: a mixed-methodology study in the US of young children's requests for advertised products', *Journal of Children and Media*, 5(3), pp 298–317.

Page 159 'Social media is also gaining popularity with children and there are targeted advertisements that users consume that are ...' Speers SE, Harris JL, Schwartz MB 2011, 'Child and adolescent exposure to food and beverage brand appearances during prime-time television programming', *American Journal of Preventative Medicine*, 41, pp 291–296.

Page 160 'Harris, Bargh and Brownell found that children who watched cartoons with food commercials ...' Harris JL, Bargh JA, Brownell KD 2009, 'Priming effects of television food advertising on eating behavior', *Health Psychology*, 28, pp 404–413.

Page 160 'In a 2015 poll conducted by the American Speech-Language-Hearing Association ...' American Speech–Language–Hearing Association 2015, *Parent Poll: Better Hearing and Speech Month* (Spring 2015), retrieved 12 July 2015, <http://www.asha.org/uploadedFiles/BHSM-Parent-Poll.pdf>.

Page 162 'Between 1995 and 2005 the prevalence of disordered eating doubled amongst both males and females.' The National Eating Disorders Collaboration 2012, *An Integrated Response to Complexity – National Eating Disorders Framework*, Retrieved 26 March 2014 <http://www.nedc.com.au/files/pdfs/National%20Framework%20An%20integrated%20Response%20to%20Complexity%202012%20-%20Final.pdf>.

Page 162 'Research by Becker and others suggests that media consumption is associated with dangerous methods of weight reduction.' Becker A E 1995, *Body, Self, and Society: the View from Fiji*. University of Pennsylvania Press, Philadelphia.

Page 164 'Increasingly, researchers are discovering that a child's capacity to develop executive-function skills ...' Bull R, Espy KA & Wiebe SA 2008, 'Short-term memory, working memory and executive functioning in preschoolers: longitudinal predictors of mathematical achievement at age seven years', *Developmental Neuropsychology*, 33(3), pp 205–228.

Clark CA, Pritchard VE & Woodward LJ 2010, 'Preschool executive functioning abilities predict early mathematics achievement', *Developmental Psychology*, 46(5), pp 1176.

McClelland MM, Acock AC & Morrison FJ 2006, 'The impact of kindergarten learning-related skills on academic trajectories at the end of elementary school', *Early Childhood Research Quarterly*, 21(4), pp 471–490.

Page 167 'A study conducted by Ashman-East sought to determine whether low-achieving primary school students ...' Ashman-East S 2015, *The effect of computerized cognitive training on the working memory and mathematics achievement of low achievers* (doctoral dissertation), Nova Southeastern University, NSUWorks, Graduate School of Computer and Information Sciences, retrieved 3 September 2015, <http://nsuworks.nova.edu/gscis_etd/25>.

Page 167 'In a 2012 study, 2500 teachers were surveyed and they acknowledged that the ability to instantly access information ...' Common Sense Media 2012, *Children, teens and entertainment media: the view from the classroom*, retrieved 15 November 2012, <https://www.commonsensemedia.org/about-us/news/press-releases/entertainment-media-diets-of-children-and-adolescents-may-impact>.

Page 168 'There are compelling arguments and a growing body of research in different journals ...' Davis DM, Hayes DM, Jeffrey A 2012, 'What are the benefits of mindfulness: a wealth of new research has explored this age old practice. Here's a look at its benefits for both clients and psychologists', *American Psychological Association*, 43(7), p 64.

Diamond A & Lee K 2011, 'Interventions shown to aid executive function development in children 4–12 years old', *Science*, 333(6045), pp 959–964.

Chiesa A, Serretti A & Jakobsen JC 2013, 'Mindfulness: top–down or bottom–up emotion regulation strategy?' *Clinical Psychology Review*, 33(1), pp 82–96.

Hölzel BK, Carmody J, Vangel M, Congleton C, Yerramsetti SM, Gard T, Lazar SW 2011, 'Mindfulness practice leads to increases in regional brain gray-matter density', *Psychiatry Research: Neuroimaging*, January 30; 191(1), pp 36–4.

Page 168 'As Weare proposes, while the research on the effectiveness of mindfulness for children is still in its infancy ...' Weare K 2012, *Evidence for the impact of mindfulness on children and young people*, The Mindfulness in Schools Project in association with Mood Disorders Centre.

Page 169 'Research published by Davis and others has shown that physical activities ...' Davis CL, Tomporowski PD, Boyle CA, Waller JL, Miller PH, Naglieri JA & Gregoski M 2007, 'Effects of aerobic exercise on overweight children's cognitive functioning: a randomized controlled trial' *Research Quarterly for Exercise and Sport*, 78(5), pp 510–519.

Page 169 'Three studies published between 2002 and 2014 have found that video games can improve older students' mental ...' Oei AC & Patterson MD 2014, 'Playing a puzzle video game with changing requirements improves executive functions', *Computers in Human Behavior*, 37, pp 216–228.

Pillay H 2002, 'An investigation of cognitive processes engaged in by recreational computer game players: Implications for skills of the future', *Journal of Research on Technology in Education*, 34(3), pp 336–350.

Rueda MR, Posner MI & Rothbart MK 2005, 'The development of executive attention: contributions to the emergence of self-regulation' *Developmental Neuropsychology*, 28(2), pp 573–594.

Page 171 'Research by Bordwell revealed that TV programs made in the 1930s to 1960s ...' Bordwell D 2006, *The way Hollywood tells it: story and style in modern movies*, University of California Press.

Page 171 'Two separate studies, both published in 2012 by Pew internet & American Life Project and Common Sense Media ...' Common Sense Media 2012, *Children, teens and entertainment media: the view from the classroom*, retrieved 19 August 2013, <https://www.commonsensemedia.org/about-us/news/press-releases/entertainment-media-diets-of-children-and-adolescents-may-impact>.

Purcell K, Rainie L, Heaps A, Buchanan J, Friedrich L, Jacklin A & Zickuhr K 2012, *How teens do research in the digital world*, Pew Internet & American Life Project.

Page 172 'In another study published by Common Sense Media, nearly three-quarters of the teacher survey respondents believed ...' Common Sense Media 2012, *Children, teens and entertainment media: the view from the classroom*, retrieved 19 August 2013, <https://www.commonsensemedia.org/about-us/news/press-releases/entertainment-media-diets-of-children-and-adolescents-may-impact>.

Page 172 'A 2009 study presented by Ophir, Nass, and Wagner found that multi-tasking overloaded children's working memory, caused fatigue, divided students ...' Ophir E, Nass C & Wagner AD 2009, 'Cognitive control in media multitaskers', *Proceedings of the National Academy of Sciences*, 106(37), pp 15583–15587.

Page 173 'A 2010 study found that children aged 8–18 were spending an average of 7.5 ...' Rideout VJ, Foehr UG & Roberts DF 2010, *Generation M: media in the lives of 8-to 18-year-olds*, Henry J. Kaiser Family Foundation, California.

Page 173 'Even though children think they're capable of multi-tasking ...' Rosen LD, Carrier LM & Cheever NA 2013, 'Facebook and texting made me do it: media-induced task-switching while studying', *Computers in Human Behavior*, 29(3), pp 948–958.

Page 173 'Multi-tasking impairs performance, especially for heavy multi-taskers.' Reynol D & Cotton SR 2012, 'The relationship between multitasking and academic performance', *Computers & Education*, 59(2) pp 505–514.

Ophir, E, Nass, C & Wagner, A. D 2009, Cognitive control in media multitaskers. *Proceedings of the National Academy of Sciences*, 106(37), 15583–15587.

Page 173 'Multi-tasking has cognitive costs – it disrupts attention, results in increased error rates and decreases academic performance ...' Ophir E, Nass C & Wagner AD 2009, 'Cognitive control in media multitaskers', *Proceedings of the National Academy of Sciences*, 106(37), pp 15583–15587.

Page 173 'Multi-tasking also appears to overload our working memory and divide attention — it can also be a predictor of depression and social anxiety ...' Becker M W, Alzahabi R, & Hopwood C J 2012, 'Media multitasking is associated with symptoms of depression and social anxiety', *Cyberpsychology, Behavior, and Social Networking, 16*(2), pp. 132-135.

Page 174 'Nicholas Carr likens this shallow processing to being a jet-ski rider.' Carr, N G 2010 *The Shallows: How the Internet is Changing the Way We Think, Read and Remember*, Atlantic Books, New York.

'Now I zip along the surface like a guy on a jet ski.'

Page 175 'When students' attention spans are depleted and they face information overload, their learning suffers according to work published in 2009 and 2012...' Ophir, E, Nass, C & Wagner, A. D 2009, Cognitive control in media multitaskers. *Proceedings of the National Academy of Sciences*, 106(37), 15583–15587.

Reynol D & Cotton SR 2012, 'The relationship between multitasking and academic performance', *Computers & Education*, 59(2) pp 505–514.

Ophir, E, Nass, C & Wagner, A. D 2009, Cognitive control in media multitaskers. *Proceedings of the National Academy of Sciences*, 106(37), 15583–15587.

Page 175 **'The attention restoration theory suggests that time in nature also increases the release of the neurotransmitter dopamine ...'** Herzog T R, Black A, Fountaine K A, & Knotts D J 1997, 'Reflection and attentional recovery as distinctive benefits of restorative environments', *Journal of Environmental Psychology*, 17(2), pp. 165-170.

Page 177 **'Levitin claims that in 2011 we were consuming five times more information on a daily basis (about 174 newspapers worth of data each day) than we were in 1986 ...'** Levitin, D. J. (2014) *The organized mind: Thinking straight in the age of information overload*, Penguin, New York.

Page 177 **'The Google Effect was first coined in 2011 after a study conducted by Harvard psychologists Daniel Wegner and Adrian Ward.'** Bohannon J 2011, 'Searching for the Google effect on people's memory', *Science*, 333(6040), pp 277–277.

Page 186 **'It is currently under consideration for the *Diagnostic and Statistical Manual of Mental Disorders (DSM)* as a mental disorder ...'** American Psychiatric Association 2013, *Diagnostic and Statistical Manual of Mental Disorders (DSM-5®)*, American Psychiatric Publication, Arlington, VA.

Page 187 **'In their 2010 descriptive review of the existing research evidence, Chakraborty ...'** Chakraborty K, Basu D, Kumar K 2010, 'Internet addiction: consensus, controversies and the way ahead', *East Asian Archives of Psychiatry*, 20(3), pp 123–32.

Page 189 **'Following are some signs that children may be forming unhealthy media habits ...'** Cash H, Rae CD, Steel AH & Winkler A 2012, 'Internet addiction: a brief summary of research and practice', *Current Psychiatry Reviews*, 8(4), p 292.

Page 191 **'In fact a 2016 study by the Action for Children organisation found that 23 per cent of parents surveyed struggled to get their children to unplug from television, phones and computer screens.'** Action for Children 2016, 'Unplugging' from technology, retrieved 11 January 2016, <https://www.actionforchildren.org.uk/news-and-opinion/latest-news/2016/january/unplugging-from-technology/>.

Page 199 **'A 2014 study by Jago and others found strong associations between children's screen time and parents' screen time.'** Jago R, Thompson JL, Sebire SJ, Wood L, Pool L, Zahra J & Lawlor DA 2014, 'Cross-sectional associations between the screen-time of parents and young children: differences by parent and child gender and day of the week', *International Journal of Behavioral Nutrition and Physical Activity*, 11(54), p 29.

Page 211 **'research on Cancer (IARC) classified radiofrequency electromagnetic fields as a 'type 2B possible carcinogen ...'** International Agency for Research on Cancer, 2011, IARC classifies radiofrequency electromagnetic fields as possibly carcinogenic to humans, retrieved 21 May 2013 <http://www.iarc.fr/en/media-centre/pr/2011/pdfs/pr208_E.pdf>.

Page 209 **'A 2009 study published in the *Journal of Clinical Oncology* linked mobile phone use to an increased risk of tumors.'** Myung SK, Ju W, McDonnell DD, Lee YJ, Kazinets G, Cheng CT & Moskowitz JM 2009, 'Mobile phone use and risk of tumors: a meta-analysis', *Journal of Clinical Oncology*, 27(33), pp 5565–5572.

Page 213 **'A 2012 study published in *Electromagnetic Biology and Medicine* estimated that five year olds absorb almost 60 per cent ...'** Gandhi OP, Morgan LL, de Salles AA, Han YY, Herberman RB & Davis DL 2012, 'Exposure limits: the underestimation of absorbed cell phone radiation, especially in children', *Electromagnetic Biology and Medicine*, 31(1), pp 34–51.

Page 215 'A 2015 Common Sense Media report found that media …' Pai S & Schryver K 2015, *Children, teens, media, and body image: a Common Sense Media research brief*, Common Sense Media, San Francisco, retrieved 19 August 2015, <https://www.commonsensemedia.org/research/children-teens-media-and-body-image>.

Page 217 'A 2013 study published in the journal *Photochemistry and Photobiology* found that …' Chamorro E, BonninArias C, PérezCarrasco MJ, Luna JM, Vázquez D & Sánchez Ramos C 2013, 'Effects of lightemitting diode radiations on human retinal pigment epithelial cells in vitro', *Photochemistry and photobiology*, 89(2), 468–473.

Page 220 'The WHO estimates that 1.1 billion people worldwide could be affected by noise-induced hearing loss because of unsafe use of personal music devices …' World Health Organization 2015, *Make listening safe*, World Health Organization, retrieved 15 October 2015, <http://www.who.int/pbd/deafness/activities/MLS_Brochure_English_lowres_for_web.pdf>.

Page 221 'A study conducted by Lichenstein and others found that the number of pedestrians that have been killed or injured …' Lichenstein, R., Smith, D. C., Ambrose, J. L., & Moody, L. A. (2012). Headphone use and pedestrian injury and death in the United States: 2004–2011. *Injury prevention*, injuryprev-2011.

Page 223 'Research from Curtin University showed that more than 30 minutes of touch-screen time …' Coenena P, Howiea E, Campbella A & Strakera L 2015, 'Mobile touch screen device use among young Australian children–first results from a national survey' in *Proceedings 19th Triennial Congress of the IEA*, Vol. 9, p 14.

Page 224 'A 2014 study conducted by Mueller and Oppenheimer showed that university students could recall more from handwritten notes …' Mueller PA & Oppenheimer DM 2014, 'The pen is mightier than the keyboard: advantages of longhand over laptop note-taking, *Psychological Science*, 16, pp 3–34.

Page 224 'Researchers from the Department for Health at Texas A&M University and from the University of Queensland have shown that smart …' Licence, S., Smith, R., McGuigan, M. P., & Earnest, C. P. (2015). 'Gait pattern alterations during walking, texting and walking and texting during cognitively distractive tasks while negotiating common pedestrian obstacles', *PLoS one, 10*(7), e0133281.

Schabrun, SM, van den Hoorn W, Moorcroft A, Greenland C, & Hodges PW, 2014, 'Texting and walking: strategies for postural control and implications for safety', *PloS one, 9*(1), e84312.